797,885 Books

are available to read at

Forgotten Books

www.ForgottenBooks.com

Forgotten Books' App
Available for mobile, tablet & eReader

ISBN 978-1-331-06794-8
PIBN 10140572

This book is a reproduction of an important historical work. Forgotten Books uses state-of-the-art technology to digitally reconstruct the work, preserving the original format whilst repairing imperfections present in the aged copy. In rare cases, an imperfection in the original, such as a blemish or missing page, may be replicated in our edition. We do, however, repair the vast majority of imperfections successfully; any imperfections that remain are intentionally left to preserve the state of such historical works.

Forgotten Books is a registered trademark of FB &c Ltd.
Copyright © 2017 FB &c Ltd.
FB &c Ltd, Dalton House, 60 Windsor Avenue, London, SW19 2RR.
Company number 08720141. Registered in England and Wales.

For support please visit www.forgottenbooks.com

1 MONTH OF
FREE
READING

at

www.ForgottenBooks.com

By purchasing this book you are eligible for one month membership to ForgottenBooks.com, giving you unlimited access to our entire collection of over 700,000 titles via our web site and mobile apps.

To claim your free month visit:

www.forgottenbooks.com/free140572

* Offer is valid for 45 days from date of purchase. Terms and conditions apply.

English
Français
Deutsche
Italiano
Español
Português

www.forgottenbooks.com

Mythology Photography **Fiction**
Fishing Christianity **Art** Cooking
Essays Buddhism Freemasonry
Medicine **Biology** Music **Ancient Egypt** Evolution Carpentry Physics
Dance Geology **Mathematics** Fitness
Shakespeare **Folklore** Yoga Marketing
Confidence Immortality Biographies
Poetry **Psychology** Witchcraft
Electronics Chemistry History **Law**
Accounting **Philosophy** Anthropology
Alchemy Drama Quantum Mechanics
Atheism Sexual Health **Ancient History**
Entrepreneurship Languages Sport
Paleontology Needlework Islam
Metaphysics Investment Archaeology
Parenting Statistics Criminology
Motivational

TROUBLES

CONNECTED WITH

THE PRAYER BOOK OF 1549.

DOCUMENTS NOW MOSTLY FOR THE FIRST TIME PRINTED
FROM THE ORIGINALS IN THE RECORD OFFICE,
THE PETYT COLLECTION IN THE LIBRARY OF THE INNER TEMPLE,
THE COUNCIL BOOK,
AND THE BRITISH MUSEUM.

EDITED BY

NICHOLAS POCOCK, M.A.,

LATE MICHEL FELLOW OF QUEEN'S COLLEGE, OXFORD.

PRINTED FOR THE CAMDEN SOCIETY.

M.DCCC.LXXXIV.

WESTMINSTER:
PRINTED BY NICHOLS AND SONS,
25, PARLIAMENT STREET.

[NEW SERIES XXXVII.]

COUNCIL OF THE CAMDEN SOCIETY
FOR THE YEAR 1883-4.

President,

THE RIGHT HON. THE EARL OF VERULAM, F.R.G.S.
J. J. CARTWRIGHT, ESQ., M.A., F.S.A., *Treasurer.*
WILLIAM CHAPPELL, ESQ., F.S.A.
F. W. COSENS, ESQ., F.S.A.
THE HON. HAROLD DILLON, F.S.A.
JAMES E. DOYLE, ESQ.
REV. J. WOODFALL EBSWORTH, M.A., F.S.A.
JAMES GAIRDNER, ESQ.
SAMUEL RAWSON GARDINER, ESQ., LL.D., *Director.*
J. W. HALES, ESQ., M.A.
ALFRED KINGSTON, ESQ., *Secretary.*
ALEXANDER MACMILLAN, ESQ., F.S.A.
STUART A. MOORE, ESQ., F.S.A.
THE EARL OF POWIS, LL.D.
REV. W. SPARROW SIMPSON, D.D., F.S.A.
WILLIAM JOHN THOMS, ESQ., F.S.A.

The COUNCIL of the CAMDEN SOCIETY desire it to be understood that they are not answerable for any opinions or observations that may appear in the Society's publications; the Editors of the several Works being alone responsible for the same.

PREFACE.

THE documents here printed form part of a large collection originally intended for a continuation of the *Records of the Reformation*, the first part of which was published at Oxford by the Delegates of the Clarendon Press in 1870. Owing to the limited sale which these volumes met with, the Delegates were unwilling to continue the publication, and no bookseller or publisher would undertake the risk of printing a series of papers for which there was no hope of a remunerative sale. Under these circumstances these documents have remained in manuscript as they were copied together with several epitomes of the scarce pamphlets and volumes of the period, which throw light upon the history of the changes in religion. Nearly all of them belong to the reign of Edward VI., for the editor had long ago abandoned his intention of publishing a second part of the Records, which would have continued the history of ecclesiastical affairs from 1533 to the end of the reign of Henry VIII., and purposed devoting his attention to the following reign —from 1547 to 1553. The reason for this was that the late Mr. Brewer's volumes of the State Papers and Documents of that reign were rapidly progressing, and seemed likely soon to reach this period, and his accounts of all important papers were so full and accurate that it would not have been worth while to publish a selection of ecclesiastical documents which would for all practical purposes have appeared in these volumes sufficiently epitomised. But there was no danger of such interference as regards the reign of Edward VI.; for, though the foreign papers of that reign in the Record Office had been admirably executed by the late Mr. Turnbull, there yet remained an immense mass of documents in the Cottonian Library and elsewhere which had been left unnoticed, and many of them perhaps entirely unknown to historians, the perusal of which would have been indispensable for any one who would take an accurate survey of the transactions of the period. And, what is much to be regretted, the Domestic Papers had been epitomised in the most meagre way in the first volume of the Domestic Series, which begins with the year 1547 and ends with 1580.

No reflection is intended by this remark on the labours or skill of the editor of the first volume, which extends over the reigns of Edward, Mary, and part of Elizabeth. The papers are perfectly well represented by Mr. Robert Lemon, but he, probably following his instructions, has just given the heads of the matters treated in each paper, so as to afford a perfect method of identifying the paper, but not so as to supersede the necessity of referring to the document itself. The mistake seems to have been discovered after its publication, for in all subsequent volumes of the series the plan has been changed; and even as regards the omitted documents of the earlier period, which have been from time to time published as appendices to Mrs. Green's volumes, the analysis of papers has been on a much more extended scale.

It is much to be regretted that the same permission, granted to Mr. Brewer as regards the State Papers of the reign of Henry VIII.

was not extended to the other calendarers of succeeding reigns, for the number of such papers which exist in other collections probably greatly exceeds that of the documents now in the Public Record Office; and it is not yet too late to add a collection of documents of the reigns of Edward and Mary from the Cottonian and other libraries to that valuable series. Meanwhile the contents of the following volume, which are almost entirely new, may not be unacceptable to readers who wish to form a fair estimate of the means by which the reformation of religion was effected and the characters of those who were the chief instruments in bringing it about.

With the view of enabling the reader to understand the subject, a considerable number of notes has been added at the foot of the text, which serve to explain who the principal actors in the affairs of this reign were and what were their objects. These notes do not profess to give anything like a complete life of the persons to whom they refer, but only so much of their actions as may serve to illustrate the character, and the changes of belief, whether real, or professed, or of a mixed character, by which they were actuated.

The papers here published will tend to show how untenable is the theory that the principal agents in the Reformation of the reign of Edward VI. ever intended to stop short with the first Prayer Book of 1549; they are a link in the evidence, which is tolerably complete perhaps without it, that there was a systematic attempt from the first on the part of Somerset and his colleagues to bring doctrine to the state in which it appears in the second Prayer Book of 1552, which there is reason to think would have been further carried out in a third Prayer Book, if the premature death of the King had not put a stop to all their proceedings. Most of the papers here printed are connected with the attempt to establish the first Prayer Book; but to understand the true view of the case it would be necessary to compare the gradual changes introduced, first in "The order of the Communion," published on the 8th of March, 1548, with its preliminary Proclamation by the King, acting, as he states, "under the advice of our most dear Uncle and other of our Privy Council," with the further advance of the Book of Common Prayer, printed exactly a year afterwards, and the more advanced Protestantism of the second book, published in the autumn of 1552.

These, together with the entries relating to Church matters in the Council Book of the reign, will show that the bishops of the time were mere tools in the hands of the Council, whilst those who resisted the changes, or having given a reluctant consent and then withdrawn from the affair, were deprived, and others substituted in their places, after an agreement made to part with some of the revenues of their sees.

No one who had read the evidence of all this to be found in the Council Book, and in Rymer's *Fœdera*, could suppose that the principal agents in the Reformation of this reign were influenced by any feelings of religion in their reckless dealing with Church doctrine and spoliation of Church property. Somerset himself was, probably, a firm believer in the system of Calvin, and may have encouraged himself in the idea that he was one of the elect who could not fall from grace. His successor, Northumberland, was certainly, during the whole of this reign, playing the part of a hypocrite, appearing on the Protestant side, though all along believing, if he believed anything, in the articles of the old faith— if his own assertion at his execution is to be taken for the truth.

PREFACE.

Some faint show of resistance was sometimes made by the bishops, but they were easily overpowered. For a considerable part of the reign there were only two who had seats in the Council—Cranmer, of Canterbury, and Tunstall, of Durham; but Tunstall seems scarcely ever to have been present, and Goodrich, Bishop of Ely, who appears to have been made a councillor some time before he was chancellor, would not have had the slightest influence, even if he had had any inclination to exert himself, to stem the tide of innovation. Cranmer's name appears frequently in the Council books, and may be seen repeatedly in the following records. But, though the main features of the life of the other agents in these transactions have been detailed, it has not been thought worth while to repeat what is now tolerably well known of the compliant temper of the Archbishop, who was content to celebrate the office of the mass at the very time when he believed it to be idolatrous and blasphemous—having passed through the phase of Lutheranism, and settled down into the Zwinglianism which is represented in the second Prayer Book of 1552. For those who want to form an estimate of his character, without the trouble of wading through the history of the Reformation, it will be sufficient to give a reference to Lord Macaulay's account of him in his review of Hallam's Constitutional History of England, or to an article in the *Saturday Review* for July 25, 1868.

Neither has it been thought worth while to give any account of Cardinal Pole, whose name appears in these papers, in the request of the Commons of Devonshire and Cornwall that he should be recalled and placed in the Privy Council. But it may be well to refer the reader to the letters which passed in the course of this year between the cardinal and the Protector, which Tytler seems

vi   PREFACE.

to have misunderstood. Pole wrote from Rome to the Earl of
Warwick, April 6th, 1549, a letter which, though expressed in
ambiguous terms, evidently means that he is anxious and willing to
co-operate with the Council in uniting both parties in the realm.
He mentions that on the same day he had sent to Somerset two
messengers, giving him information and advice about the state of
the country. On the 6th of May, Pole wrote again to Somerset a
letter, which Somerset replied to on the 4th of June. This reply
is so important that we have thought it well to insert it here :

SOMERSET'S LETTER TO POLE OF JUNE 4, 1549, IN REPLY TO
A COMMUNICATION OF POLE TO SOMERSET, which is alluded
to in Pole's letter to Warwick, April 6th, 1549.

To the Cardynal Pole.

Having received and perused your letters of the sixt of Maie, we
took some hope and comfort as though at the last you, perceiving
the abuses of Rome [the deceit and hypocrisy wherewithal the
world hath been of long time blinded, and the abominations there
used and frequented as well in life as doctrine], had now had an
eye and respect unto your natural country ye were born in [and] a
regard of your duty to your sovereign and liege lord the King's
Majesty, and to the light of Christ's word in this realm truly and
sincerely taught. And upon that consideration had directed down
your messengers, written your letters, and given instructions [such
as had become you] that ye would have used the mercy, softness,
and clemency of the king's highness' reign, and have claimed the
lenity of these times. And according to his Majesty's most gracious
liberal and free pardon had desired to have come home, and at the
last relinquished all thoughts and purposes the which had been to
the contrary, and have done the duty of a true and faithful subject

as a good Christian man ought to do. But when afterwards we read your instructions we did perceive the thing to be far otherwise, and nothing else to come from Rome than heretofore hath been wont, under colour of holiness, things neither convenient nor expedient to the king's highness and the realm. Wherefore, saving only that we had and yet have a persuasion that it may be that you did this of a sincere mind and of a will indeed such as is pretended, that is to say, to do and say such things as ye thought expedient for the realm; and hereupon whatsoever it is that you have written for that cause is of us to be taken in good part (the will meriting pardon or thanks), whatsoever the deed doth deserve, we had greatly repented us that ever we would so much yield ourself as once to hear ministers or read your writings. The which, although they made no answer, yet we cannot well omit as well friendly to declare again unto you how much you do mistake things that be here as ye boldly dare write of them that which is neither true nor convenient.

And first in all your whole process it appeareth to us [that you] take upon you, as it were, a part; and as ye were a foreign prince to encontre and face the king's majesty whom, if you could make afraid with your vain terrors, ye would offer a place where ye would be content to talk with him or his commissioners to that intent sent. Marye ye will have the choice of the ground indifferently. And as his Majesty must have his realm to talk or send unto you his subject and owing natural duty and obedience unto him, so you would be bold to borrow ground of another prince to bring your natural prince or his commissioners thither where ye might talk with his highness or his commissioners on an equality.

It is so long ago sith by the great grace of God we have forsaken that usurped power of the state of Rome that these things seemeth to us very strange and unmete, as we suppose they ought to do to every faithful heart of an obedient subject.

As to your terrors, first ye object that the king's majesty is a child; it is truth, in age; but then you must add, endued with such grace, so much aided by the providence and gift of Almighty God, so roborrated and strengthened with faithful, true, loving, and well-agreeing counsellors and subjects; that, as it may well appear by the success of things hitherto, either to defend his own or to repress the injuries of others, no prince of any age this many years before hath been more able.

The which as we take to be the favourable gift of Almighty God, so we do see no cause why this should be a terror unto us. In Scripture, Josiah was no old king even when he died and was so sore lamented, no nor yet Salomon when he best reigned and was most praised. And because ye retort us as it were to examples at home, ye do mistake King Henrie the Sixth's reign, whose childhood was more honorable and victorious than was his man's estate. And King Edward's children could have been no example unto you if their father's brother had not been so greedy of the crown. But when God will plague and scourge his people of Englond, we see as well not only seditions and insurrections, but also depositions and murders of old Kings in this realm by Herold, Edward and Richard the Seconds and Henrie the Sixt, as we do of kings being children. And if the histories of Chronicles be searched, far more examples both in number and weight of old kings murdered and deposed than of kings of young age. But we, not mistrusting the Lord, put our whole confidence in him, who is able and doth defend our King and prince, his elect vessel, against all his enemies, as well in childhood as we trust his grace shall do in his majesty's man's estate.

.Where ye touch our own private grief and sorrow, the same might have chanced at any age of the King's majesty. If God leave a nobleman to himself and withdraw his grace from him as hath too often (if it had otherwise pleased God) chanced in this realm at all ages of kings: We for our part impute it to the malice of the devil and unfortunateness and lack of grace of our brother (as indeed it is to be imputed), not to the tender age of our sovereign, which is no cause why any man should offend.

Your other discourse of the princes, that be our next neighbours, is as derogatory to the honour of them as the rest is to the King's majesty.

First for the emperor's honor, it appeareth smally regarded of you, if you think after such amities, leagues and treaties made, so firmly sworn to and bound, so long and so inviolably kept and observed on both the parties, under a pretence of justice he should invade another King's realm and go about open injuries and wrongs. And if he should, do ye not think that God would aid the unjustly vexed? and overthrow the unrighteous going about to oppress the innocent? For as for the weakness of that quarrel of the dowager's divorce, which is so long ago past, such amity and leagues coming between doth declare a will and a desire of some men to break the amity if it might be, and to bring his majesty upon the realm with some pretence, as it is not denied, and ye know that it hath been so travailed in. But yet it appeareth even by the same how much matter malice doth lack where God defendeth and princes regardeth their honour.

As touching France and Scotland (God be thanked!), experience sheweth nothing lost on our behalf nor won on their parts, either by open enmity or doubtful friendship. And as it is no news to England to have war with both those nations and not to lose; so there is no cause why that, when it shall please God so to incline princes' hearts, there may not be a friendship and peace concluded betwixt us and them without all such doubt as ye do move.

Your last peril of giving a colour to princes by the schism, as ye call it, from the see of Rome, hath been by the great and common author and chief cause of disobedience of subjects and dissention amongst princes so often attempted and so vainly (God always assisting and defending his servants, sticking to his holy word and pure and sincere teaching of the gospel) that we have hope that all other princes shall rather come to the true knowledge of their authority and the detestation of the usurped power of the see of Rome, than any one for that quarrel would attempt the hasard of battle and war with those men whom God, as we trust, hath taken under his protection.

The conclusion, and that that ye make the extreme peril and danger, may peradventure be known to you at Rome, of a dissension amongst our bishops upon the chiefest points of religion. We here do know no such thing; but, on the contrary, by a common agreement of all the chief learned men in the realm the thing of long time and maturely debated among them which had most opinion of learning in the Scriptures of God and were likeliest to give least to affection, as well bishops as other equally and indifferently chosen of judgment, not coacted with superior authority nor otherwise invited, but of a common agreement amongst themselves, there was first agreement on points and then the same coming to the judgment of the whole parliament, not severally divided, but all men admitted to the hearing and debating at large, before all states and persons hearing what could be said against it, by one whole consent of the upper and nether house of the parliament finally concluded and approved; and so a form and rite of service, a creed and doctrine of religion by that authority and after that sort allowed, set forth, and established by act and statute, and so published and divulged to so great a quiet as ever was in England and as gladly received of all partes. Whereof ye yourself, if ye had been here and did bear that affection ye pretend to your country, should have had great cause to rejoice. If yet in a school point or two some one or two peradventure will be singular in opinion, and not be satisfied in things which be not in that book, whether he be bishop or other, as ever hitherto it hath been seen in all meetings of learned men; what doth that derogate the quiet of the realm when they receive the law and be obedient unto it? Which if else they should not, the law will apprehend them before they can or shall make any disturbance or disquiet in this realm and punish the faulty according to justice.

Thus the public peril being but vain. and none in deed, which you with words doth so much exaggerate, it must needs follow that

that colloquy or parliament which you speak of and would so fain invite us unto, for remedy of those perils is superfluous and nothing necessary. Besides that, that is neither honorable nor convenient. A prince of an absolute power to go out of his own realm or send to treaty [*of such matters*]^a with his natural subject and specially of such matters, the which are already composed and set in order, and if they were not, yet, thanks be to God, there wanteth neither learned men nor good men in the realm to discuss, examine, compose, and perfect all such things as concerning these matters which might heretofore be accounted doubtful. And yet your device were not the best or likeliest, whereof the sum is that there should be indifferent men chosen betwixt the realm and the church of Rome. And you are one, a man indifferent, and therefore ye labour much to be one. These indifferent men should set an order first for the indifferentness. If the controversy be of taking away abuses, superstition, idolatry, the which should be indifferent in that to bring them in again or to keep them out still; We may peradventure in the way of reasoning grant them to be indifferent towards men, but surely to Godwards, which is the true trial and judge, they be ungodly, devilish, and wicked.

If it be for a superiority and a temporal rule that the Pope should have, as a man may safely guess that to be the very meaning of this colloquy ye would have, it is marvel how you should be indifferent on their behalf; to whom ye have sworne, and unto whose power and authority (as ye write) ye have resigned yourself. For our parts, that are true Englishmen, and faithful subjects to the king's majesty, we suppose there is no one indifferent man in that point. And we would be sorry there should ; but we will all live and die in his highness' quarrel; and sooner spend all our lives and goods than his majesty should lose of his regality and imperial power one jot. And, therefore, we do profess no indifferency in

^a The part within brackets and underlined has been struck through.

those matters; but if we knew any such indifferent man as you speak on in the king's majesty's realm, it should not be long before he should have as he deserveth. [*And if we should forswear and neglect our duties therein the common people would pluck him in pieces, to whom the name of the Pope is as odious as the name of the devil himself.*]^a For even to the end, touching that cause to have any superiority or authority away from the king, is so odious, that in no case they may abide to hear of it. So that, [*indeed,*]^b for that point, if the colloquy shall rest till indifferent men be found, it is like to sleep this good while. And, except there be more need than we see, it may sleep well enough, and be no more spoken of.

After this, ye declare private perils, as ye call them, both of the king's majesty, us, and the rest of the Council, and travail much in that the redress might be made in the king's majesty's minority. And here ye go about to bring in doubt his highness' title to the crown, which being so just, so clear, so without all manner of suspicion of doubt, if that see can find the means to fetter itself so that it can trust to have a pretence to make it doubtful, and so to persuade other, it is no marvel though the most prudent prince, the late king of famous memory, did conceive a just hatred unto it. And so ought all other princes do who doth look to the safety and security of the reign of their posterity. For when the king our sovereign lord and master's title can be thought by that see to be brought to ambiguity, let never prince think his posterity sure by any title where the Bishop of Rome may have the interpretation. Wherefore, things being here so composed and set in order as they be, the realm established in this most godly and civil policy that it is already in, no wisdom will counsel us to hear or to go about any mutation or change, especially from the better to the worse, and though man's wisdom would so move, yet the truth of God's word,

---

^a The parts bracketed and underlined have been struck through.
^b The word "indeed" is struck through.

PREFACE. xiii

with safe conscience, will not suffer us to admit any such dangerous and inconvenient counsels.

But forasmuch as ye naming both to be partial striveth to seek out a mean way of indifferency, and of a counsell, parliament, or colloquy so gathered, if there were or might be a counsell so gathered of good, wise, discreet men, learned in the lawes of God, and not affectionate, who would suffer the gospel and the word of God, not the decrees and constitutions of the bishop of Rome, to be the Judge, we never would refuse them, but do not doubt in that judgment to have the over hand. And as much as any man we do desire such a counsell or colloquy to be universal, as we trust it hath been here with us particular. And this for the truth and justness of our cause.

As for reconciling and appointments betwixt the realm and the bishop of Rome or other foreign kings and princes which ye make so hard because they differ from us in some mean points of religion concerning extern rites and other ceremonies or superiorities, though they do so, seeing we agree in one God and one Christ, why should that let us of amity and league, and why should that be occasion of enmity and war? Why should it break amity which before this time . . . . .[a] some bishops of Rome, emperors, and kings hath had with the Turk and kept the same faith[fully].[a]

And to the intent ye may the better know of our doings we have delivered to those which brought your [*bokes*][b] letters the book of Common Service, the same whereof here before we have spoken agreed upon in the parliament. In the which if ye can find any fault we shall gladly receive your letters and hear your judgment given thereupon, and shall as gently cause the reasons to be rendered unto you, wherein we do not fear ye shall be satisfied.

But if the love of your country do now move you, and ye have a remorse and desire after so long exile to return your old age into

---

[a] Torn.   [b] The word "bokes" is struck through.

the quietness of the motherly soil and air of that region which first did breed you up, to whom you owe a duty and a natural instinct and zeal to reconcile yourself, which next unto God hath most to claim of you, we shall be content to be mediator for your return. And if herein peradventure the long tarrying abroad in a foreign country do make a vain fear of conscience unto you, we shall not refuse but that ye may come hither upon licence obtained before. And we shall appoint therein some to confer with you. Not doubting but sufficient reason grounded upon God's word shall be given unto you for every point betwixt us and you in variance. And we are not in much fear but that it may well be if ye did see things here with your eyes and conferred with learned men the reasons and causes of our doings, the which now ye do not learn but by report, which in time and distance increaseth and, made of them which favoreth not the thing, is exaggerated to the worse, Ye would peradventure condescend yourself and be in all points satisfied as at this present many both of bishops and other learned men be which at the first did much repine. [*And thus*]^a fare you well.

From Greenwich, the 4th of June, 1549.

Your loving friend, if
ye acknowledge your
dutie to the king's majesty,
E. S.

Endorsed:
    To Cardinall Pole.

Pole's reply to this letter has been lost, but there is an epitome of it given in the late Mr. Rawdon Browne's Venetian Calendar, abridged from the Italian translation of it in St. Mark's library at Venice. It is not dated, but Mr. Rawdon Browne assigns it con-

---

^a The words " And thus " are struck through.

jecturally to Sept. 7, and thinks it was written from Rome. It is very long, and occupies twenty-six pages. The cardinal begins by contrasting the Protector's want of courtesy with the conduct of the late king when Pole had first opened to him his mind about the divorce of his first wife. He mentions, in the course of his letter, that Henry VIII. had restored to his mother the greater part of her property on condition of her pardoning king Henry VII. the death of her brother, the innocent earl of Warwick. He then proceeds to warn him of the danger of the emperor making war with England, and threatens him with the speedy vengeance of God should he persist in his irreligious course and his insolent language. He then accuses him of an impudent lie concerning the agreement of the bishops on the new book of Common Prayer, and denial of the popular commotions on this account, noticing how notorious are the dissensions both amongst the bishops and the people, and how the bishop of Winchester is detained a prisoner in the Tower. Towards the end of the letter he says that he had written thus far before the tidings of the great popular insurrection of the summer of 1549 had reached him; and as he was on the point of giving him his opinion, as requested, on the new book of Common Prayer, he now supersedes the doing so in order to advise Somerset to be wise in time, adding that he will always be able to assist the people, so long as they keep within the limits of their just and religious demands as they have hitherto done; and then alludes to the demand made by the people in their 12th article, saying that he will act for the benefit of the Protector's honour and dignity, so far as is consistent with the common weal and advantage. He ends by reminding his correspondent that what he had prophesied as regards internal commotions had already come to pass; saying that if his first offer of conferring with the Council about the restoration of the Catholic religion had been accepted, the whole cause of the rebellion would have been avoided, and that now it may be possible that a foreign power, called in to the assistance of one of the parties, might eventually crush them both. The letter is more than usually diffuse and prolix, even for cardinal Pole, who seems to have had a particular talent for spinning out his letters to an unnecessary length.

As regards the actual breaking out of the insurrections, to which the following papers refer, probably the earliest contemporary record is contained in a memorandum in *Wriothesley's Chronicle*, vol. ii. p. 13. He says:—" In the month of May there was a commotion of the commons in Somersetshire and Lincolnshire concerning a proclamation for enclosures, and they broke down certain parks of Sir William Harbertes and lord Stourton's, which said Sir William Harberd was sent into Wales for rescue, and slew to death divers of the rebels. Also at Bristowe and divers other shires likewise the commons arose and pulled down parks, and by good policy of the Council and other noblemen of the country they were pacified."

Whether this breaking out was connected at all, or how much it was concerned with the matter of the changes in religion, does not appear from this chronicle; neither does the writer of the diary connect the next insurrection with the order for substituting the Prayer Book of 1549 for the ancient offices of the Church. He notices at p. 15 that in the same year in July—" The commons of Essex and Kent, Suffolk and Norfolk, made insurrections against inclosures, and pulled down divers parks and houses in divers places, and did much hurt;" and adds that—" Also in Devonshire about Exeter, the Devonshire men and Cornish men made insurrections against the king's proceedings, to maintain the Mass and other ceremonies of the pope's law; which were a great number, and camped about the city of Exeter."

The risings do not seem to have been arranged with any previous concert on the part of the different counties, though they were very general throughout the country. There had been one in April of the previous year, 1548, in Cornwall, which was more immediately connected with the apprehended changes in religion. This was speedily suppressed, and a proclamation of pardon issued May 17 to the ringleaders and others, with the exception of the following names:—John Williams, William and John Kilter, John Delion, Richard Trewela, William Annies, John Chikoste, Alene Rowe, Lawrence Britton, Michaiel Dion, Britton, Olyver Ryce, John Tregena, Richard Rowe, Pascoe Trevian, Martin Raffe, Jeremie Roberts, Henrie Tyrleven, John Tribo the elder, Thomas Thyrland, Dion Michaell, John Moryce, Tryball, Sir Martin Gefferye Priest, John Pierre, mariner, William Thomas alias Nenis, Richard Hodge, Tribo the younger, Edmund Irishe and Hugh Mascue alias Waxers alias Parker. The excepted names are printed here because they have been omitted by all historians of the period. A copy of this proclamation is in the Cottonian Library, Titus B II. fol. 25. There is also a copy in the collection of the Society of Antiquaries.

The insurrection in the west was apparently more considerable than any that preceded it. There were no less than three documents drawn up in reply to the requisitions of the insurgents. The first of these may be seen in Holinshed and Foxe, and was printed at the time in a small pamphlet bearing date 8 July, 1549. A first draft of it in abridgment was printed from one of three copies now existing in the Record Office by Tytler, vol. i. p. 178.

This reply, together with the articles as printed, seems to imply that the insurgents afterwards enlarged their demands into fifteen articles, which were answered by Cranmer, a copy of which answer may be seen in the editions of the archbishop's works published at Oxford by Jelf, and in the Parker Society edition. Another answer by Dr. Nicholas Udall is here for the first time printed from the copy in the royal MSS. But Foxe seems to imply that he had seen an answer given by the commons to the king's answer of July 8. Whether any copy of this exists the present editor is unable to say, but that there was such a reply is plainly proved by the fact that a French translation of it is now in the Grenville Library, No. 11,903. The answers given are so sensible and to the point that probably they did not suit Foxe's purpose to produce them. The volume consists of six sheets in fours, *a, b, c, d, e, f*, the last having only three leaves. The preface consists of an eulogium on the people of England for rising against four articles which had been demanded of them by people not understanding the mysteries of religion, to which it says they had made a christian answer, and had risen in arms in defence of their religion, and that the king might not be drawn into error in his young age. The pamphlet itself, which seems very politely written, begins by thanking the king for his reply, which the writers think cannot be his own, but must have been written by those who had long abused his name for the ruin of the country and the oppression of the poor, and who designated the insurgents as traitors, rebels, heretics, and schismatics, after reducing them to slavery and endeavouring to force their souls the way to damnation. They receive the letter with respect as bearing his majesty's name, though having nothing of his spirit in it. They reduce the charges made against them to four heads.

The accusation of rebellion they dispose of by asserting that their governors had passed all limits, performing duties reserved to bishops; the religion of 1200 years is changed at the caprice of two or three. The bishops might have been consulted instead of intimidated; and they answer to the allegation that all must be ordered according to scripture, that they find in scripture submission in temporal things to magistrates, and in things belonging to the soul, obedience to bishops and priests inculcated, and they offer their souls as due to God, and their bodies in dutiful allegiance to the king.

The second article, which treats of five points of doctrine, they regard as an interference with matters which can only be settled by the consent of the whole of Christendom. As regards the restrictions on baptism, poor people cannot always procure sponsors, and will have to break the law if they cannot; as regards the sacrament of the altar they cannot understand how it can nourish the soul, spiritually, except it be miraculously the body and blood of Christ as has been believed for 1,500 years. And as to other ordinances of his majesty, which appear to have some show of reason, they ought to be annulled as scandalous and curious, as having been made by one who has neither authority nor power to manage such matters. As regards the third and fourth articles, in which they are charged with ignorance and rebellion, they refer to various precedents of governors of kings in their nonage who had mismanaged affairs, and had been resisted by the people, and allege that, under the present Council, England was no longer respected as formerly, and had been plunged into unnecessary wars and expenses, and they allude to the possibility of the Emperor's interfering for the restoration of the old religion, the Council having reduced the nation to a state of poverty and paganism. How was it possible for them to be governors who taught the king to despise religion and protect himself by foreign troops? They ask for no pardon because they are rising in defence of the king and against his governors. They conclude in the following words:

Suffer not, sacred Majesty, that their perverse heresy and unhappy opinion of the faith should constrain us to change the religion so holily and happily preserved by your predecessors. And accept your very humble and very obedient subjects whose desire is to be the dogs appointed to keep your house and your kingdom, and the oxen to cultivate your lands, the asses to carry your burdens, which for the defence of your person and of what belongs to you shall be ordained by your commands. We will pray the Lord God, who holds and turns the hearts of kings where He wills, to watch over and conduct your young age to such perfection of sense, of learning, and of virtue as shall be for the salvation of your soul, the comfort and tranquillity of your subjects, the increase and reputation of the glory of God and the weal of Christendom.

The most curious feature about the work is its date. It bears an imprimatur 25 Oct. 1550, more than a year subsequent to the suppression of all the insurrections.

Udall's answer to the rebels, which has never appeared in print, must have been written at the time of the Rebellion, but the present editor knows nothing more about it than can be gathered from internal evidence.

The author, Nicholas Udall, has been hitherto principally known as the person who superintended the publication of the first volume of Erasmus's paraphrase on the New Testament in an English translation, which appeared in 1548-9, in two volumes folio. Udall was himself the translator of the Gospel of S. Luke. The Preface to S. Luke dated " Sept. 30, 1545," is full of compliments to the Queen Dowager for having set on foot the publication, and to the King, " the elected instrumente of God to plucke down the Idolle of the Romishe Antichriste"; and of magnifying the Scriptures as a clear fountain compared with " the muddie lakes and puddles purposely infected with the filthie dregges of our Philistines the Papistes." He speaks as if the translation of S. Luke alone had been entrusted to him by the Queen, and as if he had made a new translation. Yet he for the most part follows the Great Bible of 1539 or Cranmer's of 1540. In the dedication of S. John to the Queen Dowager, which is without date, but which cannot be earlier than 1547, he again compliments the Queen, and then proceeds to compliment the princess Mary, whom he speaks of as being the translator of the commencement of part of the paraphrase, the completion of which she consigned to Dr. Francis Malet; but this dedication contains no vulgar abuse of the Pope or Papists.

In the dedication of the Acts, which is also to the Queen Dowager, he alludes to the recent publication of the " Homilies," and speaks of his having superintended the translation, as he had that of S. Matthew, adding that he had not interfered with the Gospel of S. John because, as he expresses it, " I knew the translatours thereof with whose exquisite dooyngs I might not without the cryme of great arrogancie and presumpcion bee buisee to entremedle."

Udall had long since adopted the opinions of the men of the new learning. He is mentioned as Nicholas Udall of Corpus Christi College, in the narrative of Anthony Dalaber, as amongst those who were in 1528 " suspected to be infected of heresy, from having purchased such books of God's truth as were brought to Oxford by Thomas Garret, fellow of Magdalen College and curate of Honey Lane in London;" and his first appearance in the world of literature is at the coronation of Anne Boleyn, for which he composed some English Verses and Ditties, which were sung partly " at the pageant representing the Progeny of Saint Anne exhibited at Cornhill, besides Leadenhall," partly " at the Conduit in Cornhill," where " was exhibited a Pageant of the Three Graces," and " partly at the little Conduit in Cheapside," where " was exhibited the Judgement of Paris."

They are preserved among the Royal MSS. in the British Museum Library, with the press mark " 18 A. LXIV." and their title is entered in Mr. Gairdner's Calendar on May 31, 1533, as " Verses composed by Nic. Udall and spoken at the pageants in Cornhill, Leadenhall, and Cheapside, at Queen Anne's procession through the city." They are in Latin and English, pp. 29, with an endorsement, " Versis and dities made at the Coronation of Quene Anne." Mr. Gairdner has only printed the heading, which is as follows:—

" Hereafter ensueth a copy of divers and sundry verses, as well in Latin as in English, devised and made partly by John Leland and partly by Nicholas Vuedale, whereof some were set up and some other were spoken and pronounced unto the most high and excellent Queen the lady Anne, wife unto our sovereign lord King Henry the Eight, in many goodly and costely pageants exhibited and showed by the mayor and citizens of the famous city of London, at such time as her Grace rode from the Tower of London through the said city to her most glorious coronation at the monastery of Westminster on Whitson eve in the xxvth year of the reign of our said sovereign lord."

Several of these verses were printed by Mr. Arber in his *English Garner*, vol. ii. p. 52; but they do not possess much merit. It is to be regretted that the whole manuscript was not reproduced. The volume is dated "1 Nov. 1879." Ten years before, he had reprinted Nicholas Udall's "Comedy of Roister Doister," by which his name has become more notorious than it had hitherto been.

Yet he was a man of considerable note in his day, and he forms no exception to the usual description of character, illustrated in the notes which follow, of persons who sailed with the tide and accommodated themselves to all the changes of the reigns of Henry, Edward, and Mary. He was born in Hampshire and belonged to a family who were settled at Wykeham. The date of his birth is uncertain, but it must have been about the beginning of the sixteenth century, probably about 1506. He was elected scholar of Corpus Christi College, Oxford in 1520; four years afterwards he took his degree and was admitted fellow, but seems to have been refused his degree of M.A. in 1526, as Wood thinks, because he was addicted to Lutheranism; but if this was so, he managed to get over the difficulty, and took his degree of M.A. in 1534. He was head master of Eton from 1534 to 1541, when he was dismissed for supposed complicity in a robbery of plate and images by two Eton scholars, J. Hoorde and T. Cheney, assisted by Udall's servant Gregory. The account of this matter, given in the Council Book, is as follows:—

At Westminster, the 14th of March, [1541], being present the duke of Suffolk, the Lord Privy Seal, the Great Chamberlain of England, the Vice Chamberlayn, Sir Thomas Wriothesley, Secretary, Sir Ralph Sadleyr, Secretary.

Nicholas Uvedale, schoolmaster of Eton, being sent for as suspect to be counsel of a robbery lately committed at Eton by Thomas Cheney, John Horde, scholars of the said school, and ..... Gregory, servant to the said schoolmaster, and having certain interrogatories ministered unto him touching the said fact and other felonious trespasses whereof he was suspected, did confess that he did commit buggery with the said Cheney sundry times heretofore and of late, the 6th day of this present month in this present year, at London, whereupon he was committed to the Marshalsea.—Nicolas's *Proceedings of the Council*, vol. vii. p. 153.

He had previously in 1537 been appointed to the vicarage of Braintree, which he held till 1544. At Edward's accession he was made Canon of Windsor, and seems to have been in high favour with Mary, and in her reign was appointed head master of Westminster School. He died in 1556. The following warrant from Queen Mary is reprinted from Kempe's *Loseley MSS.* p. 63:—

By the Quene.

Marye the Quene.

Trustie and welbeloved, we greete you well.

And wheras our welbeloved Nicolas Udall hath at soondrie seasons convenient heretofore shewed, and myndeth hereafter to shewe his dilligence in setting foorth of Dialogues and Enterludes before us fo' ou' regell disporte and recreacion, to th'entent that he maye bee in the better readinesse at all time whan yt shall be our pleasure to call, we will and comaunde you and every of you that at all and every such tyme and tymes, so oft and whan soever he shall nede and require yt for shewing of any thing before us, ye deliver or cause to bee delivered to the said Udall, or to the bringer herof in his name out of our office of revelles, such apparell for his use as he shal thinke necessarie and requisite for the furnisshinge and condigne setting forthe of his devises before us, and suche as maye bee semely to bee shewed in our royall presence, and the same to be restored and redelivered by the said Udall into yo' hande and custodie again. And that ye faile not thus to dooe from time to time as ye tendre oure pleasure till ye shall receive expresse commaundement from us to the contrary herof. And this shal be your sufficient waraunte in this behalf.

Geven under our signett the iii daye of Decembre in the seconde yere of ou' reigne.

To the maister and yeoman of the office of our Revells for the time being, and to their deputie or deputies theire and to ev'ye of them.

In 1553 he was zealous enough for the restored form of religion to be one of those who endeavoured to make Thomas Mountain recant his Protestantism, as appears from Nichols's *Narratives of the Days of the Reformation,* p. 178. In this year he printed a translation of Geminus's *Anatomia,* and afterwards in 1560 published *Floures for Latine speakyng, gathered oute of Terence.* This, together with the translation of the *Apophthegmata* of Erasmus, which appeared in 1542, was published with the initials " N. U.," as was also his translation of Peter Martyr's treatise *Concerning the Sacrament of the Lordes Supper,* which is without date.

The names of the persons who subscribed these articles—are spelt somewhat differently in Grafton and Holinshed and Foxe. The latter gives the names of those who " were taken and apprehended, the chieftains and ringleaders of that mischievous dance, whereof the principal were Humfrey Arundel, Berry, Thomas Underhil, John Soleman, W. Segar, Tempson, and Barret, two priests, Henrye Bray, Henrye Lee, two mayors, with divers other more above specified; all which accordingly afterward were executed." In a previous catalogue of the chief gentlemen, captains, he enumerates "Humfrey Arundell, esquire, governour of the Mount, James Rosogan, John Rosogan, John Payne, Thomas Underhil, John Soleman, William Segar;" and then adds: "Of priests, which were principal stirrers, and some of them governors of the camps, and afterwards executed, were to the number of eight, whose names were Robert Bochim, John Tompson, Roger Barret, John Wolcoke, Wil. Asa, James Mourton, John Barow, Rich. Benet, besides a multitude of other popish priests, which to the same faction were adjoined. The number of the whole rebellion, speaking with the least, mounted little less than to the sum of ten thousand stout traitors."

Grafton's Chronicle gives the names of their first captains as Humfrey Arondell, Wynslade, Holmes, and Bery, or Bury, who, he says, "were taken and sent to London, and there, according to their deserts, had judgment as traitors, and were drawn, hanged, and quartered at Tiborne." Where he adds, that "many of the people of that country that were doers or maintainers of this rebellion were executed among themselves, and many put to great fines and loss of offices and livings, as they had well deserved." Vol. ii. p. 519, ed. 1809, *Fabyan's Chronicle*, gives a somewhat different account. He says: "Their chief captains were taken and brought to the Tower of London, and the 26 day of January after was drawn, hanged, and quartered, and three more at Tiburne. In the chronicle of the Grey Friars the entry relating to this matter is:—

Item, the 27th day of the same month was drawn from the Tower of London unto Tyborne four persons, and there hanged and quartered, and their quarters set about London on every gate; these was of them that did rise in the West country.

The person who signs his name as Henry Braye, mayor of Bodmin, is by mistake called Bowyer by Grafton; who gives the account of his execution, which it did not suit Foxe's purpose to relate. It is as follows:—

" And among other the offenders in this rebellion I thought it well to note twain; for the manner of their execution seemed strange. The first was one Bowyer, who was mayor of a town in Cornwall called Bodmyn. This mayor had been busy among the rebels; but some that loved him said that he was forced thereunto, and that if he had not consented to them they would have destroyed him and his house. But, howsoever it was, this was his end. On a certain day Sir Anthony Kingston, with his company, came, and were right heartily welcomed to the Mayor. And before they sat down to dinner, Sir Anthony, calling the mayor aside, showed him that there must be execution done in that town, and therefore willed him with speed to cause a pair of gallows to be made, that the same might be ready by the end of dinner. The mayor went diligently about it, and caused the same to be done. When dinner was ended, Sir Anthony called the mayor unto him, and asked him if that were ready that he spake to him of, and he answered it was ready. Then he took the mayor by the hand, and prayed him to bring him to the place where the same was and he so did. And when Sir Anthony saw them, he said unto the mayor, 'Think you they be strong enough?' 'Yea, sir,' said he, 'that they are.' 'Well, then,' said Sir Anthony, 'get you even up to them, for they are provided for you.' The mayor cried, 'I trust you mean no such thing to me.' 'Sir,' saith he, 'there is no remedy. You have been a busy rebel, and, therefore, this is appointed for your reward.' So that without longer respite or tarrying then was the mayor hanged. At the same time, also, and near unto the place, there was a miller who had been a very busy varlet in that rebellion, whom, also, Sir Anthony Kingston sought for. But the miller had warning, and he, having a good tall fellow to his servant, called him unto him and said: 'I must go forth; if there come any to ask for me, say that thou art the owner of the mill, and that thou hast kept the same this four years, and in no wise name not me.' The servant promised his master so to do. Afterwards came Sir Anthony Kingston to the miller's house, and called for the miller. The servant answered that he was the miller. 'Then,' said Master Kingston, 'how long has thou kept this mill?' and he answered, 'three years.' 'Well, then,' said he, 'come on, thou must go with me,' and caused his servants to lay hands on him, and brought him to the next tree, saying: 'You have been a rebellious knave, and therefore here shall you hang.' Then cried he, and said that he was not the miller, but the miller's servant. 'Well, then,' said he, 'you are a false knave to be in two tales; therefore hang him up,' said he, and so he was hanged. After he was hanged, one being by, said to Sir Anthony Kingstone, "Surely this was but the miller's man.' 'What, then,' said he, 'could he ever have done his master better service than to hang for him?'"—*Grafton's Chronicle*, p. 520, ed. 1809.

The editor had not intended at first to insert any documents of a later period, but having found two letters of Cranmer's, which have escaped the researches of historians and the editors of Cranmer's works, he thought it well to insert them, as there is no probability of there ever being again an edition of the Archbishop's works printed. The first contains a direction to Dr. Matthew Parker to preach on the 4th Sunday in Lent, 1550, and somewhat resembles the letter of the 12th of February, dated also 1550, directing him to preach on Sunday the 22nd of March, the 6th Sunday in Lent, but though apparently dated in the same year the first belongs to the year 1550 and the other to 1551, showing that Cranmer sometimes used the English and sometimes the foreign style of commencing the year on the 25th of March or the 1st of January respectively.

The other is a letter of some importance as showing how much deference was paid to Bucer's opinion. It has here been printed from a copy, but the English translation appears in Dr. Jenkyns's edition of Cranmer's works as well as in that published by the Parker Society. The addition of the two letters from Dr. William Turner will also throw some light on the character of one who, acting as physician and chaplain in the Protector's family, had more indirect influence on the proceedings of the time than has been commonly thought.

The extracts from the Privy Council Register with which this part of the volume concludes complete the account of ecclesiastical affairs which has partly been given in the last Oxford edition of Burnet's *Reformation* and partly in the *Archaeologia*.

The editor has thought that this preface may be fitly concluded with a specimen of the teaching of the last year of Edward VI. It is a very scarce tract, which he has copied from the only copy he has ever seen. It was written by Martin Micron, the colleague of Alasco, as minister to the Dutch Church, the services of which were intended to be a model for those of the Church of England. The treatise is noticed by Lowndes, who gives a title which differs somewhat in spelling from that of this copy. It is a small volume of sixteen pages, in the British Museum, with the press mark 4326a, in beautiful preservation, and bound in purple morocco—lettered

Micron. A short Instruction, &c. The date, as will be seen, is December 8, 1552. It is entered under the head of C. (T.), and that of Micron, in the recently-published Catalogue of Books in the Library of the British Museum to the year 1640, as being published [London, 1560?] 8vo. Micron was one of the exiles who accompanied Alasco on his departure from England, September 1558, when they were refused admittance into Lutheran assemblies on the ground that they were the Devil's Martyrs.

A short and faythful
Instruction, gathered out of holy Scripture, composed in Questions and An-
sweres, for the edifyeng and comfort
of the symple Christianes, whych
intende worthely to receyve
the holy Supper of the
Lorde.

1 . Corin. xi.
℣ Who so euer shall eate of thys Bread
& drinke of the Cuppe of the Lorde
unworthely, shalbe gylty of
the body and bloud
of the Lorde.

2 . Corin. 4.
℣ I beleve, and therfore I speake. .

℣ To the faythful congregacion of the
Dutch Churche at London. Grace
and peace from God the father, and from our Lor-
de Jesus Christe.

FORasmuche as our Lorde Jesus
Christ hath cōmaunded all true
Christiãs to observe, holde and
use hys holy Supper in remem
braunce of hym tyl his cōmyng
agayne : & seying also that all they whiche-
A   accor

according to the rule of holy scripture neither do examyn, trye nor proue them selves ryghtly before ye recept of the sayd holy supper, neither yet do truly iudge & discerne the difference of it frō other pro phane bankettes, are gyltie of the body and bloude of Christ: and seying also that no man can accordyngly other trye and proue hymselfe, or ryghtly iudge and discerne the body of the Lorde, except he first knowe and understande the foūdacion and groūde of the Christen fayth and religion: Therfore haue we (as they whych are carefull for the health of your soules) wryttē this brefe & shorte sūmary of the moste nedefull and principall partes of the christen religion, to your moste profytable instruction & comforte to thentent that no mā other through ignoraunce shulde despise that cōmaundement of Christ: or els thorough stubburnes should[e] othe[r] not regarde the recepte of that holy Supper, or in any wyse slaunderously or unworthely abuse it. In consideracion whereof we humbly beseche you of charitie and for Christ Jesus sake, that you wyll thankfully take thys my labour, and wyth all diligēce imbrace it, to the furtheraūce of your owne saluaciō, and our ioye in the daye of the Lorde. Gyven in London by
your

your welwyllyng Minister. Marten Micron. 8. Decemb. 1552.

Question. Welbeloved brother or syster N. seyng that thou intēdest to receave with us the holy Supper of the Lorde Jesus Christe, so before all thynges (yf otherwyse thou wylt not make thy self gyltie of hys bodye and bloud) thou muste be a christian : therefore we aske of thee. Wherby knowest thou, that thou arte a Christian.

Answere. Two maner of wayes : fyrste bycause the holy ghost by the witnesse of fayth certifieth me in myne herte & sealeth my conscience, that I am the chylde of God alonly through the merite of Jesus Christe. Secondarely, because that I thorowe the same spirite (as touching the inwarde man) am moued wyllyngly and gladly to the due obedience of god des holy cōmaundementes. *Rom.* 8.
2 Cor. 1.

Question. Whych are the cōmaūdemētes. Answere Those whych God hymselfe cōmaūded, & Moses in the .xx Cha. of Exo. wrote, in maner and forme folowyng.

¶ The ten cōmaundementes.

I am the Lorde thy God, which brought the out of the lande of Egypte out of the house of bondage :
Thou shalt haue none other Goddes but me.

A 2　　Thou

2. Thou shalt not make unto thy selfe any graven ymage, nor the lykenesse of any thynge that is in heaven aboue, or in the earth beneth, nor in the water under the earth, thou shalt not bowe downe to thē nor worship them: for I the Lorde thy God am a gelouse God, and viset the sinnes of the fathers upon the chyldren unto the thyrd and fourth generacion of them that hate me, & shewe mercy unto thousandes in them that loue me and kepe my commaundementes.

3. ⁋ Thou shalte not take the name of the Lorde thy God in vayne. For the Lorde wyll not holde hym gyltlesse that taketh hys name in vayne.

4. ⁋ Remember that thou kepe holy ye Sabboth daye. Sixe dayes shalt thou labour and do all that thou haste to do, but the seventh day is the sabboth of the Lorde thy God. In it thou shalt do no maner of worke, thou and thy sone, & thy doughter, thy man servaunt and thy mayd servaunt, thy cattel, and the straunger that is wythin thy gates, for in syxe dayes the Lorde made heaven and earthe, the sea and all that in them is, and rested the seuenth day. Wherfore the Lorde blessed the seuenth daye, and halowed it.

5. ⁋ Honour thy father & thy mother, that thy dayes maye be longe in the lande whych

whych the Lorde thy God gyveth the.
¶ Thou shalt do no murther. 6
¶ Thou shalt not cōmitte adultery. 7
¶ Thou shalt not steale. 8
¶ Thou shalt not beare false wytnesse a- 9
gaynst thy neyghbour.
¶ Thou shalt not couet thy neyghbours 10
house, y^u shalt not couet thy neyghbours
wyfe, nor hys servaunt, nor hys mayde,
nor hys Oxe, nor his Asse, nor anything
that is hys.

Question. Howe are these cōmaundement-
tes deuyded?

Answere. Into two tables, whereof the first   Ex. 23, 34.
pertayneth to God, and the other to oure   Deute. 9.
neyghbour.

Question. What learnest thou in the foure
fyrst cōmaundementes whyche belonge
alonly unto God?

Answere. That I shall set my fayth, truste   Esa. 44.
and confidence upon no creature, but up   Psal. 115.
on God alone. And hym not wyth yma-   Mat. 15.
ge service or any other counterfayt wor-   Exo. 25.
shippyng, but alone in spirite and truthe   1 Reg. 15.
shall worship and serue, & shall also day-   Joh. 4.
lye prayse hys holye name, and exercyse   Esa. 48.
my selfe diligently not onely in hearyng   Ephe. 5.
hys holy worde, but also in the use of his   Luk. 8, 10.
Sacramentes.

Question. What learnest thou in the sixe cōmaundementes folowynge, whyche be-

longe

longe to our neyghbour?

Answere. That I shalbe obediēt unto thē whome God hathe set over me, and that I shal by no maner of meanes be hurtfull to my neyghbour in hys body, wyfe, famylie, goodes, honour, name, fame or estimacion, no not so muche as w^t any euel lust, but in al godly and honest thin ges shalbe to hym an helpe and furtherāce.

Question. Haste thou these cōmaundemen tes in all pointes so perfytlye fulfylled, that y^u art able to stande in the iudgemēt?

Answere. Och naye: for seyng that ye lawe is spiritual, and I am carnal, I can not but confesse my selfe in many thingis a gaynst that holy lawe to have offended, not onelye in leauyng undone that that is therin cōmaunded, but also in doynge that, that is therin forbydden.

Deute. 27.
Gala. 3.
Jaco. 2.

Question. Seyng that man because of one synne by the sentence of the lawe is condemned and excluded out of the kyngdōe of God, howe shalt thou then be saued, for asmuche as in many thynges thou hast synned, and because that no man can entre into Goddes kyngdom unlesse he be cleane from all synne?

Answere. My saluacion dependeth onely of mere mercy and grace thorowe Jesus Christ, whyche wythout al my deseruing hath taken and accepted me for one of
hys

hys members, & also hath made me partaker of all hys gracious merites & good dedes, because wyth a repentaunt herte I beleve undoutedly to be saued thorow hym.

Question. Seying the grounde of thy fayth is set alone upō Jesus Christe, wylt thou shortlye declare, what thou belevest on Christe?

Answere. I beleve that Jesus Christ in one persone is very God of God: and very mā of man: and also that he is my only mediatour, aduocate, intercessour, hyghe preest, kynge and Prophete, whyche hath taken upon hym my curse and condempnacion, and hath to me agayne re-restored frely hys holynes and righteous nes, as it is most briefly comprysed in the chiefe articles of our Christen fayth.

Rom. 1. 9.
John. 1. 3.
1. Joh. 2.
1. Tim. 2.
Heb. 7. 8.
Deute. 18.
Act 3. 7.
Gala. 3.
Roma. 8.

Question. Whyche are the chief articles of the Christen fayth? *Answere.*
❡ I beleue in God the father almyghty, maker of heaven and earth, &c.

Question. What understāndest thou by that worde (*I beleue*) as thou confessest sayeing: I beleue in God the Father: I beleue in God the Sonne: I beleue in God the holy Ghost.

Answere. I meane thys, that I set all my fayth, truste and confidence in God the father who hathe made me and all the

A 4 worlde

worlde: In God the Sonne, who hathe redemed me and all mankynde: and in God the holy Ghost, who sanctifieth me and all the chosen people of God.

Question. Belevest thou then, that God the father, the sonne, and the holy Ghost are one true God?

Answere. Yea moste surely, for so all the holy scripture teacheth us, and therof are we admonyshed in our baptym wherin we are baptysed in the name of ye father and of the sonne, and of the holy Ghoste.

Question. Hathe Christ ordened no sure outward exercises and certaine markes and tokens wherby hys congregacion maye be knowen and discerned from all other churches and sectes?

Answere. Yes doutles, and that because of oure weaknesse, that we throwe them maye be exercysed and strengthened in a sure fayth, & also by the due administracion of them may so muche the better be styrred up to the due obedience of the forsayd cōmaundementes of God.

⁌ Sure markes and tokens of
Christes true Churche.

Question. What are ye sure exercises markes & tokēs of the true church of Christ?

1. *Answere.* The fyrst is, the syncere preachyng of Goddes holy worde.

2. The seconde is, the ryght use of the Sa-

cra-

cramentes instituted and ordeyned of Christe.

And the thyrde is, the christen correccio 3 of the congregacion. In whych thre thinges all true christianes ordenarely with all diligence and obedience ought to exercyse them selves, whereby also they are seperated & disseuered frō al other sectes.

Question. Wherein standeth the syncere preachyng of the holy worde of God.

Answere. In the ryght declarynge of the lawe, and of the holy gospel, whereof hytherto I have made my confession.

❡ Of the Sacramentes.

Question. What are the Sacramentes?

Answere. They are holy exercises, seales & effectual tokens of remembraunce, ordeyned of the Lorde himselfe for the comforte of his congregacion. In wych exercyses the free forgevenesse of synnes in and by Christ Jesus, before our eyes, and that most clearly and euidentlye is set out and sealed. And besyde that, we are thereby admonyshed of our duty both towardes God, and to our neyghbour.

Question. How many such Sacramentes are there?

Answere. Two, that is: Baptyme. And the holy Supper of the Lorde.

❡ Of Baptyme.

Question. What is Baptyme?

A 5   Answer

Answere. It is an holy ordinaūce of Christ in the recept whereof all the membres of hys congregacion (in whych yonge children are conteyned also) are baptysed wᵗ water in the name of the father, and of the Sonne, and of the holy Ghost.

Question. What comforte hast thou of thy Baptyme?

Answere. Great cōforte. For albeit of nature I am uncleane & the child of wrath, yet neverthelesse by fayth in the promyses of mercy am I fully persuaded, that thorowe Jesus Christe I am assuredly & certeynleye accepted and taken into the grace and favour of God, as my body in the recept of baptyme is besprenkled and wasshed wyth water.

Question. What more comforte haste thou of Baptyme?

Answere. Forsoth thys: that I may all my lyfe longe haue a contenuall forgeuenes of my synnes, into the whych thorow the devels temptacion & myne owne weaknes and fraylnes I may chaunce to fall: whensoever I wyth a repētant hert in spirite and fayth thorow Jesus Christ do praye and aske pardon and forgevenesse of the same.

Question. Whereof moreover arte thou admonished in thy baptyme?

Answere. Truly that I shal al my life lōge for-

Gala. 3

forsake the devell, the worlde, and all the fylthy lustes of my fleshe, and wyth al diligence continually walke in a new and godly lyfe.

⁋ Of Christes holy Supper.

Question. What is the holy Supper of the Lorde?

Answere. It is an holy soule banket, ordened of Jesus Christe, for an effectuall remembraūce of hys death, especially that he upon the crosse once for all offered up hys innocent bodye, and there also shed hys moste precious bloude for the forgevenes of synnes. Math. 26. 1 Cor. 10. He. 7. 10.

Question. Wherefore intendest thou to receyue the holy Supper of our Lorde Jesus Christe?

Answere. Because my Lorde and Maister Jesus Christe hath wylled, ordeined and cōmaunded it to be receyued in remembraunce of hys death, for the synguler cō forte, profyt and cōmoditie of me, and of all the worthy receyuers of it. Math. 28. Mar. 14. 1 Cor. 11.

Question. What profyt and comforte fyndest thou in the due and worthye recepte therof.

Answere. Truely, in the ryght ministracion therof, it is lyuely and effectually set out to me myserable synner as it were before myne eyes, beaten into my remēbraunce, yea wytnessed and sealed to my

feble

feble conscience through the holy Ghost, that Christ hath once for al upŏ the crosse made an euerlastyng full and parfyte oblacion and sacrifice for my synnes, and that I also beleuynge in hym haue thorough hȳs death and oblaciō once made, forgyvenes of my synnes wyth comfort and full truste of euerlastynge lyfe as ve rely, truly and certeinlye as I at hys table eate of the breade broken and drinke of the cuppe of the Lorde, whyche (after the use of holy scripture and maner of Sacramentes) he ealleth his body and bloude.

Question. What fourme, maner, and propertie of speakyng useth the holy scriptu re in all Sacramentes?

Answere. Verely, that the outwarde partes or matter of the Sacramentes in the holy scripture are decked, bewtifyed and adourned wyth the names of the mysteries and hyd thynges, whych they signifye: to thentent it myght be knowē wher unto they were pperly ordeined, and wherfore they shulde be receyued. As circumcision is called the Covenaunt of God: the Paschlambe is intitled the Passeover or passe by: Baptyme is named ye washing away of synne or bath of the new byrth. Even so the holy Supper is called the body of Christ broken for us, and his bloud shedde for us.

Heb. 7. 10.

Gen. 17.
Exo. 12.
Tit. 3.
Actu. 22.
1 Pet. 3.
1 Cor. 10 and 11.

Question

Questi. Is yᵉ very natural body & bloud of Christ necessarely present here upō erth, so that in yᵉ supper it may be catē & drōkē. *Answere.* Nay truely: For fyrst it were utterly contrary to the nature & propertie of al Sacramentes. Againe, the opinion of corporal presence obscureth the spiritual eating & drinkyng of the body and bloud of Christ, whych al the old fathers (as S. Paul sayeth) dyd: whych spiritual eatyng and drynkyng alone in holy scripture is required unto saluaciō. Besyde that, it defaceth and in a manner blotteth out the very true nature & propertie of Christes body, whyche was made of the substance of the virgine Mary hys mother, and not of breade. Further it maketh the preestly office of Christe of none effecte, or at the least unsufficient. For in that office he once for all offred hys body and shed hys bloud for our redempcion, and doth not yet dayly seperate & diuide his bloud from his glorified body again Moreover, thys corporal presence is contrary to the article of hys ascension and our continuall lokyngs for hys returne at the last daye. Finally, this fond ymaginacion of Christes bodely presence setteth out & describeth to us suche a Christ as in the wrytynges of the prophetes & apostles is utterly unknowen.

1 *Syxe reasons agaynst the corporal presēce of Christ in the supper.*

2

1 Cor. 10.

3

4

5

6

Question

Question. Wherof els art thou admonished in the use of Christ's holy Supper?

Answere. Truly, that I w^t all myne herte shall thanke my Lorde Jesus Christ for thys great benefite of my redemption.

And this thankefulnesse by hys gracious favoure, wyth pacience, loue, mortificacion of carnall desyres, sobernesse of lyfe and conuersacion, and finally wyth a continual and free cōfession of hys holy name, shal I signifye and declare unto my lyues ende.

⁋ Of Christen correccion.

Question. Where is the correccion of the Churche commaunded of Christ?

Answere. Verely in the .18. cha. of S. Mat. gospel under these wordes: yf thy brother trespase against the. Go & tel hē hys faut betweene hym & thee alone. yf he heare the, thou hast woune thy brother. But yf he heare the not, then take yet with thee one or two, that in the mouthe of two or thre wytnesses euery matter may be stablyshed. yf he heare not them: tel it unto the congregacion. yf he heare not the cō gregacion, let hym be unto the as an hea then man, & as a publican. Verily I say unto you: what so ever ye bynd on earth shalbe bounde in heauen: and what so euer, ye lose on earth, shalbe losed in heaven

ven. Thys ordinaunce of Christ S. Paul
also confirmeth & putteth in use as appea 1 Cor. 5.
reth in the 1. epistle unto the Corinthes.
Question. What is the correccion of the
Churche of Christ.
Answere. It is an ordinaunce of Christ, Math. 18.
through which euery christian is bound Luke. 17.
orderly after the worde of God, lovingly Rom. 15.
Collo. 3.
to admonishe hys brother of hys faute : & Heb. 3. 12.
also agayne willingly & gladly to receive Jaco. 5.
and take admonicion, warnyng & chari- 1 Cor. 5.
table rebukes for the same. Or els yf he 1 Thes. 5.
refuse and utterly despyse all suche godly
admoniciōs and warnynges (so that ac-
cordynge unto Christes rule they be orderly done) then by the authoritie of goddes worde he ought to be excōmunicated
& put out of the cōgregation & delyuered
to sathan : and as an heythen & publican
to be estemed, reputed & taken, unto such
a tyme he returne, amēde & recōcile him
selfe agayne unto the congregation.
Question. Seying that subtile sathā seketh 1 Petri. 5.
al wayes & meanes to pluck awaye man
from hys fayth and obedience to Jesus
Christ, how shalt thou thē be able to stāde
in thy profession.
Answere. By the only grace of God & such Mar. 13.
meanes as he hath ordeined, which are : Ephe. 6.
Jaco. 4.
watchyng, resistyng and prayeng &c.
Question. To whom prayest thou ? & howe ?
Answere

Answere. To God onely throwe Jesus Christ, in spirite and truthe.

Question. For what thinge prayest thou?

Answere. I praye fyrste for those thynges that are to the preferrement and aduancement of goddes glory & our owne soules health. And then for suche thinges as are profytable and necessary for the susteynyng of thys lyfe, but so as they agre and stande wyth the wyl and pleasure of God: And finally, that it may please god to delyver and defende us from all thynges that are to the hynderaūce of his glorye & to the decay of the health of our soules. Al whych thynges are cōprised in the praier which Christ taught his disciples: which is: Our father which art in he. &c.

1.

2.

3.

Question. Wylt thou accordyng to this cō fession of thy fayth lyve: And wyth al diligēce obserue the discipline of the church, and bond of charitie: & also (al envie, malice & hatred of herte set aparte) wilt thou reconcile thy selfe & be at one with al mē with whome thou arte at variaunce?

Answere. Yea by the grace of God, so farre as is possible to thys myne infirmitie & weaknes, yᵉ whych I shal earnestly pray unto God to strengthen me dayly more and more. Amen.

⁋ Translated out of Dutch into Englyshe, By T. C.

CONTENTS.

	PAGE
I.—Letter from the Duke of Somerset to the Marquis of Dorset and the Earl of Huntingdon	1
II.—Dr. William Turner's Letter to Cecil, complaining that the Deanery of Winchester is given to another	3
III.—Draft of Memorial to the Sheriffs	4
IV.—Licence to Mr. Gregory to preach under instructions from the Lord Privy Seal	6
V.—Similar Licence to Dr. Reynolds	7
VI.—Instructions to Lord Russell from the Council	8
VII.—Lord Russell's Letter to the Duke of Somerset explaining the state of affairs in the west country, written in June, 1549	11
VIII.—Memorial of the Council to the Justices of Peace in Devonshire, of the 26th of June, 1549	12
IX.—Letter from Lord Arundel to Secretary Petre, June 29, 1549	14
X.—Letter from the Council to the Lord Privy Seal, advising him how to act	15
XI.—Supplication to the Council from Staines deprecating the destruction of their Bridge, June, 1549	19
XII.—Letter of the Council to the Princess Mary of the 7th July, 1549, sent after the appearance before them of Dr. Hopton her chaplain	20
XIII.—Letter from the King to the Princess Mary on the subject of the Mass	21
XIV.—Letter from the Council to Lord Russell announcing re-inforcements, July 10, 1549	22
XV.—Somerset to the Lord Privy Seal, promising to send Lord Grey de Wilton	25
XVI.—Letter from Somerset to Lord Russell, of the 17th July, mentioning the Rebellion in Norfolk	27
XVII.—The Council to Lord Russell again promising help by Lord Grey de Wilton	29

CONTENTS.

	PAGE
XVIII.—Letter from Somerset and the Council to Lord Russell promising help by Lord Warwick	30
XIX.—Letter from the Council to Lord Russell in answer to his of July 22	34
XX.—Letter from the Council to Lord Russell announcing the mission of Sir William Herbert	35
XXI.—Letter from the Council in answer to the supplication of the Commons of Cornwall	36
XXII.—Letter from the Council to Lord Russell giving an account of the examination of Sir John Arundel	38
XXIII.—Letter from the Council to Lord Russell with further instructions	39
XXIV.—Proclamation to Justices of Peace issued in July, 1549	43
XXV.—Letter from the Council to Lord Russell declining to send him more troops	44
XXVI.—Letter from Somerset to Lord Russell, announcing the Declaration of War by the French King	46
XXVII.—Letter from the Council to Lord Russell advising him to diminish his forces	47
XXVIII.—Letter of Thanks from the Council to Lord Russell	50
XXIX.—Another Letter of the Council to Lord Russell, limiting the number of his advisers	52
XXX.—Letter from Somerset to Lord Russell, directing him how to act as regards the Insurgents	53
XXXI.—Letter from the Council to Lord Russell dwelling on the dangers from an apprehended French Invasion	56
XXXII.—Letter from the Council to Lord Russell, authorising him to bestow Knighthood on such as he thought deserving of the honour	60
XXXIII.—Letter from the Council to Lord Russell desiring him to send up the Ringleaders for trial	63
XXXIV.—Letter from the Council to Lord Russell, requiring him to thank those who had contributed to the victory over the rebels	65
XXXV.—Letter from the Council to Lord Russell directing him how to act as regards pardoning the rebels	65
XXXVI.—Letter from the Council to Lord Russell complaining of his having exceeded his instructions	68
XXXVII.—Letter from the Council to Lord Russell, ordering him to take down the Bells from the Churches	73

CONTENTS.

PAGE

XXXVIII.—Letter from Somerset to Lord Russell, blaming him for not having executed Paget - - - - 74
XXXIX.—The Protector's Letter to Lord Russell recommending merciful dealing with the rebels - - - - 74
XL.—The King's Letter summoning his subjects to defend him and his Uncle. Written Oct. 5th, 1549 - - - - 76
XLI.—Warrant of the King to Sir Harry Seymour to raise Men and bring them to Hampton Court to defend him from the Conspiracy. An original, signed by Edward and Somerset - - - - - - - 77
XLII.—Letter from Somerset to Lord Russell and Sir William Herbert, summoning them to Hampton Court - - 78
XLIII.—Another Letter from Somerset to Lord Russell and Sir William Herbert with instructions to be given by the bearer, Lord Edward Seymour - - - - - 79
XLIV.—Letter from the King to Lord Russell and Sir William Herbert begging them to come to him for his defence - 79
XLV.—Letter from the Council at London summoning the people to their assistance against Somerset - - - - 80
XLVI.—Letter from Somerset to Lord Russell urging him to come to Windsor as speedily as possible. Written Oct. 6, 1549 - 82
XLVII.—Letter from the Council at London to the King detailing their grievance against Somerset. Draft partly in Petre's, partly in Wriothesley's hand - - - - 83
XLVIII.—Original draft of a Letter from the Lords of the Council in London to the Council at Windsor intimating their intention to remove Somerset from the office of Protector - 86
XLIX.—Letter from Somerset to the Council at London expressing wonder at the detention of Secretary Petre - - 88
L.—Lord Russell's and Sir William Herbert's letter to the Duke of Somerset expressing disapproval of his line of action - 90
LI.—Circular Letter from the Council at London to Sheriffs and Justices of Peace of the Counties - - - - 92
LII.—Letter from Lord Morley to the Council in London taking part with them - - - - - - - 94
LIII.—A Proclamacion set forth by the state and bodie of the Kynge's Maiestes Counsayle now assembled at London, conteinyng the very trouth of the Duke of Somerset's evel Government, and false and detestable Procedinges - - 95
LIV.—Letter from the King to the Council in London deprecating extreme measures against Somerset - - - 102

CONTENTS.

	PAGE
LV.—Letter of the Lords of the Council at London to the Council at Windsor	104
LVI.—Letter from Sir Thomas Smith to Secretary Petre stating his difficulties	106
LVII.—Draft of a Proclamation offering a Reward to any who shall give information of Maintainers of the Duke of Somerset's Traitorous proceedings	108
LVIII.—Letter from Christopher Mount to the Duke of Somerset on the progress of Lutheranism, written from Strasburg, Oct. 10, 1549	110
LIX.—Letter from Lord Russell and Sir William Herbert to Somerset, in answer to his letter of the 5th of October	112
LX.—Minute of the Despatch to the Ambassadors denouncing Somerset	113
LXI.—Letter from Warwick and the other Lords acting with him countermanding the previous order to repair to them	118
LXII.—Draft of a Letter from the Council to the Lieutenant of the Tower ordering the close confinement of the servants of the prisoners	120
LXIII.—Inventory of Goods conveyed away by the Duke of Somerset's Servants and others	120
LXIV.—Account of the King's Goods taken by the Duke of Somerset	123
LXV.—A List of Prisoners in the Tower at the end of October or beginning of November, 1549	124
LXVI.—Edward's Letter to the Bishops ordering them to call in and destroy the old Books of the Church	127
LXVII.—Cranmer's Letter to Parker ordering him to preach at Paul's Cross on March 16, 1550	130
LXVIII.—Cranmer's Letter to Bucer about the use of vestments	130
LXIX.—Letter from Dr. William Turner to Cecil, asking for the Presidentship of Magdalen College, Oxford	131
LXX.—Letter from Dr. William Turner to Cecil about Preferment, Jan. 5, 1551	133
LXXI.—Letter from Warwick to Paget, suggesting that Russell, now Earl of Bedford, should be made acquainted with what was going on	134
LXXII.—Extracts from the Council Book of Edward VI. relating to Church matters	135

UDALL'S ANSWER TO THE COMMONERS OF DEVONSHIRE AND CORNWALL - - - - - - - - 141

TROUBLES CONNECTED WITH THE PRAYER BOOK OF 1549.

I.—LETTER FROM THE DUKE OF SOMERSET TO THE MARQUIS OF DORSET AND THE EARL OF HUNTINGDON.

[Domestic Papers of Edward VI. vol. vii. art. 31.]

After our right harty commendacions to your good L. Wheras in the most parties of the Realme sundry lewde persons have attempted t'assemble themselfs, and first seking redresse of enclosures,[a] have in some places by seditious priests and other yvel peple set forth to seke restitucion of tholde bluddy lawes; and some fall to spoile to prevent all inconvenyences with you, we pray you

[a] The earliest notice of these rebellions is in Wriothesley's *Chronicle*, vol. ii. p. 13, where he says: "In the month of May there was a commotion of the commons in Somersetshire and Lincolnshire concerning a proclamation for enclosures, and they broke down certain parks of Sir William Harbertes and Lord Stourtons, which said Sir William Harberte was sent into Wales for rescue, and slew and put to death divers of the rebels. Also at Bristowe and divers other shires, likewise the commons arose and pulled down parks, but by good policy of the Council and other noblemen of the county they were pacified." The following extract from the Council Book throws some further light on the proceedings of the Council:—

"3 Junii.—To the Commissioners in Cornwall to proceed with as convenient speed as might be to the execution of the traitors there as they tendered the King's majesty's pleasure. Albeit some of them thought the number appointed to be executed there was over great, yet they were required to proceed to the execution of his Majesty's commandment without delay; and to the intent they might be certain of the number and persons appointed to suffer, and in what places the same should be executed, there was another bill of the same sent, enclosed herein."

to cause the proclamation sent herewith to be published by the sheriffs which shal withstand yvel brutes, for yorself and the gentlemen of the shire of Leycestre by your admonicion.

We pray you to be holly in a redynes to represse th'attempts in the beginneng if any chaunce there. Mary lest the peple shulde by brutes conceyve ye wolde overrunne them before they commit yvel, it shalbe good ye and the gentlemen doo kepe a sundre at your severall dwellings, wherby also ye shalbe at the less charge.

Thus fare your good L. right hartely well.

From Syon the xjth of June, 1549.

Your L. assured frende,

E. SOMERSET.[a]

To our veric good lords
the lord Marques
Dorcett and Th'erle
of Huntington.[b]

---

[a] This was the Lord Protector, Edward Seymour, the brother of Jane Seymour, the third wife of Henry VIII. created Viscount Beauchamp in 1536, and Earl of Hertford in 1537. He was made a Privy Councillor and Knight of the Garter in 1541, Captain of Jersey and Lord Admiral in 1542, and afterwards in the same year Lord Warden of the Scottish border, Lord Chamberlain in 1543, Commander at Boulogne in 1545, lieutenant in the North in the same year, and in 1546 the King's lieutenant in parts beyond the sea. Lastly in 1547, Duke of Somerset and Earl Marshall of England.

[b] The first person addressed in this letter is Henry Grey, third Marquis of Dorset, who succeeded his father Thomas in 1530, and was created Duke of Suffolk Oct. 11, 1551, and afterwards beheaded Feb. 23, 1554. He had married Frances, eldest daughter of Charles Brandon, Duke of Suffolk, whose two brothers (sons of the Duke by his last wife) had died of the plague, both having succeeded to the dukedom, July 14, 1551. She was the daughter of Mary Tudor, the French Queen, and mother of Lady Jane Grey. The other is Francis Hastings, Earl of Huntingdon, who succeeded to the title on the death of his father George in 1544, and died in 1561.

II.—Dr. William Turner's[a] Letter to Cecil, complaining that the Deanery of Winchester is given to another.

[Domestic Papers of Edward VI. vol. vii. art. 32, P. 276.]

To his singulare good and Christiane frende master W. Cicell[b] be this letter delyvered.

Master Cicell,

i thank yow for your paynes tayken about the obteynyng of my lycence, which if i had sealed i wold shortly occupi in Yorkshyre, for the Archbishop of York[c] hathe writen unto me to cum to

---

[a] Dr. William Turner was domestic physician to the Protector Somerset, and appears to have been in deacon's orders, but was not ordained priest for more than three years after this, by Ridley, December 21, 1552. He was a licensed preacher. He wrote several works on medical and other subjects. His principal theological work is a Dialogue against the Mass and the Priesthood, published without date. He died July 7, 1568.

[b] William Cecil, afterwards created Baron Burleigh, Feb. 25, 1571, was at this time Secretary of State, having been appointed to that office in September of the preceding year, 1548. He was now in his 29th year, having been born Sept. 13, 1520. His introduction to the Protector's notice was through Sir John Cheke, whose sister Mary he had married, August 8, 1541. This lady died, Feb. 22, 1543, and he soon afterwards married Mildred, the daughter of Sir Anthony Cook, the King's tutor. This strengthened his interest with the Protector, and he was thrown with him into prison, in November, 1549. After his release he served under the Duke of Northumberland, and his signature is appended to the device for making Lady Jane Grey Queen, he himself vindicating his conduct in this, by saying that he signed merely as witness of the King's signature at Edward's earnest intercession. He managed to keep in with all parties till his death on the 4th of August, 1598.

[c] This was Robert Holgate, who succeeded Edward Lee in the Archbishopric of York in 1544, and was deprived at the beginning of the reign of Queen Mary. He had been provincial of the monks of the order of Sempringham, and is chiefly known as having been brought before the Council to answer to a charge brought against him by one Norman of having taken away his wife from him. Harpsfield describes him as being at that time of about fourscore years of age, and says that the lady was a young girl of fourteen or fifteen. He speaks of her not as the wife, but " as a person betrothed to another man, and by very force kept from him, as I have heard the party myself confess and complain in this Queen's time, and that he intended to procure process out for him. But whether the Archbishop's death or some composition stayed the suit or to what end the matter came I know not."

hym with all the spede that may be, whiche thyng i wold gladly do, if i had theyr to my lordis gracis consent who (as i heard yow say) intended that i shulde go to Winchester to be occupied theyr. If that i myght have a lyvyng for me and myne there i wold gladly do as my lordis grace requirethe, but that an other man[a] shuld have the deanery and do nothyng and i shuld be bound to be a workman, *sola spe venturæ, nescio quando, præbendæ, alendus,* the love that i bear unto my wyfe and chylder will not suffer me. My chylder have bene fed so long with hope that they ar very leane; i wold fayne have them fatter, if it were possible. I pray you know of my lordis grace what is hys gracis pleasure in thys mater; i cannot dwell here all thys next cummyng wynter. Sy[r] i hear say that ye have certayn howses to let in London; if that they be not all promysed i pray you let mastres auder my mother in law (whom i thynk ye know) have one of them, for as myche as ye wold take of another. She intendeth to dwell by hyr chylder in London. i trust that ye shall be honestly payed it that she promiseth you.

Fare well from Ken,
the xi. of iune [1549].

By me WYLLYAM TURNER.

III.—DRAFT OF MEMORIAL TO THE SHERIFFS.
[Domestic Papers of Edward VI. vol. vii. art. 37.]

Trustie and welbeloved we great you well.

And where we are advertised that Certaigne of our Subjects hath of late in that our county of Devon repyned and rebelled agaynst the

---

[a] Sir John Mason, Knight, had been appointed to the deanery of Winchester in succession to William Kingesmyll in 1549, and held it till the beginning of Queen Mary's reign. The mother-in-law alluded to in the letter is the wife of George Auder, an alderman of Cambridge, whose daughter Jane was first married to Turner, and afterwards to Richard Cox, Bishop of Ely.

most godlie procedyngs [*in the last sessions*] of parliament at Westm. in the last sessions thereof, concernyng the boke set furth by our authorite in full parlament of the rite and ceremonies to be used in our churche of England and Ireland and all our domynions, of which we do mych marvell that eny of our subjects should be so ignoraunt, disobedient, and dysloiall unto us to gaynsay thact of all our hole realm and the common agreement of both our spiritualtie and temporalite there gathered together, and altho the same doth deserve most extreme punishment as agaynst Rebelles and Traitors; yet of our abondaunt mercye [*with th'advice of our most entierly beloved*] are desirous to shew to all our lovyng subjects by th'advice of our most entierly beloved uncle the L. P. governor of our person and protector of all our realms, dominions and subjects, and the rest of our privy Council, we are content to accept this hitherto done to have been done rather of ignoraunce then of malice, and at the mocion of some light and naughty persons then of any evill will that our loving subjects doth bear to us or to our procedyngs.

And therefor at the sute of diverse gentlemen who hath made humble sut for them by thadvis aforsaid have pardoned, and by these presents do pardon, all the said contempts and offences heretofore past. So that the said offenders shall never hereafter be trobled nor vexed for eny such offence hereafter paste and done, upon condycion that hereafter they do behave themself towards us as the dewty is of lovyng and obedyent subjects. In obeyeing the godly lawes and statutes by our authorite promulgated and set forth. The which thyng we will ye shall promulgat and declare accordyngly, willyng, and streigthly chargyng you and every of you yf eny maner person after this our writing, pardon, and commandment shall eftsones attempt to repugne or resist our godly procedyngs in the lawes by us and our parliament made by gathering or assembling in companyes or otherwise to apprehend the same. And to se our lawes and statuts duely and severcly executed agaynst all such offendors as apperteyneth.

In witnes whereof we have signed this present with our hand. By us under our signet at our manor of Richmond the xx[th] of June, 1549, and in the third year of our reigne.

Endorsed as follows :—

xxth of June, 1549. M. to the Sheriffs, Justices of peace and rest of the gentlemen in Devonshire touching them that would not reade the booke of prairs.[a]

IV.—LICENCE TO MR. GREGORY TO PREACH UNDER INSTRUCTIONS FROM THE LORD PRIVY SEAL.

[Petyt MSS. No. 538, vol. xlvi. fol. 431.]

The Lord Protector and the Counsell the xxiij[th] of June to Mr. Gregorye.

After our hartie commendations: Forasmoche as yt is acceptable to God to have his people leade theyre lyves in the feare and knowledge of hym and thereuppon also folowythe as by good order quyet and [due] obedyence of all people to theyr prynces and heds, the which no wyse so convenyently can be brought to passe as to have frequent and dyscrete preaching of his hollie word and commandement; we have thought yt mete s[ence] our verie good Lord the lord pryvie Seall i[s] appoynted under the Kyngs Ma[tie] to have the [whole] governaunce of that west parte of realme durin[g] his Mai[ties] pleas[r], that ye shuld both be lycens[ed], and commanded by us on the Kyngs Ma[ties] beh[alf] to preache and

[a] After the following memorial there are three pages vacant. Then follow two leaves belonging to it, on the back of the second of which is the endorsement and date, and on the obverse of the first is—

"Fynally, the sayd L. Russell shall ones every [*moneth at lest he do*] moneth att the lest advertise hither of the state of the countreys committed to his governance, and as any other maters of importance shall occurre to sygnifie oftener, whereupon order shall be gyven as shall appertayn."

oppenly declayre with sincerytye the word of god in su[ch] publyke place and auditorye as the same lord pr[yvie] Scall shall solycyte you, whose dyscryssyone [and] grave wysdome the Kyngs Matie and we so [myche] esteme that wythout his order and certen know[ledge] we will ye take no labour uppon you. [And for] your delygence and studye herein, although the same be your dewtie, and of god prescrybed, yet [we] will have yt in good remembraunce and rewarde y[ou] to your contentation.

And so we b[id you] far[e] well. From Richemound the xxiii^th d[ay of] June, A° 1549.

[Your lo]ving ffreinds,

E. SOMERSET.

W. SANCT JOHN.

R. RICHE CANC.   A WYNGFELD.

F. SHREWESBURY.   ARRENDELL.

EDWARD MOUNTAGU.

CICILL.[a]

V.—SIMILAR LICENCE TO DR. REYNOLDS.

[Petyt MSS. No. 538, vol. xlvi. fol. 431.]

The lorde protector and the Counsell, the xxiiij^th of June to Mr. Doctor Reynolds.[b]

After our hartie commendacions: For as myche as yt is most acceptable to have his people leade theyre lyves in the feare and knowledge of hym and there uppon also folowythe as by good ordre, quyet, and due obedyence of all people to theyr prynces and

---

[a] This document was printed with several errors of copying by Strype in his *Memorials,* vol. ii. p. 168.

[b] If we may judge from the account given by the author of the *Troubles as Frankfort,* neither Mr. Gregory nor Dr. Reynolds did much service in their capacity of preachers. He says: "If you call to remembrance who hazarded his life with that old honourable Earl of Bedford, when, as he was sent to subdue the popish rebels of the west, you shall find that none of the clergy were hasty to take that service in hand but only old Father Coverdale (P. 196)."

heddes, the whiche no wise so convenyntly can be brought to passe as to have frequent and dyscrete preaching of his hollye word and commandement, we have thought yt mete, sence our verie good lord the lord pryvie Seall is appoynted under the kyngs Matie to have the governaunce of that west part of the realme during his Maties pleasure, That ye shall bothe be lycensed and commanded by us, on the Kyngs Maties behalf, to preache and oppenly declare with syncerytie the word of God in suche publyke place and audytorye as the same Lord pryvie seall shall solycyte you, whose dyscressyon and grave wysdome the Kyngs Matie and we so myche esteme that wytheout his ordre and certen knowledge we will ye take no labor upon you. And for your delygence and studye herein, although the same be your duetie and of god prescribed, yet we will have yt in good remembrance and reward to your contentation.

And thus fayre you hartely well.

Frome Rychmount the xxiiijth of June, 1549.

Your loving frends,

E. SOMERSET.
  R. RICHE CAUNC.   W. SANCT JOHN.
    F. SHREWESBURY.   EDWARD MONTAGU.

VI.—INSTRUCTIONS TO LORD RUSSELL FROM THE COUNCIL.

[Domestic Papers of Edward VI. vol. vii. art. 40.]

A Memoriall for the Lord Russell, Lord Privie Seale, for the purposes ensuing.

Whereas the K. M^y by the advice of us the lord protector and Council hath thought mete to appoint the said Lord Russell to reside for a time in the west parts of this his Majesty's realm as well for the good governance of his highness' counties of Devon, Cornwall, Somerset and Dorsett, in good order and quiet, as also for the better defence of his highnes loving subjects in the same shyres in case of any invasion or other attemptats by forregn ennemies, His highness' pleasure is that he the said lord Russell repairing to his charge shall at his fyrst coming to every of the sayd shyres call unto him the justices of peax and such other of them and of the most grate and honest men of every of the said counties as he shall think convenient, by whom and by as many other waies and meanes as he may, he shall informe himself of the state and ordder of every of the said shyres; and finding the same to be in good ease and quietness he shall take such further order for the good continuance thereof as to him with their advises shall be thought most expedient.

But if the people shall be out of frame and not in such order of obedience as were convenient, the said lord Russell, consulting with the said justices for this purpose and others, as is aforesaid, informe himself of the causes of their said unquietness, shall travel by all ways and means possible both to remedy the causes aforesaid, bring the people with gentilnes to such conformitie as [*to bringe them . . . . . and obedient subjects*] appertayneth by travayl and gentle persuasions [*which way if it shall*]: if they shall nott bee reduced to the knowledge of their duties, his hyghnes pleasure is the sayd l. p. seall shall, by force of his majesty's comyssion to him addressed for this purpose, assemble [*the power of there for the better*] such nombers of men, within the limits of his commission, as may be hable both to repress the obstinatt and willful doings, [*and*] bring them to the knowledging of ther bounden dueties, and be also an example to others to attempt the like [*repressing of such as obstinately shall trouble the good quiet of the countre, conducing of the rest to an order and thacknowlegeng of their bounden duties in this behalf*]. And in case of any invasion by th'ennemies, the said lord Russell, leving his Mat^{ies} subjects as is aforesayd, shall extend all his good dexteritie and courage for repulse of them and defence of the countree to th'uttermost; and to th'intent the same may be in better order for defence if any such thing shuld chaunce he shall give order, if it be not alredy don, for the setting up and watching of the beacons in all necessary places accustomed, [*according to thorder heretofore*] especially reysed by the costs in such places and after such order as heretofore hath byn prescribed for that mater. [*In the meane time to thintent things may be in good*] And for the better exchuing of all occasions of troble and inquietude at home in the sayd shyres, [*order we ourselves*] his Ma^{tes} pleasure is the said lord Russell shall have a speciall regard to giving speciall charge to M^{rs} and fathers to have an earnest continuall regard to the good governance of their children and servants, and to the quiet of the countrey; for seing that clothiars, dyars, wevars, fullers, and all other artificers be kept occupied, and that all occasions of unlawfull assemblies be avoyded as moche as may be [*and in any case any shall attempt the breache of the lawes or otherwise use any kinde of misorder to se thoffendors punished to thexample of others*].

His highnes pleasure also is that amongs other things the said lord privie seale shall have a speciall respect to se [*the kin*] his Ma^{tes} procedings [a*nd order*] touching matters of religion well obeyed and executed according to the order lately set forth in that behalf.

Finally [*It hath byn also thought good that ones every*] And if any light seditions or vayn brutes and rumors shall be spredd in any of the countries under the rule of the said Lord Russell he shall endevor hymself by all the wayes and meanes he may, to know the begynnars and fyrst settars forth.

And bycause we know thatt [*great, thatt no one thing doth often*] sondry ill and seditious persones for the better atcheving of ther devellysh purpose have many tymes used to spredd abrod [*sondry*] such lewd and ontrue brutes and rumors as they Imagine may best sett forth ther [*said*] naughty purposes, the sayd lord Russell [*shall*] (who may well assure himself to be ondelaydly advertised from us of all occurrants of importance) shall endevor him self from tyme to tyme to search out the authors or spredda^{rs} of the sayd rumours, causing them to be apprehended and committed to ward [*ther to remayn*] and after furthar punished according to ther deservings.

Endorsed :—
    M. of my lord
      privie seales,
        memorall xxiiij° Junii, 1549.

VII.—LORD RUSSELL'S LETTER TO THE DUKE OF SOMERSET EXPLAINING THE STATE OF AFFAIRS IN THE WEST COUNTRY: WRITTEN IN JUNE 1549.

[Domestic Papers of Edward VI. vol. vii. art. 41.]

It cannot appear to our Judgments that the town off Sherburn doth stand upon any such strayte, as the same with any meane force shall be a stay to the passage of the rebels eastward, nor that they can be well impeched of the said passage by any other strayts of that Countrey, otherwyse than by an army abyll to withstand them in the face. For first it appeareth that the distance between the river which goeth by Dorchester and that which goeth by Bridgwater is xx^{ti} myles.

And over the river w^h goeth by Dorchester men may ryde almost in all places.

The countrey from Lamport to Brydgewater and so down to the sea side, which is about 8 miles, is very strong, but that countrey is not for horsemen to do servyce in.

And betwixt those two rivers they may pass in all places. As the countrey lyeth the town of Sherburn standeth directly between the said two rivers, saving that the said town beareth somewhat more eastward. And an army may pass over every side of the said town eyther between the same and the town of Bruton off the one side through Somersydeshyre, or by Dorsydeshire between the said town off Sherburn and the south sea without any stay to impeche them, other than the low country off Blackemore which beareth not above two miles in brede from the said town, but that town is a convenient place for a strength of men to lye in for the indifferent stay as well of Somersideshyre and Wylshire, as Dorsydeshire during the time that these rebels shall not pass the bonds of Devonshyre.

And if we be driven to retire it standeth uncertayn to us hitherto, by what quarter we shall most conveniently use the same until their determinations of proceeding more evidently appear, but your grace may be assured that therein we shall omit nothing undone that may empeche or molest them by all ways possible as far as our power shall extend.

J. RUSSELL.[a]

Endorsed :—

The answer to the instructions for the situation of the country, and again

The answer to the effect of the instructions sent by Mr. Dudley and Mr. Travers.

VIII.—MEMORIAL OF THE COUNCIL TO THE JUSTICES OF PEACE IN DEVONSHIRE, OF THE 26TH OF JUNE, 1549.

[Domestic Papers of Edward VI. vol. vii. No. 42, fol. 138.]

After o^r right harty commendations.

Wee have receyvyd yor tres of the xxiiijth of June, by the w^h wee doo understand that those lewd psonnes of whom you wrote before, being ons well quieted by you^r good meannes, bee now agayn assembled in a farre greatter nomber thorough the psuasions of some seditious persones such as desier a styrre more then quietnes. For remedie wherof, albeit you may understand partly o^r mynde by o^r former tres wryten un to you, yet, considering thatt as this and such lyke mysorders be for the more part easely holpen att the begynnyng so they may with tyme grow to further inconvenience, if the declaration of such mater as we signefied un to you before shall nott satysfye them, we require you to traveyll by thayr meannes eyther

---

[a] The writer was the Sir John Russell who first appears in history 1513, as a gentleman of the King's privy chamber. He was created a peer in 1539, with the title of Baron Russell. He served various offices, and became Lord Privy Seal, Dec. 3, 1542, and Lord High Steward in 1547. He was afterwards created Earl of Bedford in 1550, and died in 1554. He was the bearer of the ring from the King to Wolsey, Nov. 1, 1529, and had been sent against the northern rebels in the insurrection of 1536, and was employed in the West in 1545.

openly with the hole world [*and traveyll to induce them by fayre meanes*], or els apart with the ringleaders by all the best ways you can devise to induce them to retyre to ther houses, putting them [*or such a th*] and especially the cheff doers [*ringleaders*] among them in remembrance what an onnaturall dealing this is of subjects to rise against ther soveraigne lord. What onkindnes his Ma^t may herafter justly conceyve herof sens these things be attempted in his mynorite. Whatt dyshonor and onsuertie to the hole realme may grow by these attemptats. Whatt courage the [*our enemyes the the shall*] hearing therof shall administer to the Ff men, Scots [*and such others as*] o^r enemyes, to putt them in remembraunce thatt the parts of good and obedient subjects hadd byñ ffyrst to have sued for remedie att the hands of ther soveraign lord, and nott to take uppon them selfs the swerd and authorite to redresse as they list, especially those maters w^h being allredye establisshed by a law and consent of the hole realme can nott (if any thing was to be reformed) bee otherwise altered then by a law agayn. By these or such other good words you may fyrst assay to asswage them wherin if you shall not be hable to satisfie them, yett shall you by these meannes somewhat mitigate their furor, and use the meannes you possably can best devyse to stay the comÿng of gretter nombers un to them, and in the mean tyme putt yor selfs w^h such of yor tenaunts and servants as you best trust, secretly ordered to attend such further direction as o^r very good lord, the lord pryvey seall, who is now in journey towards you, shall farthar prescribe as for the delay of a tyme for th'execution of the statute. Of the shepe & cloth we have written more amply to you by our former letters, and this eftsones requiring you to joyn wysely and manly together in these things, we bydd you hartily farewell. From Syon.

Endorsed:—
M. to Sr Thomas Denys, peter courteney, and Antony Harvy, justices of peax in Devon, xxvith of June, 1549.

IX.—Letter from Lord Arundel to Secretary Petre, June 29, 1549.

[Domestic Papers of Edward VI. vol. vi. art. 44.]

Ye shall understand that these parts remayn as well as may be in a quaveryng quyet; the honest promes faythefully to serve the kyng, the rest I trust wyll folow yf the devysses shall soon...... ..... be now shortely to be usyd.

Sir, I here that the persone of Sr Willm George is out for the commyssyon of oyer and determyner. His fame soundeth not amongst the pepull for the just admynystratyon of Justyce. I thought good to write this much unto you by casse I have sens o^r departure from my lords grace herd this much, praying you to revelle the same unto him and to none other. Also thynkyng this mater meter to be openyd by you my frend then by myne own letters unto his grace, I trust you therwith, and end with comẽdatyons in this letter, and wyll begin the next with acõdynglye,

From Geldford, the xxix of June, 1549.

Yo^r assuryd frend,
ARRUNDELL.[a]

Endorsed as follows :—

    To my veric loving
      ffrend Sr Willm Peter
      knight, one of the kings
      Maties twoo principall
      Secretaryes.

Therle of Arundell,
    xxix° Junii, 1549.

[a] The writer of this letter was Henry Fitzalan, Earl of Arundel from 1543 to 1579. As Lord Maltravers he was one of the panel of Peers returned for the trial of Lord Dacre, July 9, 1534, when he was unanimously aquitted of the charge of treason. He was made Knight of the Garter in 1544, and Lord Chamberlain 1546. He went as Lord Deputy to Calais in April, 1540, and in the following year Somerset, then Earl of Hertford, was sent over to aid him in settling certain disputed points as to the boundary of the pale.

X.—Letter from the Council to the Lord Privy Seal, advising him how to act.

[Petyt MSS. No. 538, vol. 46, fol. 432.]

From my Lord Protector the xxix[th] of June to my L. Pryvie Seall.

After our hartie commendations to your good Lordshipp. The same shall understand that we have receyved your letters frome Salysburie wth other lres out of the west partes brought by one Stowell, of whome we harde at leugh the hole state and procedyngs of the busie people in Devonshire. For answere wherof, Fyrst, we geve your L. most hartie thanks for your paynes and great delygence, used as well, by the waye, as also for your stodye towardes the end of your journey, not doubting but at your comyng in to those parties your wysdome and good polycie shall we fynish those styrres.

For the proceding wherein we have thought mete to let you knowe our advyse, as we have upon the understandyng of the matter conceyved yt best, remytting neverthelesse the alteracon therof as good occasion shall serve to your wysdome. Fyrst for the appesing of the multytude assembled at Sampford Cortney, we thinke your lordshipp Assembling your power of horsemen and some convenyent nombre of hagbutes footmen, The towne of Excester being left in good sauftie for all purposes of your returne, you maie resorte nye to the sayd towne of Sampford, tarying also w you half a dosen or double bases, and before you shall attempt any entreprise against them to lett them understand theyr dysobeydyence and the causes of theyr greyffes to be only devysed of veyry falshed by such as mynde trayterously to the Kyng's Ma[tie] and theyr utter dystructyon, and therefore vt is thought that the greate number of them be but seduced and deceyved wth false rumors, So that yf they will depte to theyr houses, lyke good subjects, And remyte the redresse of theyr greyfs to the King's Ma[tie], who hath only power that to do, and none more redie, then they shalbe taken as the kyng's subjects, having erred by ignorance. And yf other wyse they will maynteyne them selves in any assembles they shalbe sure to be used as high traytor[s] and rabelles to the kyng's Ma[tie] and the croune. And that shall they feele furthw[th], without any extremytie to be spayred. And in the treating hereof thay maie be answered, to certen theyr spetiall brutes and rumors; as to that thay say, After the payment for shepe thay should paie for theyr geese and piggs and such like, the same is not only utterly false, but a thing never mente by the kyng, the counsyall, nor any wyse man leving, being founde oute by some sedytious traytor, as in the end will fully appeare; and for the artycle of Baptysme, of not baptysing theyr cheldren frome sonday to sondaie, the same is lykewise false, as may appere by the kyng's Ma[ties] book, even in the last sentence of the fyrst syde of the leafe entreating of baptysme, and so lyke wyse maie thay credyt all them that spred suche rumors bythe try all of that one, yf thay will puse the book.

We wold also ye caused before your depture to be publysshed and bruted Abrode sondrye wyse, that these men thus assembled, be wonderfully abused, and that by the provocation only of certen popyshe prests, whiche color all theyr doyngs with other sedytyous rumors, and meane nothing ells but to subdue the people to the pope by whome they leved as in a kyngdome, And all other the kyngs loving subjects in a thraldome.

And yf in this and lyke maner thay be not paycified, but will stand to theyr former purpose, then our meanyng is ye shuld proced this other or lykewyse as ye maie Thenk best. Your horsemen may lye a loufe, making nowe and then offers to the towne, and sending certen harcquebutters of horseback to the places of adventayg, to the intent the rebellors may be draune to the utter ptes of the towne, where thay have cheyned upp theyr passages. And then, your bases being fyrst placed, x or xii score frome the towne behynde your horsemen, Agaynst the same passages shall redely after the retorne of your horsemen annoye them, and slay suche numbers of them, as we thynke playnly the press therof will cause them sodenly to gyve over and shrincke, and yf not but that they shall break or yssue out upon you, then we doubt not but that your horsemen, being instructed before of your L. good pollyce, shall utterly dystrysse them and overthrow them. And in consyderacõn of the hole matter we dyssyer especyally those Syxe men wch do solyc[it] the causes of theyr complying unto one especiall man Steple in the same towne, and the same man also may be apprehended to be ponyshed above all others for example sake.

We wold also ye used this pollycie before your tyme of enterpryse agaynst them ij or iij dayes, that ij or iij trustie lykly persons may be addressed thether wth good wyse instructyons to be come ptaker of the said multytude, and to professe moche ernestnes therein, to the intent to gytt some credet and authorytie amongst them, and so to procede two or iij dayes, as ye shall appoynt them, And afterward uppon the rumors to be brought of your L. power thyther and upon the brute of their offences, the terror of comytting treason, the feare of a kyng's execution, ye and upon knowledg that they have been seduced by false dysposed people, And furthermore upon the feare of theyr owne lives, the same men so suburned maie waxe fañt and so fall to fearre by degrees, that yt maie be without suspect and not only to begyñe to flee themselves, but also to move all others that to do. And in the night And lykwyse for the more annoyaũce of them we wold ye dystressed all maner of victualls nigh to the towne, And by good watch provede that theyr victualls maie be intercepted, wch thing wthout any other force to be attẽpted may chaũse cause them geve over at the fyrst.

For the furder order of things a mysse wthin the cyrcute of your comission we will shortly send unto your Lordshipp two comyssyons. And A proclamacõn, the one of the Commissiones to be for oyer and determyner of all roytts, etc., thother for the inquery of decayes and unlawfull inclosures. The proclamacõn for the assessing and taxing of excessyve pryses of victuals, thexecution whereof we praie your Lordshipp consyder shall serve to great purpose. And so being weyed we pray your L. to use all convenynt deligence and industrie.

Furthermore understandyng by enformaĉon that there is one Mr. Blakston, an Eccleasticall Commissarie, whose credett as yt is to moche, so yt is abused in sedusing the kings people by dysparsyng Amongst them false and sedycyous advertisements of thalteraĉon of Relygyon; We thenke yt verie mete that ye earnestly treat wth the same ptie, that by his letters, preaching, and otherwise as ye shall think cõvenyent, do sturre and provoke all maner Curats and other people wthin his Jurysdiction to be obedyent, and to let them knowe that they be dyssayved in theyr opinyons, and that nothing more earnestly ment towarde them then trewe and good establyshing of theyr faithe and the proffit of the cõmon wealthe. And so fynally to order that people maie be revoked to more quiet or the sayd cõmyssion^r to be brought out of his credytt, where as yf he shuld remayne wthout Amendyng, moche harme might folowe. For the suburnyng of your men and the dysparsyng of convenyent rumors to appease theyr false rumors, our meanyng is the same shuld be used iij or iiij dayes before your pceding towardes them, for that we thynk therbye theyr power will waxe daylye lesse and lesse.

And yf the man kepyng his fonde office in the steple, and vj. othe^r wch be referendaries of causes to hym maie be cõvenyently apprehended, we wold, yf otherwyse than by rack or terror they will not confesse the fyrst and orygynall begynnyngs hereof, they were sent hether upp to us, as also we wold the lyke, yf your L. shall think so mete, that anye others wold upon the rack or terror confesse Authors or begynnynges hereof, wch thing to knowe as a verye necessayrie we dysyre. Thus most hartely we byd your good Lordshipp fare well.

For the syttyng of postes According to your desyre We have all redie gyven order.

From Richmond, the xxix[th] of June,[a] 1549.

Y[or] L. assured loving Frends,

E. SOMERSET.

A. WINGFELD.

WILLM. PETRE.

A. DENNY.

XI.—SUPPLICATION TO THE COUNCIL FROM STAINES DEPRECATING THE DESTRUCTION OF THEIR BRIDGE. JUNE, 1549.

[Domestic Papers of Edward VI. vol. vii. art. 46.]

To the right honorable lords of the King's Ma[ties] most honorable privie Councill.

In their moost humble wise besechen and shewen unto your good lordshipps your orators thinhabitants of the towne of Stanys, in the countie of Midd[s]. That where your said orators have received comandement frome my lorde protector, in the king's graces name, to pluck upp the Comen bridge at Stanys, for the saufgarde of the Realme, as they allege frome enymyes, whiche ys and wilbe to thutter undoyng and distruccion of all the hoole Towne and countrie thereabouts; and the said Bridge is yett staied parte of it, upon that the said Towne of Stanys hathe promysed to send out a Scowte to discrye yf any armye be comyng that waie. In consideracõn wherof it may please your good lordshipps to signifie unto your said orators your lordshipps pleasure herin and what your said

[a] Between the letters of the 29th June and the 10th of July there is a document entitled " The King's Majesty's Answer to the Supplication made in the name of his Highness's subjects of Devon and Cornwall." This has been printed by Tytler in his *England under the Reigns of Edward VI. and Mary*, vol. i. p. 178, who says, " There are in the State Paper Office three contemporary drafts of this answer, none of them signed by Edward or Somerset. This is dated July 8th, and on the same day Sir William Paget wrote from Brussels to Secretary Petre, shewing how soon tidings of the mutiny had reached the Continent."

Orators shall do therin. And your said orators shall dailly praie unto Almyghtie Jhesu for the prosperous preservacion of your good lordshipps.

Endorsed :—

The supplicaçõn of the men of Stanes.

XII.—LETTER OF THE COUNCIL TO THE PRINCESS MARY OF THE 7TH JULY, 1549, SENT AFTER THE APPEARANCE BEFORE THEM OF DR. HOPTON HER CHAPLAIN.[a]

[Petyt MSS. No. 538, vol. 46, fol. 4.]

After due commendations to your grace.

The same may by these presents understand that we have heard your chaplain Doctor Hopton and in like manner informed him for the declaration of such things as we have instructed him to utter unto you, whom we require your grace to credit therein accordingly. Thus we pray God conserve your grace in health.

From Richemond, the 7th of July, 1549.

Your grace's assured,

E. SOMERSET.

T. CANT.^{r} H. RICHE CANC. W. SEINT JOHN. J. WARWICK.
H. ARUNDELL. WILLM. PETRE, S^y. A. DENNY.
EDWARD NORTH. P. SADLEYR.

To my lady Marye's grace.

[a] It appears from the Council Book that a letter on the subject of conformity to the new Prayer Book was issued by the Council on Trinity Sunday, June 16, and sent to the Princess Mary, commanding her to send her comptroller and Dr. Hopton, her chaplain, to them. See Harl. MS. 2308, fol. 92b. The entry is as follow :—

" Upon information made to the Lord Protector's grace and Council that the lady Mary's grace, contrary to the king's Majesty's proceedings and the laws of the realm established on that behalf by the last act of parliament, did use to have mass said openly in her house, refusing to have there celebrated the service of the Communion, whereby it appeared to his grace and their lordships it might be thought she might seem to the world to disallow and be offended with the proceedings of the king's

XIII.—LETTER FROM THE KING TO THE PRINCESS MARY ON THE SUBJECT OF THE MASS.

[Petyt MSS. No. 538, vol 46, fol. 7.]

Edward.   By the King.

Right dear and entirely beloved sister we greet you well.

And late you wite that having presently addressed our right trusty and right well beloved counsellor the lord Riche our Chancellor of England, and our trusty and right well beloved counsellor Sir Willm Petre, knight, one of our principal Secretaries, to open unto you certain things on our behalf we have thought good by the advice of our counsell both to pray and require you not only to give credence unto them but also to shew yourself conformable in that which on our behalf shall by them be proponed unto you.

Given under our signet at our palace of Westminster the 22th of July, in the 4th yere of our reign,

E. SOMERSET.   W. WILTESHIRE.   J. WARWYK.
       J. BEDFORD.   W. NORTHT.
G. COBHAM.   H. ARYNDELL.   W. HERBERT.
               EDWARD NORTH.

Endorsed:—
    To our right dear and entirely well beloved sister the Lady Mary.[a]

Majesty her brother: Their lordships wrote to her grace on that behalf giving to her advice to be comfortable and obedient to the observation of his Majesty's laws to give order that the mass should be no more used in her house, that she would embrace and cause to be celebrated in her said house the Communion and other divine services set forth by his Majesty, and that her grace would send to the said Lord Protector and Council her comptroller and Doctor Hopton, her chaplain, by whom her grace should be advertised for their lordships more amply of their minds and advices to be both her contentation and honour."

Mary's answer of June 22, with the Council's rejoinder of June 24, and her final reply of June 27, may be seen in *Foxe* and in the appendix to Tierney's edition of Dod's *Church History*.

[a] Nearly all the letters that passed between the Princess Mary and the Council on the same subject may be seen in the Appendix to vol. ii. of Canon Tierney's

XIV.—LETTER FROM THE COUNCIL TO LORD RUSSELL ANNOUNCING RE-INFORCEMENTS. JULY 10, 1549.

[Petyt MSS. No. 538, vol. 46, fol. 435.]

From my l. protector and the Counsiall the xth of Julii.

After our most hartie comendacions unto your good lordship, We have seen your severall tres of the viij of this present, by the wch and the reporte of the berar we do understand at good lenght your contynuall travaill for the staye of the Rabells in those partes, for the wch we do gyve you our most hartie thankes. And for the better encoragement of those gentilmen wch you comend and do serve under you, lyke as we have thought good to send them our letters of thanks wch shall come to your Lordshipp wth these, So in respect of your comendacion we have wrytten to the mynt of Brystall for a hundred pounds to be delyvered to your Lordshipp to be bestowed amongs those gentilmens servaunts as you shall thynk good: mary you may by no meanes gyve ne promyse to any more wages then the Kyngs Matie hathe heretofore usually gyven, wch is as your Lordshipp knowythe is vj d. to a foteman and ix d. for a light horsseman by the daye. As for the place of yo^{ur} owne Abode by cause yor L may there bothe best cõsyder wch waie the rabells may be most annoyed and the rest of the countres adjoyning well preserved in quiet, and will, we doubt not, wth all your possible delygence employe your self, Accordenly, we do remytt the place to your L. And during your abode nyhand the sayd rabells you

---

edition of Dod's *Church History*. They range from the date of June 22, 1549, to July 16, 1551. The story is continued to the 29th of August, 1551, by extracts from the proceedings of the Privy Council, reprinted from the *Archaeologia* and from Foxe. There is a gap, however, in the correspondence of nearly a year and a-half, between June 27, 1549, and December 2, 1550. The letter here printed from the Petyt Manuscripts shows that during that interval there was no intermission in the persecution of the princess on the score of her religion.

maie by cutting a waie the victualls not only bring them to a greate mesery, But also by spreding abrode rumors of theyr develyshe behavours, crueltye, abhomynable levings, Robberies, murders and such lyke bring suche a detestation of them amongs the comon people and fewe we thenk will repayre towardes them.

And where your Lordshipp dyssyreth to have a number of fotemen, all beyt we thenke yt wold be veric hard to send you in a short tyme suche a nomber of fotemen as wth playne force might be hable to mete with the rabells and attempt the settyng on without a suffycent force yt wold be also dengerous, yet do we put in order wth all the spede we maye cl Italyan harquebutters, wch furthwth repayre towards you; we do lykewyse geve order for three or foure hundreth horssemen under the leyding of the lord graie to repayre towards Salysburye and so forward towards you as occasyon shall require, besydes other iiij^c horssemen strangers and one thossand almaynes fotmen, wch we mynd lykwise to send towards you yf nede shall so require. We have also wrytten to Mr. Harbert[a] to be in a Redynes wth the force of Wiltshyre and Glocester. And because we understand that Sr John Arondell, being sent for by youe, hath refused to come, and besydes that, usythe hymself other wyse then besemethe a good subject, we wold yor Lordshipp, yf the prymisses be trewe, shuld for example sake cause hym to be sent frome thence to Mr. Harbert, and frome hym to us, to be forther used according to Justice.

---

[a] This was Sir William Herbert, son and heir of Sir Richard Herbert, an illegitimate son of William Herbert, who was created Earl of Pembroke 27th May, 1468, and beheaded in 1469. Sir William was one of the sixteen executors of the will of King Henry the Eighth, and was afterwards created Baron Herbert of Cardiff Oct. 10, 1551, and on the following day Earl of Pembroke. He married Anne, sister of Queen Catherine Parr. His eldest son, Lord Herbert, married Catherine, the younger sister of Lady Jane Grey, in 1553. In May of this year 1549 he had dispersed the rising in Wiltshire. He was afterwards one of the peers who sat on the trial of Somerset in 1551, and was one of the conspirators who proclaimed Lady Jane Grey as Queen, but turned with the tide in favour of Mary, and afterwards was one of Elizabeth's Privy Council.

Fynally by cause yor Lordshipp wryteth that the rabells and others in those pties do sprede rumors of the tumults in these countres; You shall understand that nowe, thanks be unto god, they be appeased and throughly quieted in all places, saving only in Buckingham shyre, there a fewe lyght persons nuely assembled, whome we trust to have also appeased wthin two or three dayes. And thus one thing we assure your Lordship, that in all places thay have not only confessed theyr faults wth verie lowlye submission, but also for rellygyon declared themselves in Suff., Essex, Kent, Hampshire, Surry, and many other places so well pswayded as, hearing of your rabells, thaye dyssyre to dye agaynst them in that matter. We mynde send shortly unto you a proclamation wch we think shall bothe sett a terror and dyvysyon amongs the rabells themselves.

And thus we bid yor Lordshipp most hartely fayre well frome Syon the xth of Julii.^a

Yo^r L. assured frends,

E. SOMERSET.

R. RICHE CANC^r. W. SAINT JOHN.

W. PETRE.

R. SADLEYR. JOHN BAKER.

Postscript.—Yo^r Lordshipp herewth the warrant to brustell for v^c lb wch you maie send thyther and so receyve the monye: your L. may also puse the letter herein closed, and after shall yt cause yt be dd to gentilmen nowe attendyng yor Lordshipp.

^a A long letter from the Protector and Council, of July 4, 1549, to Paget, the ambassador at Brussels, was published by Strype in his *Memorials*, vol. ii. Appendix, p. 101. It is very incorrectly transcribed, and omits altogether the concluding part, which contains the following allusion to the insurrections of this year :—

"And where some light persons before your departing had solicited some others like themselves for plucking down of pales and inclosures, and such like matters, you shall understand that sithens your departing hence the like stirs have been renewed in Essex, Kent, Hampshire, and Devonshire, whereof part be already quietly appeased and the rest in good towardness also to return peac[eably] to their

XV.—Somerset to the Lord Privy Seal, promising to send Lord Grey de Wilton.

[Petyt MSS. No. 538, vol. 46, fol. 436.]

From my lord protector to my lord privie Sealle the xiith of Julii.

After our right hartie comendacõns to your good L.

This shalbe to signifie unto you that we have receyved your letters of the tenth of this present and harde the declaration of the haralde, berer of the same; and for the doubt ye make of Excester and your determynatoñ to levey two thoussands of fottmen wythe whome and your horsemen gyve the adventer for the relyef of that towne; by yor former tres we understand that the towne was not hable to kepe yt self two daies for lack of victuall; sythens pceyving that the towne was furnyshed eight dayes, yf we hade at the beginning knowne so myche, we had not stock to have releyved the matter otherwyse; for when ye wrotte ye were not hable to have any fotmen to whome to trust; howe could ye then for the shortnes of the tyme, Of the townes victualling and their power tauld greate, have bene hable to adventre the succors wth only y^r horsemen? Your owne tres were the cause of our staye, but pceyving nowe ye maie have fotmen, we remytt yt unto you to do yor uttermost wth the number m^l vj^c yea yf yt be m^l vij^c,^a we styck not at yt; for as th'ympossibilitie to have men stayed hytherto, So p̃ntly by this your freshe advertysement to mynd to take fotmen, we have geven order to the Treasouro^r or Comptroler of the mynt of Brystowe the Kyng's Receyvor to Croche our Receyvor, to present upon your bill, that ye shall lyke to demand. In lyke manner

houses; so as there is no likelihood of any gr[eat] matter to ensue thereof. And yet having experience [how] slanderously these small tumults shall be divulged [and] spread by the Frenchmen, we have thought good [thus] to advertize you by these and other letters of the full t[ruth] of these matters. Upon the knowledge whereof you may answer these untrue and vain brutes as you shall think good."

^a These numbers are somewhat uncertain.

what ye cane gytt of marchaunts to be repayed here, take yt. Yt shalbe aunswered wth thanks. When gentelmen of the countrye come to you ye maie use them, but onles ye knowe them fully perswayded for the matier in contraversie of relygyon gyve them not to moche credytt, but so use yt Nevertheles as being wth you thay maie be unsuspected to their owne appayrance. Thay speake to have to do in the governaunce of the kyng's Matie thaie shall knowe or thay come any thing nerer thay shall bothe be lett of that porpose, And the substance of suche rank Traytors receyve theire deserts on the waye For appoyntment of Counsayllors wherin ye require Sir Peter and Sir Gawen Carewe, we referre yt to your self to chose whome ye think mete to be called unto you for advise and for understanding of the state of the cõntrey. As to Sr John Arrendell yf he should be sodenly sent for he wold padventer refuse us and so shall enter despacon. Therefore we will wink at the matter for the tyme, and so shall ye do well to doo also, onles ye can pceyve according to our former Letters that he maie be quyetly delyverid unto thandes of Sr Willm̃ Harbert to be conveyed hether: we had determyned to send downe to you the lord Graye^a wth a band of horsmen and some hagbuters footmen. But that uppon occasyon of a sturr here in Bucks and Oxfordshire by instigacõn of sundery preists (kepe it to your self), for these matyers of religion, we have been forced to kepe him a while and yett we

---

^{a} This was William Lord Grey de Wilton 1529-62, who had been one of the council at Calais in 1540, lieutenant of Hampnes Castle 1539, governor of Boulogne 1546. He had been in the unsuccessful expedition against Scotland in the preceding year, and was supplanted by the Earl of Rutland, and had just been sent against the rebels of Oxfordshire, whom he dispersed with 1500 men under his command. He was sent to the Tower with Somerset, October 17th, 1549, and was pardoned and released June 10th, 1553; and on September 23rd of the same year was appointed deputy of Calais in place of Lord Willoughby, and afterwards captain of Guisnes October 6th, being succeeded at Calais by Lord William Howard. He was afterwards, in Elizabeth's reign, sent to Scotland in the year 1560. He has earned an infamous notoriety by his order of July 19th, 1549, for the execution of rebels in Oxfordshire and other counties, such amongst them as were priests to be hanged on the top of the steeples of their own churches.

trust w^{th}in a vj daies matyer shall he chaystice them, and then shall we send him unto you. Thus fayre yor good L. ryght hartely well, from Syon the xij^{th} of Julii, 1549.

Your L. assured frend.

After the wryting hereof arreyved your other letters of the xi^{th} of this pñt c̃oteynĩg the service of footmen necesarie, wherein what we mynt of your relyef by footemen ye pceyve as above. What ye maie do specyally in the meane tyme for the helpe of the Towne to stand, do yt.

Your fyrst lres of the greatnes of theyr nombers of footemen and your impossabilitie to have any to trust to, moved by your owne instigac̃on our accompt service by horsemen and no other cause had we to myslyke footmen yf they might have been had. And that ye had not doubted them we assure yo^u suche care we have to the repryssion of the most rank Trayto^rs That thus wth hedy matyers waic nothing wth us in respeck of them. And therefore shall ye have the sayd L. Graie and his nombers or yt be long wth you and the onlye stay for the tyme is this lewde matier of Bucks and Oxfordshire.

Your Lordshipps assured,
E. SOMERSET.

XVI.—LETTER FROM SOMERSET TO LORD RUSSELL, OF THE 17TH OF JULY, MENTIONING THE REBELLION IN NORFOLK.

[Petyt MSS. No. 538, vol. 46, fol. 438.]

From my L. Protector to my L. Prevye Seall the xvii^{th} of Julii.

After our right hartie c̃omendac̃ons to your good lordshipp the same shall understand that we have receaved your lres, and fyrst to the suyts of Sr Andrewe Dudley and Sr Thomas Dyer we wilbe glad to cõsyder them in that we maie convenyently doo them good. Hitherto the case of Sr John Arrendell is not so certeyn as that we cane make any certayn accompt whereunto it tende, wherin we praie you gyve us notyce of the full wherwi^th to charge him our former letters. To your owne sute for the heire of Sr Thomas Trencherd we be pleased wth the same, and have taken order wth the lord greate M^r for the satysfaction of your desyre.

To the estate of these parties God be thanked yt is presently on good termes of obydence, saving some of the light sorte remayning tyckle, but no great nombre, namlye at and abowte Norwhich, whither the m^rques of Northampton is goon hence for stay of the contrey and repression of the evill. And yett theyre we trust ther shalbe no great matyer, for psentlye are there come hither half a dozen chosen of theyr compayny who seke the kyngs Maties mercie and redresse of things, and be returned to receyve pardon by dyreccons of the m^rques siche as will seke yt at his handes. We have for the mean tyme bounde Sr Arrendell by greate suyrties and somes not to passe a mile frome London. We have pntly write to the lord Gray our cotentations to allowe hym xl^s by daie for him self and his horsemen to be payd as others of theyr quality, to have no place of name but a consyallor's to gyve advise or texecute according as shuld be concluded, and that you wold in favor preferre him, which we pray you. Thus wyshing you, the Contenuance of yor prosperus procedings we bid yor Lordshipp right hartely farewell.

From West_r the xxvij^th of Julii,[a] 1549.

Your L. assurd frend,

E. Somersett.

[a] A mistake of the writer for July 17.

XVII.—The Council to Lord Russell again promising help by Lord Grey de Wilton.

[Petyt MSS. No. 538, vol. 46, fol. 438.]

From my lord protector and the Counseall, the xviijth of Julii.

After our hartie cõmendacõns to your good lordshipp the same shall understand that we have receyved your letters of the xvth of this present, and as to thalmaiynes ye require to have, we wold gladly have holpen you with them, but ptlye for the disorder of these parties hereabouts, and namely for that thay be odyous to our people abrode, in so moche as we cane hardly move them to receyve them without quarell here at hande, we do deferre the sending of them; the strangers, horsemen, and Italyan hacbutters, footemen shalbe wth you as sone as thay cane possabelye, being alredye in the waie thyther. For the ordynance of Purbeck, wch ye declare to lye daungerously, and that the rabells threaten to recover, we referre to your cõsyderaton eythe^r to appoynt yt to be brought to the Castell of Corfe or unto Poole yf ye consider yt maie in any of these places be in strength and out of theyr possession. At lest wayes we wold that the smalle ordynaunce should be taken thence and the powder also; wch being done the great ordenance shall stand them in small stede. In cace Mr. Herberd shall not come unto you but chaunce otherwyse to be employd ye shall be furnished of ayde of a skylfull man on horseback, The lord Graie, who by advertysement even nowe we pceyve to have chased the Rebells of Bucks, Oxfordshire, and these parties to their houses, and taken cc of them and a dosen of the ring leders delyverid unto him whereof pte at least shall suffer paynes of death to the example of all malefactors.

As to your devise to have lyke pclamacõns to Cornewall as was lately sent to you for Devonshyre we have taken ordre to have them out of hande, and do send them downe unto you for satysfaccõn of your dysyre in that behalf.

Piers is arryved here, and we have sent for Sr John Arrendell to Portsmouthe to be conveyd hither.

Thus fare yor good L. right hartely well.
Frome Westm^r the xxviij^th of Julii,^a 1549.
                Your assured frends,.
  E. Somerset.
  T. Cant.   R. Riche Canc^r.
            W. Sanct John.
                      ·J. Warwyk.

XVIII.—Letter from Somerset and the Council to Lord Russell promising help by Lord Warwick.

[Petyt MSS. No. 538, vol. 46, fol. 439.]

Frome my L. protecto^r and the counsiall to my lord previe seall.

After our hartie comendacons to you the same shall understand that we have receyved your letters of the xviij^th of this present and wth the same your articles of answere, And the letters out of Cornewall conteynyng the state of those countres, tharryvall of Mr. Dudley and Mr. Travers and your demand of a mayne force, and so forther as the same your letters do p^rport.

And fyrst where you note the smallness of your owne power, the dayly encrease of the rabells nombers and the necessytie to have a mayne force, wythout wch you aledge in one part of yor lres that neyther can the cytie be relevyd ne the Rebells either assalted or resisted, And in an other pt ye make a clere impossabilitie; We be sorye to here frome you as men having experyence anye suche desperation and impossabillities made, wch being trewe can not be redubbed, and yf force maie do yt and that sodenly things cannot be had hens, ye do wisely cōsider not t'adventure the overthrowe for the smalnes of yor power, in wch cace there might ensewe great unsurytie to your charge and dyshoner to the Kyngs Matie. But in the meane season you maie nevertheles us yor dyscryssyon as you shall se cause. Wherein, for a forther helpe having nowe viij^xx

---

^a This was a mistake of the writer for 18th of July.

good Hagbutters strangers sent unto you maie put them on horseback, gytting horses out of the countreye for them, whosoever one them, the C^{aPens} becoming by your word and credyt answerable for theyr delyvery ; ye shall so encrease your strenth and deceye them by yt of so many horses yf they wold mynde to use them, besydes we wold sett on horseback as many others as ye can gytt that ye maie trust unto. And by that meane shall ye avoyde thennemy from gytting of horses out of Somersetshyre, and those parties that they wold els have taken. And being thus furnished, though they be x^t tymes so many in nombre, for ye shall wth v^c horse chosen th'advantage of the countrey, and dysposing some reasonable nombre of fotemen at places mette as uppon straights of passages, both out of their vitaill and skirmyshing, ayde of your hagbuters bickering wth them in there marche, take A greatt advantage on them of theyr victualls and other wyse as shalbe to them impeschment, and yet at all tymes when yt shall appear by the renforce of thennemies convenyent to retyre, they maie draw themselfs back and the footmen also wth them in surytie. And in this wise thennymies encountred by force of horse, men, hagbutters, and politique handling of the matyer by interruption of theyre vitaill, thay shalbe wery of theyr lyeng and a bate theyr pryde after thay have mett wth men of conduict.

The mayne force purposed by my L. of Warwik[a] cannot yet for

---

[a] This was Sir John Dudley, son of Edmund Dudley, who had been executed Aug. 10, 1510. He was created Viscount Lisle March 12, 1542, and was one of the sixteen executors of the will of Henry VIII. On the 17th of February, 1547, he was created Earl of Warwick, and made Great Chamberlain of England. It is remarkable how absent he was from the Council during the latter part of 1547 and till the middle of 1549. He seems to have been waiting his time to upset Somerset. After Somerset's fall he appears to have become reconciled to him, when his eldest son married Lady Anne Seymour, Somerset's daughter. He became Duke of Northumberland in 1551, and was chief manager for placing Lady Jane Grey on the throne. His attempt to show loyalty to Queen Mary, when Lady Jane Grey's cause was hopeless, did not succeed, and he was executed on the 21st of August, 1553, professing that he had been all along a Catholic at heart; though, for political ends, he had professed agreement with the men of the new learning.

a tyme be sent unto you, for no lenger then yesterdaye sume of the Countres hereabouts as Essex, Suff. Norff. and Kent were not in so good ordre and quiet as we wold wyshe, though theyr articles be not suche as your matters, raves, and spoyling of Townes ; also other yet be thaie to say to you in counsaill things of comon ordre, as to have one man to have but one ferme lands at theyr owne prych, and suche lyke ; they stand for p̄nt reformation and yet must they tary a playment tyme.

When those things be ended he shalbe in order to come to you wth comÿssyon of Wiltshire and Glocester to amend your force, besydes those he bringeth hens, and for the which ye shall have my L. Graye, who hath ccl. horse and the viij^{xx} hagbutters sent by Spinola. Ye saye out of Dorset and Somerset shires ye loke not to have above M^l fotemen, and that yor number of horses exced not vi or vij^c, yett do the Rebells bragg that they will have x^{ml} to seat on your backs out of those shires, as the awe of theyr nombers is so great, so be your nombers mencyoned so moche under foote. It were strange to us that they shuld not at least be hable to make iiij^{ml} or more, and to prevent frome Joyning wth the rebells, yea to make them serve wth you. We have devysed that ye make wth all spede p̄clamac̄on for those shyres moche of th'effect of that last sent for Cornewall for forfecture of lands, etc., adding in yt that If they shall not come unto you to serve according to theyr dewties and obedyence to their souvereign lord, and show themselves as prest and redie to fight against those rank rebells and papists of Devon as be c̄ometh good subjects, they shalbe bothe demed and for Trators and forfect theyr landes, Copiholds and goods wthout redempc̄on to themselves, wyfes and children, and be wthout all hope of p̄don to the p̄petuall dysherison of them selfs, and all that depend uppon them, the matyer of Copiholds being so generall a leving to the nomber of those shires, shalbe as moche a terror as anye other thing that can be possibly devised.

The rebells have used this practice wth you to send a nomber under color to submyt themselves t'explore your doings, and t'understand your force and numbers. Whi shuld not ye agayn gytt two or three, such as may be trusted, to do the lyke for your pte amonges them, wherby to take the advantage of service. To the power gathered in Cornewall as joyne with the rebells, the Proclamacon being all redie sent downe shalbe some stay unto them, yf yt will not, we think to put it to execute, as uppon their going t'entre upon theyr lands and goods, so maie ye paventur withdrawe them back to save theyr owne. A better psonage to execute yt can not be devised then Sr Willm. Godolphin, who hath bene a frontier man. And therefore we would ye gave ordre wth hym in it: let him cause yt to be pclaymed by face of the proclamacõns. As to shott whereof ye[a] to have lack, shyft is to be made there bylede, whereof we doubt not there is plentie within the lymyts of your comyssion, and for powder the same hath been sent hence unto you. In those pties of your comyssion where ye cannot trust the men that should possess them, we think mete ye cause to be gathered together all the hagbutters, Bowes, arrowes, shott, powder, and other municõn, and bestowe them in some castell as at Bristowe or elswher ye shall think best to put them, wherby thay maye be out of t'hands of th'ennymes. Upon knowledge of the treason wrought by the mayor of Plymouthe in the yelding upp of the towne to the rebells, we have geven ordre with Cotten to passe with certen of his shippes and gallyes that waic, and fyrst to attempt by all good meanes to wynne the possession of the castell, and to place Hawkyns with some other men there to apprehend the Mayor, and so gyve good order for the towne; according to your request we have sent another Trumpet and a Guyder of the Kyngs Armes to leade the people. Thus fare your good L. right hartely well.

From Richmõnd the xxijth of Julii, 1549.

We praie you also uppon the arryvall of Willm. Graye with his two hundreth of Ryding men you will t'extend favor to hym.

---

[a] *Complain* omitted by accident of copying.

Y_o_r lordshipp's assured frends,
E. SOMERSETT.
W. SANCT JOHN.[a]
A. WINGFELD.
W. PETRE, S_y_.
T. SMYTH.

Post Script.—Wythin these two dayes we hope my L. of Warwick shalbe in ordre to depte towards you; we shall els lack of our will.

XVI.—LETTER FROM THE COUNCIL TO LORD RUSSELL IN ANSWER TO HIS OF JULY 22.

[Petyt MSS. No. 538, vol. 46, fol. 442.]

From my lord protector and the cõsiall to my lord pryvie seall the Kyngs Maties Lieutant in the west parties.

After our right hartie cõmendacõns unto yo_r_ good L. We have receyved your letters of the **xxij** of this Instant, and herde the report of Mr. Travers, and have be right glad of your good begyn-

---

[a] This was Sir William Paulet, Baron St. John of Basing, March 9, 1539, one of the most constant attendants at the Council during the whole of this period. He was created Earl of Wiltshire, Jan. 19, 1550, and on the 12th of October, 1551, Marquis of Winchester. He was one of the executors of the will of Henry VIII., and received the great seal March 7, 1547, when Wriothesley was deprived of the chancellorship. He sealed the letters patent which made Somerset Protector, and held the seal till All Saints Day, when Rich was appointed Lord Chancellor. He stood by Somerset till his fall was certain, and then cast in his lot with Warwick, and presided at Somerset's trial in 1551. He afterwards took the part of Lady Jane Grey, but deserted her cause, and went over to Queen Mary's side; but afterwards conformed to the changes in religion under Elizabeth, and kept his place of Lord High Treasurer through the reigns of Edward, Mary, and Elizabeth, till his death in 1572, at the age of 96.

ning, and geve therefore to you the King's Maties and our right hartie thanks, requiring you to imparte the same to suche gentilmen and others as at this pñt have done the Kyngs Matie good, faythfull, and paynefull servis. And trust of as good successe to folowe to the Kyng's highness and all the realmes comfort.

For your further relefe we have given order for supplying of your wants, wch shall wth all spede arryve wth you according as Mr. Travers shall further showe unto you to your contentacõn. And for men we have geven to Mr. Aleurg^a Coffmyssyon as well out of South Walles as out of Glocestre Shyre, and other who shall wth nomber sufficyent we trust Relyef you with all speede. Where ye require footemen, and we heretofore have sent horsemen, Th'occasyon was of you That we made so moche doubt, that ye shuld not be hable to kepe them in the streits. And then yf they shuld come abrode horsemen shuld have done most ease. Nowe we trust ye shall have enught of both to encontre and subdewe the rebells.

For the Mayor of Plymmoth, we ar glad to here the mater of the towne not to be so evill as we herde, but thend shall shewe all, and we have geven order as by the tyme we think you knowe and lyke well your devise therein.

XVII.—Letter from the Council to Lord Russell announcing the mission of Sir William Herbert.

[Petyt MSS. No. 538, vol. 46, fol. 442.]

From my L. Protector and the counsiall the xxiiij of Julii.

After our right hartie coffmendacõns to yor good lordshipp. For the more spedie aide of you we have wrytten to Sr William Herbert, who shall Immedyatlye wth all spede repayre unto you w^th

---

^a This name is doubtful.

a convenyent nomber and power of men, and that so great as it shall please you to appoynt, for Mr. Herbert is of such curage, that he sayth he is hable rather to bring to manye then to fewe and so redie to do. We do not doubt neyther of the good will and stomake that ye have to the Maties service, nor yett of your good husbandrye in so moch as maie be done for his hynes at this p̃sent.

And therefore have com̃ytted the order and appoyntment of the nombers and all other such things unto you. And so praye you to sertyffie Mr. Herbert of yor mynde herein wth all spede, and so bid you right hartely fare well. From Westm^r, the xxiiij^th of Julii, 1549.

Yor Lordshipp's loving frends,
E. Somerset.

T. Cant.   R. Riche Canc.ᵃ

W. Sant John.

W. Noortht.   J. Warwick.   A. Wyngfeld.

Post Script.—We have resayved a l^re here inclosed the wch declayreth from Mr. Hobbie the meanyng of the Frenchemen, to the takyng of some place in Corneswall, the ^wch yf you cane convenyently declare unto them, we think yt will work paventure some what in them.

ᵃ This was Richard Rich, created Baron Rich of Lecze in the county of Essex, Feb. 16, 1547. He was one of the most contemptible characters in the Council. He first sided with Somerset against his brother, and signed the warrant for Seymour's execution. He accompanied Somerset from Hampton Court to Windsor when Edward was removed there, but, finding that Somerset's party was deserting him, he took the great seal with him, and joined Warwick in October, 1549. In the dissensions of 1551, not knowing what side to take, he pretended illness, and resigned office Dec. 21, 1551. He soon recovered, and lived on till the year 1560. His treachery towards Sir Thomas More and perjury on the trial of Bishop Fisher of Rochester may be read in any history of the period.

XVIII.—LETTER FROM THE COUNCIL IN ANSWER TO THE SUPPLICATION OF THE COMMONS OF CORNWALL.

[Petyt MSS. No. 538, vol. 46, fol. 443.]

To the Commons of Cornewalles supplicacon yf thay be not sone^r repressed answer shalbe made.

To Humfrey Arundell's poyson sent a brod by his tres ye shall well occurre, yf ye make proclamacõn there in the shires about you that whosoever shall Receyve take or here any such tre or wrytting sent to incite or move, other to favor, or take pte wth them, or ayde them with vituall or otherwise, shalbe taken as Rebells and suffer forfyture Accordynly, Except immedyatly without participating or opning yt to any other they bring the same letter that they have or see to you, and then ye execute the same Proclamatoñ straytly with all severytie, as we trust eyther nowe by my L. Grays and others comyng, or els verie shortly ye shall full able in the Shyres about you, the which ye may not fayle to do. And lykewyse uppon such as shall use trayterus and rebellyous words, moving and bendyng to sedycõn or to the dysapoynting and dysfornishing of you, or to not serving the Kyngs Matie, or shall aid the rebels.

For the reteyning still of the gentilmen o^r servaunts as Mr. Phillippes and other which ye do write of, we are veyrie well content thay be with still; lykewyse of Mr. Elmer. Ther was other cause why we did send for them. Nowe we are not only cõtent that they shall remayne wth you, but we have also wrytten to other of our men and reteyners to remayne still in the shyres nere unto you to ayd you as nede shalbe. Thus we bid yor L. et^c.

Frome West., the xxvth of Julii, 1549.

Yo^r L. loving frends,

E. SOMERSET.
T. CANT.   R. RICH CANC.   WILLM SANT JOHN.
A. WYNGFELD.

EDWARD NORTH.[a]

---

[a] This was Sir Edward North, who first appears as clerk of the Parliament and afterwards as treasurer of the Court of Augmentations in 1540, and in 1546 Chan-

XIX.—LETTER FROM THE COUNCIL TO LORD RUSSELL GIVING AN ACCOUNT OF THE EXAMINATION OF SIR JOHN ARUNDEL.

[Petyt MSS. No. 538; vol. 46, fol. 443.]

From my L. Protector and the Counseall to my L. previe seall, the Kyngs Matie lieut̃ant in the west p̃ties.

After our right hartie com̃endac̃õns unto your good L. Sr John Arendell, who hath all this while remayned in safe costodie, was yesterdaie before us the lord protector and the rest of the Counsiall, where, being examyned upon suche things as we had to charge hym withall, he sayde that at suche tyme he was fyrst sent for by y^r lordshipp he was verie sicke, and not hable to travell; the seconde t̃res sent from you he shewid us, and more t̃res he sayd he had not nor anye cõmandement other then These two frome y^r L. He sayth forther he was not com̃anded upon his allegeaunce, and that he mynded to have come unto you upon y^r t̃res as sone as he shuld have been able. As for men he sayth he was hable to make no number, being but a stranger in the countrey where he lay. And for hering of Masse he sayth That upon occasyon of the light talk

---

cellor of the same court. He was one of the sixteen executors of the will of Henry VIII., and one of the three sent with Lord Seymour and Sir Anthony Browne to take the great seal from Wriothesley. He was one of the twenty-six appointed Councillors to Somerset, March 12, 1547, by the commission which excluded Wriothesley, and was one of the nine conspirators against Somerset who met at Ely House, Oct. 6, 1549. His name does not appear on the Council's subscription to Edward's limitation of the crown, but he signed the answer to Mary's letter, announcing to her that Lady Jane Grey was queen, July 9, 1553, and also the letters to the sheriff of Nottingham and Derby written from the Tower, July 12, calling Mary a rebel and a bastard. Yet he was raised to the peerage by Mary, April 7, 1554, and bore the sword before Philip, Nov. 24, 1554, on his meeting Cardinal Pole, and it appears from a State Paper of April 29, 1554, that the French ambassador had then lodged at Lord North's house for six months. Elizabeth, on her journey from Hatfield to the Tower, stayed at his house from Nov. 23rd to 28th, 1558. He died Dec. 31, 1564.

of the people at the fyrst rysing of Rebells in Devonshire he caused two masses to be sayd, which he sayd he did only to appease the people, and ever sythens he hath harde and caused to be sayd the servis according to the kyngs Maties order. Procession he sayth he caused to be had upon Corpus Christi day, and after procession the Com̃unyon according to the lawes, and no masse. These things we have thought good to signifie unto your Lordshipp, praying you both to examyne the full trough herof, and also to send us a playne dyscorse of all the sayd Sr John Arendell doyngs wherwith he may be charged, to th'intent we maye forther order the matter accordingly, and so we bid yor L. right hartely farewell.

From Westm^r the xxvijth of Julii, 1549.

Yo^r L. assured frends,

E. SOMERSET. T. CANT. R. RICHE.
W. SANCT JOHN. A. WINGFELD.
W. PETRE, S^y. JOHN BAKERE.[a]

---

[a] The name of Sir John Baker has appeared only once before in these papers, viz., on July 10th. He was not one of the executors of the will of Henry VIII., but one of the twelve appointed to assist them as privy councillors. He had been attorney-general from 1536 to 1540. He was one of the twenty-six councillors whose names are mentioned in the patent by which Somerset held his protectorship. He was present at the Council, Aug. 10, 1540, when Paget was made clerk of the Council, where he is designated as Chancellor of the First Fruits and Tenths. He was Speaker of the House of Commons at the time of Lord Seymour's condemnation. On the 9th of October he joined Warwick's party against Somerset. He was forced to come to the Council, June 11th, 1553, and on June 21st was one of the twenty-four who set their hands to Edward's device for the limitation of the crown, though he was very unwilling at first to do so. He was present at the Proclamation of Queen Mary, July 19, 1553. After this he disappears from history.

XX.—Letter from the Council to Lord Russell with further instructions.
[Petyt MSS. No. 538, vol. 46, fol. 444.]

Frome my l. protector and the Cõsell to my L. Pryvie Seall, lieutãnt to the Kyng's Matie in the west p̃ties.

After our hartie com̃endacõn to your lordshipp. To your letters the xxvth of Julii, we have aunswered for the most p̃te in our former letters. As to that of sending you horsemen, you must understand that ye made the keping of Excester so impossible, and the keping of them in the strights so full of desperacõn that our devyse was to make you strong with horsemen to matche them on the playne, and so we sent unto you therafter, and wrote unto you our mynde and phantysie as we thought best, nor ye must not thinke that we put eyther any doubts in your wysdome or experyence in warre or reprove your doyngs when we do wright unto you our advyse. The care which we have and cannot put from us that all shuld be well causeth us to wryte. And how wise and valyant capteyne a man is, yett to here the Counsiall of another can do no hurte. And we thinke us to have some experyence in these things. Marie we wrote as though thay had nowe passed the streights.

Ye did encounter a skirmishe with them in the streights, and therefore in dede footmen and harquebuses could do more service, and so we have provyded for you.

We lyke well your devyse for pinises to cut of theyr vytayles by sea.

Where ye declare that thoccasyon of being able to levie so fewe in Somersetshire is the evill inclynation of the people, and that there are amongs them that do not styck openly to speak such traterous words agaynst the kyng and in favor of the trayterous rebells. Ye shall hang two or three of them, and cause them to be executed lyke traytors, And that wilbe the only and the best staye of all those talks.

As to them that maketh dyverse excuses and will not serve the kyngs Matie, ye shall cause them to be noted espĩally the chiefe doers, and in your retorne thay may be ordered according to theyr deserts. Though ye think proclamaçõns can do no great good, so as we wrote unto you made, yet thay may do you some good. Hurt they can do none.

The Proclamaçõns in Cornewall, though thay have wroght no great effect in Devonshyre as yet, as long as thay be there in strenght, all which will ye knowe no man dare medle to invade theyr possessyons. And more yt will Corwall, till the nomber be depted. But when those Campes and nombers should have removed and come forward, men wold have bene redye to have stepped into theyr howses and lands. And thay wold have bene glad to have returned to the defence of theyr owne.

Ye wryte that ye are answered in termes, and that the wryter mystoke the name of shier. We do not take yt so, and we think we understand the matyer well enũgh, for a mold with you is sone made, and with a dice of Iron and leade there, ye shuld sone cast yor fytte shot. And for us here, not knowing the hight and ermatytie of your peces, how is yt possable we shuld sende you shott, we shuld paventure sent you shott as fytt as a shoe for a mans hand.

And altho' we send you sufficyent furnyture of shot for bowes, yet ye must understand that the more arrowes ye use except good heade be taken the more ye furnysh your ennymie, Who will returne your owne arrowes agayne to you, as Mr. Travers sayth ye did to them a skrymyshe. And therefore the shott of the habirgõn pelot is brust; which never returneth. The dearth of vituall which maketh that your souliers cannot lyve of theyr waigs ye maie some what ease by settyng pryce of vitayle. And the rebells using belyke the church goodes be the more lyberall. For that matyer yf nede be of geving more wages, No man knoweth the kyng's Maties necessytye better then you. Yf yt wilbe a spedy fortherance for the dyspatch of the matier use your dyscryssõn therin. But ye must therwithall what an example this wilbe hereafter. We do lyke well yor ordering of the ring leaders, and recon no lesse then you do that sharpe justice must be executed upon those sondric traytors which will learne by nothing but by the sword. We do not doubt but ye have geven theyr espiall that shuld carie the letter to be publysshed in pulpets his dewe reward, and so bidd you right heretely fayre well.

Frome Westm^r the xvijth [a] of Julii.

Post Script.—We have sent you the kyngs Maties answere to the rebells of Cornwalles supplicacōn, And also certen Proclamacons against those constables which hath bene or wold be sturrers and caryers abrode of the Rumors to bryng the people in an uprore.

Yo^r L. loving frends,

E. SOMERSET.

T. CANT.   R. RICHE.   W. SANCT JOHN.
A. WYNGFELD.[b]
W. PETRE, S^y.[c]
T. SMYTH.
JOHN BAKERE.

---

[a] A mistake of the transcriber for July 27.

[b] This was Sir Anthony Wingfield who appears as captain of the Guard in 1536. He was present at the Council, holding the office of Vice-Chamberlain when Paget was appointed clerk of the Council, Aug. 10, 1540. He was made Knight of the Garter in 1541, from which time he appears to have been in constant attendance on the king, and was nominated in his will to be of the Privy Council, who should assist the executors. He was present at the Council of Feb. 21, 1548, and signed the order for the removal of images from churches, as well as the warrant for Seymour's execution, March 17, 1549. He joined the party against Somerset on the 9th of October, 1549, and on the 11th he was sent to Windsor to secure the person of Somerset, and on the following February 2, when Arundel and Southampton were banished from the Council, he was rewarded for his services by being promoted from being captain of the Guard to the office of Lord Chamberlain of the Household in succession to Paget, who had been raised to the peerage and made Comptroller, Jan. 19, 1550. He was sent with Rich and Petre to the Princess Mary, Aug. 28, 1551, with the king's letter about the service of the mass.

[c] This was Sir William Petre who was Secretary of State, July 7, 1544. He was sent with Lord Russell, who had just been created Earl of Bedford, with Paget and

XXI.—Proclamation[a] to Justices of Peace issued in July, 1549.

[Society of Antiquaries' Collection of Proclamations.]

A Proclamation comaunding all Justices of the peace, Knights, and Gentlemen to repair home to their habitacõns and countries.

The Kings most excellent Matie by the advice of his most dearest uncle Edward Duke of Somersett, Governor of his most Roiall person and of his Realmes, Domynions, and Subjects, protector, and the rest of his privie Counsell, straightly chargeth and comaundeth all and singuler Justices of peace, Knights, and other Gentlemen inhabiting and dwelling within any County or place of this Realme of England that they and every of them with all convenient speed shall repair unto their dwelling houses to putt themselves in order and readines to serve his highnes, as they and every of them tender his Ma^{ts} pleasure, and will answere to the contrary att their uttermost perills.

Sir John Mason, as ambassador to France, January 21, 1550. He was one of the twelve appointed to assist the sixteen executors of the will of Henry VIII., and was one of the twenty-six councillors appointed in Somerset's patent as Protector. He was on the commission to examine all contemners of the Book of Common Prayer in 1549. He was on the commission with Cranmer, Ridley, Smith, and May to try Bonner, any three of them having full power to deprive him (Rymer, xv. 191); but he seems not to have sat after the first day, and Bonner was condemned by the other four. He joined the conspirators against Somerset, October 6, and afterwards was one of the commissioners who deprived Gardiner of his bishopric, April 18, 1551, and afterwards, August 28, was sent to the Princess Mary, with the Lord Chancellor and Sir Anthony Wingfield, to persuade her to give up the service of the mass, and signed the Council's letter of July 9, declaring that Lady Jane Grey was Queen, but turned with the tide and declared for Queen Mary, July 19, and was appointed one of the committee for managing affairs during Philip's absence from England in 1556, and afterwards, at the accession of Elizabeth, became one of the Queen's Council.

[a] This proclamation has been printed from the manuscript copy No. 43, in the collection of printed and manuscript Proclamations in the possession of the Society of Antiquaries. It does not appear in Grafton's edition of the Proclamations of this reign.

XXII.—Letter from the Council to Lord Russell declining to send him more troops.

[Petyt MSS. No. 538, vol. 46, fol. 446.]

From my L. P. and the counsiall the xxviiith of Julii.

After our right hartie comendacons to your lordshipp. We do perceyve by Mr. Herbert letters that he doth intend to make you x^m men on fotte, by reason that ye have so required of him. The which request semeth to us straung. For when we do consyder that Cornewall and Devonshyre both of them shuld make all theyr force is not able to make above vij^m men, tag and rag, that shuld come to fyght, and yet some we are sure thay leave behind to kepe theyr howses and the townes and one thousand of them is in Exceter. So that things, accompted as they shuld be esteymed, The rebells cannot be thought to be in the hole agaynst you past iiij^m men and the more part unarmed, as indede thay have been estemed of some that hath vewyd them; your bande alredie we take yt to be no lesse then about iiij^m more or lesse; And yet better armed with harmes and having arquibusses, which thaie have none.

And ye must consyder that yf seyng now ye c̃oplaine for want of vytayle, yf such a nomber men suche come unto you, The one of you should be redye to cate a nother for want. And ye shuld be constrayned to scale and depart peradventure before th'enterpryse done. Then agayne seing th'enemie lyeth in the strength, ye cannot occupie above ij^m at ones, thought ye wold never so fayne. So that yf ye devyde your bande and assayle them in two places at ones, yet ye shalbe sufficient, consydering the good ordre and armirae a gaynst fearfull rebells and unarmed. And yf they shall come abrode Then are ye well provyded of horsemen, which thay have not. Yf Mr. Herbert bring you two or three thousand men out of Waylles well appoynted with ij^m out of Glocestershyre and Wyltshyre, taken but of the best appoynted and most willing, ye shalbe better for your purpose then yf ye shuld have xx^m ; for the multytude shuld not only pesture you, and consume your vitayles, but of so many some doubtfull and holowe herted shuld turne to the rebells part. Ye shuld be in more daunger of your own company then of the rebells them selfes. Wherefore we pray you consyder those things amongs other. And so take ordre accordingly.

Fare you most hartily well.

Frome Westm̃ the xxviijth of Julii.[a]

Yo^r L. loving ffrends,

E. SOMERSET.

R. RICHE CANC.

W. SANCT JOHN.

A. WYNGFELD.

WJLLM. PETRE, S^y.

T. SMYTH.

---

[a] Between this letter and that of August 8 there is a letter headed with the king's name and signed by Somerset, addressed to the gentry of Essex, summoning them to assemble at Walden, in Essex, before the 17th day of August to meet the Duke of Somerset. This being Sunday, Cranmer's absence is accounted for by his probably being engaged in preaching somewhere, as he was on the preceding Sunday, 21st July, when it was noticed that he inveighed against the rebels, and celebrated in a cope without a vestment, and communicated eight persons. On Saturday, the 10th of August, he preached again at St. Paul's to the same effect. This accounts for his absence from the Council on that day also. He was expected on the 31st of August, to preach again on the subject of the suppression of all the three rebellions, but sent Dr. Joseph, his chaplain, rector of St. Mary-le-Bow, in his stead.

XXVI.—Letter from Somerset to Lord Russell, announcing the Declaration of War by the French King.

[Petyt MSS. No. 538, vol. 46, fol. 449.]

Frome my L. protector to my L. pryvie seall, Lieutenant of the west parties, the viij. Julii.[a]

After our hartie comendacōns to your Lordshipp, this daie the French Embassador hath bene with us and declared unto us that the French King hath revoked hym, and hath declared open warre agaynst the Kyngs Matie and all his subjects.

Wherefore these shalbe to will and require you to gyve ordre with all spede possible to all the ports of the Countie of Dorsett, Devon, and Cornewall, and all other places of your Jurisdyccōn, that thay have good guard and care to the ports and all places where th'ennymie may land; and also to the Countrey to be redie to the defence yf thay shuld land in any place. And that they destroy all Frenchemen's merchandises, shippes, and goods what so ever they be, being not denyzed, and theyr persons also, as enymies to the kyngs ^{m}a^{tie} and put them in sauf custodie till forther order be taken as apteyneth. Thus we pray you fayle not.

Frome Westm̃ the viijth of August 1549.

Yo^r L. loving frend,

E. Somerset.

Post scripṭ.

And forasmoche as the Frenche Kyng hath declared hym selfe open Enymie to the Kyng's Matie, highnes geveth lycence to all maner his subjects furwyth to arme them selfs and theyr vessells to the seas and to make good pryse of any Frenchemen's wayres.

---

[a] This is a mistake of copying for 8 August. This letter, which was misplaced in the MS. volume, is here restored to its proper place according to its date.

XXVII.—Letter from the Council to Lord Russell advising him to diminish his forces.

[Petyt MSS. No. 538, vol. 46, fol. 447.]

Frome my L. P. and the Counsiall to my L. prevye seall, leiutenant to the Kyngs Matie in the west pties.

After our right hartie comendacõns to your Lordshipp,

Having respect to the Kyngs Maties charges and the necessytie of this tyme, the which no man knoweth better than you, uppon this good successe[a] the Almyghtye God be your travaill hath sent the Kyngs Matie we have good t'admonishe your Lordshipp of this. Praying you to dymysse of such nombers as ye have superfluous and more, and ye thinke shall serve you espially the men of the shyres of Somersett and Dorsett; And that for two causes, thone that the same will most faȳtly fight agaynst the Devonshyre men, theyr neighbors, and had most nede to have the gentilmens and men of wysdome and dyscryssyon emongs them to rule them and kepe them due obedyence and ordre, Thother that Frannce having broken with us, it were most expedyent that there shuld be some wyse heades and power in the sayd shyres for the saffegard of them against all attempts; And espially Pole and other places upon the sea syde; and most of all consydering that such nombers as ye nowe have there, vitailes being but skarsse, must nedes be dayly more skarse. So that the great nomber shall rather hynder then forther you by consumyng of vitayles, and do you no more servis then a fewer shall.

And where we have advertysed you of this our mynde we pray you to signifie unto us agayne frome tyme to tyme what nombers ye shall have, that we may take ordre agayne for the payment of them accordyngly.

---

[a] Lord Russell had defeated the insurgents towards the end of July, and six days later, viz. on Saturday, August 3, began his march with about 1,000 men towards Exeter, which he reached on Tuesday, August 6.

And to th'entent the same may be more spedely done, we have wrytten to the mayor and the towne of Excester that for the more hastie furnyture thay make for you so moche monye as they may. And we shall repaie the same unto them eyther in London or els where they wuld leyfer have yt within eight dayes at the ferthest, theyr certyficat of the delyvery therof made and delyvered unto us, when we knowe what som yt is thay have provyded unto you. Then as the countrey shall growe more and more quiet for the more dyschargyng of the Kyngs Maties charges and great costs ye dymysse such as be ferthest of, And so by lytyll and lytill, as your wysdome shall se most expedyent, Alleviate at this tyme suche expences as possable may be spayred. The causes why we do require this nedyth not to be declared unto you.

Thus we bid your L. most hartely fare well.

Frome Westminster the tenth of August, 1549.[a]

Your l. loving ffrends.

And forsomoche as the horsemen shall do you but small servis the espially in that contrey we pray you dymisse so many horsemen as ye may, consydering that the horsemen be double charges to fottmen and being able to do so small serves shalbe Importable And vayne cost to the Kyngs highness. And Touching the straungers horsemen soncst of all to dymysse them to come to London, that we maie Imploye them more necessarie beyond the seas, where they maie do better servis. And though ye shall not padventure have mouye at that present to paie them holie, Yet ye shall cause to be reconed with them to a certeyn daie, And so dymiss them Appoynting

---

[a] There is a letter of the same date, August 10, printed by Tytler, vol. i. p. 193, from Warwick to Cecil, deprecating the substitution of himself in the place of the Marquis of Northampton, to be Commissioner for the counties of Cambridge, Bedford, Huntingdon, Northampton, Norfolk, and Suffolk; on the ground that it would be a fresh discouragement to Northampton, who had "lately by misfortune received discomfort enough." Northampton had entered the City of Norwich, July 31, and on the same night was defeated by the rebels, who burned part of the town and killed Lord Sheffield.

them shalbe payed, and we shall not fayle to take order that they shalbe fully contented and payed as aperteyneth. As for the pardon of Pomeray, the Kyngs Matie by our advises refereth the same to yor lordshipp to be graunted by you yf you shall so thynk good. Marie, we wold yt were graunted to hym secretlie, and he traveled with all that tyme of the promys therof for spiall service to be fyrst done by hym, eyther in the apprehendyng of Humfray Arandell, Underhill, or some other of the most notable. He must also declare his former popish errors to suche as have bene seduced in religion by hym; So as lyke as he was a meane to allure them to blynde supersticōn and papistry he maie also travell nowe to bryng them to knowledg of theyr dewties and trewe religion, wherein ye must travell as earnestly as ye maie.

We wold that yor L. shuld cause inquery to be made in all places as for papists, for masse bookes of th'olde superstissious service, and cause them to be brent, geving order that people do use the service appoyntid by his Matie, and that the gentilmen and Justices of peax have contynually a good eye to see the same executed accordyngly.

As for mouye required by your L. we mynde to gyve ordre for sending of a convenyent som towards you with all spede as we maie.

We require your Lordshipp to have a good respect to the suyertie of the towne and pte of Poole in Dorssetshire, And to appoynt some of your Dorsetshire men for the suyertie therof. You knowe that the takyng therof by the Frenchmen might be verie dangerous to the realme.

 E. SOMERSET.
  R. RICHE CANC^r.
   WILLIAM SANT JOHN..
    THOMAS SOUTHAMPTON.[a]

WYLLM PETRE, S^y.

[a] This is the first time in the course of these papers that the name of the Earl of Southampton appears as a councillor. He is better known by the name of Lord Chancellor Wriothesley. In 1538 he had been made Secretary of State, and had

XXVIII.—Letter of Thanks from the Council to Lord Russell.

[Petyt MSS. No. 538, vol. 46, fol. 449.]

Frome my L. Protector and the counsyall to the lord previe seall, leuteynant to the Kings Matie in the west parts.

After our most hartie comendacõns unto y^r good lordshipp,

We have seen your lres of the vijth of this instant and have the credyt of Mr. Travers, by the which, lyke as we do at good lengthe well understand your wise doings and the good and honorable successe yt hath pleased God to graunt you agaynst those rebells; So have we thought good to gyve your Lordshipp the Kings Matyes and our most hartie thankes for the same, nothing doubting but as the [same] is presently moche to your comendacõn and honor, so shall the remembrance therof so remayne in the Kyngs Matie as

always been a particular friend of Gardiner, Bishop of Winchester, and with him was chiefly concerned in the Act of the Six Articles. He was always zealous for the old learning, and, having previously been raised to the peerage, January 1, 1544, as Baron Wriothesley of Titchfield, he succeeded to Audley when he resigned the great seal, April 22, 1544, and took the oath abjuring the Papal Supremacy, April 30. Upon Audley's death he was made Lord Chancellor, May 3. He drew the king's will, and was appointed one of the sixteen executors, and was created Earl of Southampton, Feb. 16, 1547. He was the only one of the council of whom Somerset at that time was afraid, who accordingly managed to deprive him of his office March 6, 1547, as well as of his seat in the Council. Accordingly little more is heard of him for two years. It is probable he regained his seat in the Council by the influence of Warwick, who could calculate upon him as an ally in thecoming contest with Somerset, but the exact time has not been ascertained, but he signed the warrant for committing Lord Seymour to the Tower, Jan. 17, 1549. He also signed the new Statutes for Cambridge as a member of the Council, April 8, 1549 He, with Gardiner, appears to have been quite sincere in his acquiescence in the abolition of the Papal authority in England, but was opposed to all other changes in religion. From this time forward he appears as the opponent of Somerset believing that Warwick was at heart a Catholic, and died apparently disgusted with the turn affairs had taken, July 31, 1550. On Somerset's deposition he, with Northampton, Warwick, St. John, Russell, and Wentworth, was appointed to the charge of governor of the king's person.

you shall have good cause to reiose of theyse your travells and labor employed at this tyme.

We do all so understand by yor sayd lres the good servis of the lord Graie and sondrye other gentilmen, to whom we requyr yor Lordshipp not only to gyve the Kyngs Maties most hartie thank on our behalfes, but also to assure them that the Kyngs M^{atie} will not fayle to have alwaie upon any occasyon to be mynistred such consyderacōn therof as shalbe to all theyr comforts, wherof your Lordshipp may bothe assure them and shewe this parte of our lres with our hartie comendacōns and thanks for the same unto them.

We praie yor Lordshipp also to gyve thanks to Mr. Bluet, the gentilmen, Mayor and others within the cytie of Excester throught whose paynes, wisdome, and good courayge that citie hath veric honestly preserved themselfes agaynst the sayd rebells, and therby declared theyr good affections to his Matie, which you maie well assure them shall be so consydered towards every of them in any resonable suyttes hereafter as shalbe to theyr comforts. And thus with our most hartie thankes to yor Lordshipp and them all, we bid you hartely farewell.

Frome Westm̃ the xth of August,[a] 1549.

      Your l. assured loving frends,

E. SOMERSET.

        R. RICHE CANC^r.

  W. SANCT JOHN.

        THOMAS SOUTHAMPTON.

  W. PETRE.

        JO. BAKERE.

---

[a] "The 10th of August, being Saturday, the Archbishop of Canterbury made a collation in Paul's quire for the victory that the Lord Russell, Lord Privy Seal had on Monday last past against the rebels in Devonshire, which had besieged Exeter, and lain in camp before it by the space of three weeks, and like to have famished them in the town, but the said. Monday, the Lord Privy Seal entered the city and slew, hurt, and took prisoners of the said rebels 4000, and after hanged divers of them in the town, and about the country."—*Wriothesley's Chronicle*, vol. ii. p. 20.

XXIX.—Another letter of the Council to Lord Russell, limiting the number of his advisers.
[Petyt MSS. No. 538, vol. 46, fol. 450.]

From my l. p. and the counsiall the xth of August to my l. previe seale, the Kyng's Maties Leiutenant in the west pts.

After o^r most hartie comendacõns. Understanding that our verie loving frend Sr Willm Herbert and his companye, a greatt nomber gentilmen be arryved with your lordshipp, albeyt we do knowe that both amongs them and those which were with you before there be many which for theyr wysdomes, experyence, and other good qualyties bee worthie to be of his Maties counsiell with you for his highnes affayres there; Yett consydering that the having of many counseallors shall not only be trobelous to them that be called but also maie breed a confusyon in thaffayres, we have thought good to requyre yor lordshipp to use the persons underwrytten only as his Maties counsellor^s under you who be appoynted by his Matie by our advyses to be of counsyall, that is to say, my l. Gray, Mr Herbert, Sr John Pawlett, Sr Hugh Pawlett, Sr Andro Dudley, and Sr Thomas Speke, whome we doubt nothing but yor L. shall fynde them both deligent and wylling to ayde and assist you to the best of their power, And thus we bid you most hartely farewell.

From Westm^r this x^th of August, 1549.

Yo^r good L. assured frends,

E. Somerset.

W. Sanct John.

R. Riche Canc^r.

Thomas Southampton.

W. Petre.

Jo. Bakere.

XXX.—Letter from Somerset to Lord Russell, directing him how to act as regards the Insurgents.

[Petyt MSS. No. 538, vol. 46, fol. 451.]

From my l. protector to my lord pryvie seall, leiutenant to the kyngs Matie in the west partes.

After our right hartie comendacons to yor Lordshipp, We are right glad to heare by yor lres that the men about Excet^r cometh in so redelie to demaund theyr pardon, wherby we trust ye shall have the les to do w^t the rest.

As touching your proclamaçon, the copie whereof ye wryte to have sent us, yt was be lyke forgotting by your secreterie. And therefore not having yt we cane gyve no judgment of yt. We do lyke well that Orne shuld be brought in by his brother; So that yet some of that stocke semeth to be true men to the kings Matie, And so praie you that spayring the comon and mean men ye do execute the heads and cheyf styrrors of the rebellyon; And that in so dyverse places as ye maie to the more terror of the unrulie.

For Paget, for so miche as he is manyfestly knowen to have bene an heade and Captyon of rebellion, altho' Some favo^r peradventure for his brothers sake[a] some wold thynke shuld be shewyd,

[a] This brother was Sir William Paget, clerk of the Council, 1540-43, made a Privy Councillor, April 23, 1543, and one of the sixteen executors of the will of Henry VIII. He was afterwards raised to the peerage with the title of Lord Paget of Beaudesert, Jan. 19, 1550, when he resigned his office of Comptroller of the Household, which was given to Sir Anthony Wingfield. This was the same day that Russell was made Earl of Bedford and St. John Earl of Wiltshire. Two days afterwards he was sent as ambassador to France with the Earl of Bedford, Sir William Petre, and Sir John Mason. He sided with Somerset, and Oct. 10, 1549, addressed a letter from Windsor to the Lords of the Council at London, which was signed also by Cranmer and Smith. He stuck by Somerset to the last, and was sent with the Earl of Arundel to the Tower in November, 1551. On the 22nd of April, 1552, his Garter and George were taken from him, and given to the eldest son of the Duke of Northumberland. And on the following 6th of December he was deprived of the chancellorship of the Duchy of Lancaster. His name does not appear among the councillors who signed Edward's device for the succession. Pro-

Yet in this case of suche treason and rebellion as this, yt behoveth us most of all to shewe Indyfferent Justice, and especially consydering that we have not spayred our owne brother in mat^r conserning the damage of the kyngs Maties person and high treason, as our dutie was, Yt shuld mych Import us yf we should spare any other mans brother. And therefore in no wise we wold ye shuld in this case shewe any other favor then as to dyrect Justice apperteyneth, and so procede to hym with the rest.

Touching the noiacōn of the counsell before this tyme, we ar sure ye have receyved our l̃res to yor satysfaction.

We wold gladlye here of Humfray Arondells doyngs and demeanour, and how ye shall demeane yourself wth hym, whome we trust shortlye ye shall have in yor hands. Whome and Wyncestlo and Underhill, yt is for the Kyngs Maties honor not to escape due ponyshment; But that ther example shuld be terror this great while to all the countrey, And not to attempt such kynd of rebellion agayne.

We have wrytten to the towne of Excester to ayde you with so moche monye as thay cane, as by this tyme we ar suer ye knowe. And yet neverthelesse we have geven order for monye to be sent unto you so spedely as cõvenyently yt maie be.

Touching thencrease of yor nombers, in dede we are not ignorant that ye have a great noumber, and therfore we ar rather affrayed that the multytude and nõber will hynder you, so that ye shall not have vytayll suffycient. Wherfore as we have wrytten to you in our last l̃res, So eftsones we pray you as ye maie demysse of yor nomber especially and fyrst of the shyres of Somerset and Dorset for the defence of the countrey yf nede shalbe agaynst the Frenche, And

---

bably he had been deprived of his seat in the Council; and he was sent with the Earl of Arundel to Queen Mary, whose cause they had espoused on the night of July 19, 1553, and July 24th they conducted Northumberland from Cambridge to London. He seems afterwards to have been in high favour with Philip and Mary, and was made Lord Privy Seal January 1, 1556, the same day that Archbishop Heath was created Lord Chancellor.

better staye agaynst the unrulie. And though ye have not monye to dyscharge them cleane, yet ye maie dymysse them to ease the king of further charge, willing them to leave one man a peace, or twoo of a band to receyve the monie. And we thinke a good nombre of the gentilmen dyssyrous to go home wilbe right glad of that dyscharche and so to be dysmyssed. And so ever as the Cuntre more and more is subdued and brought to obedyence to dymisse theyr bandes, the strangers fyrst and horsemen and those that be forthest of, and shuld put the kyngs ^{matie} to most charge.

We do not doubt but that yor charges be greate and yor dyets costly, and, though present ordre be not geven, yet ye shall not doubt but that shall be no lesser by the Kyngs Maties servis.

Ye have done well to execute the ringleaders. Marry we wold gladly the names and the nomber of them. And thus we bid yor L. most hartely farewell.

From Westm̃ the xjth [a] of August, 1549.

Y^r L. loving frends,

E. SOMERSETT.

Post script.—That we do wryte to you of Pagett this is our meanyng ; yf he be indede and have declared him selfe a cheyftyan leder or capten of sydycõn, Then he is other to have according to Justice as reason is. Yf he have not bene a notable styrer or ringleder, Then you to use the thing according to yor dyscrycõn.

---

[a] On the same day, Sunday, August 11, there was an order of Council as follows:—

"An order was taken, that from henceforth no printer should print or put to vente any English book but such as should first be examined by Mr. Secretary Peter, Mr. Secretary Smyth, and Mr. Cicell, or the one of them, and allowed by the same, under pain," &c.

XXXI.—Letter from the Council to Lord Russell dwelling on the Dangers from an Apprehended French Invasion.

[Petyt MSS. No. 538, vol. 46, fol. 452 b.]

From my l. p and the counsiall to my lord pryvie Seall, lieutenant to the Kyngs Mā.

After our right hartie comendacõns to yor good L.

The same shall understand that we have receyved your lres of the xijth of this present grounded for answer of ours sent unto you for the demynicõn of the power there; and where ye alledge the reasons that move your staye, And so make your request for monye to be sent thither, which is thother pte of your lres. To the fyrst, for your nombers we consyder howe greate the same be of horsemen; And where ye wryte that albeyt the contrey men come in more and more by submyssyon, yet the same is not so pfect that ye thynk not meate to weaken your power, And that ye will neverthelesse in the respect of the defence of the Counties of Somerset and Dorset agaynst the enymies, do that maie be done both therefore and namely for exonoracõn of the Kyngs charge; My L. yf ye kuewe as moche as we do herein presently see (and yet ye cane well gesse yt) what dyvers and sondrye occasyons the Kyngs Matie hath temploy both men and monye, ye wold think we desyer not this demynishment of charge without good cause. His highnes hath a French Kyng, as hath been advertyssed you, for ennymie, agaynst whose yong and lustie attempts both by sea and lande all Shyfte must be made to provyde. We have the Northe, which is no small charge and daylie shall increase to prevent the worst that maie ensue ther, knowing what accompt the Frenche maketh t'annoye us and to hynder our proceedings that waie, appoynting or invasyon agaynst us bothe in Fraunce and there at an instant. The charge of the sea, the renforce of all oure forts with men, tharmy, which of force hath bene prepayred under conduccõn of my Lord of Warwik into Norff. beinge x or xii m¹ men besydes a number prepayred to attend on the Kyng's Matie about viii or x m¹ men; theis things consydered, as on thone parte yt is a plaine mater to say you that monie was never so deare, and that therfor we must avoyd all causes of the least expences, So, weying of thother side, the necessytie to imploye men in so manye places, we be movid to require at least frome you the sending of your strangers horsemen hether for spiall servis els where, besydes the dysmissing there of some others to theyre countryes, wch you maie well do, yor nomber of horsem̃ beinge so greate as yt is; we meane not to dysmysse yor footmen strangers, whose staie is so necessarie to you as thay be, and your com̃endaco͂n suche of them as the hagabut which thaie use with skill maie not be spayred frome you; and suerly what for lacke of mouye and vytayle to furnisshe so great a nomber, you must of force both abridge your nomber as sone as ye maie cõvenyently, and of y^r victorie so well begonne devyse to make some good, and with spede; for yf you shall suffer those rebells to breathe, to catche a pryde by your somewhat forbearing to followe them, and wynning tyme so to gether strong uppon you, yowe shall not do that with a great nomber that taken in tyme you might have done with a moche fewer; at the fyrst thay were in some dysmaie, and then one of your men being in array was worth three of the rebells, sythens by some lyberty to gather thay may take newe stomakes, wax desperet and strengthen them selfes agaynst you; ye peradventer thay maie so take comoditie to get some porte wherby bothe to weaken you so miche and so withal gyve an entrey by theyr desperaco͂n and mallice to forren enymyes to hold yt, and to force th'inhabitants of suche porte to take parte also expressly agaynst you; and as to lacke of your victuall, though we wold never so fayne helpe you with yt by sea, yet must some stay be for the provyssyon and shipping of yt on the way, and howe uncerteyne the wether will every daie be more and more, ye ar a sea man, ye can well ynough tell. There is cause to bestowe a force of shippes to other purposes as th'affayres be nowe you knowe, And why shuld not those countrey men be compelled to furnishe you as well as the rebells cane bring them to victuall them agaynst the Kyngs good subjects? And shall they be suffered to denye yt yow for the Kyng yf you dysperse your nombers of men to sundery pties, so nevertheles as thay maie be redic ever to joyne to gether, ye maie put to them the feare of burning and spoyeling of the cõntrey as the Rebells have done, and force them to vytaill yowe. All shyft possable must be used to furnishe yourselfe ther of that ye maye.

And though we send yowe p̃ntly a sõme of monye, such as with respect to other places we maie convenyently spare, yet cane yt not so soone arryve with you but that yf ye shuld tarry and slacke service before the comyng of yt, ther wold be a wonderfull consumption of tyme, And the thinge almost eaten out in waiges, or ever yt could be brought to be delyveryd unto them that shuld serve for yt; in the dysmissing then of suche of your men as ye send awaie, we wold not wyshe any tarring for theyr monye, but let them leave in every countrey a s̃peall man to resave yt when it cõmyth.

And nowe good my Lorde we praie yowe agayne and agayne do yow yor uttermost to folowe yor so welbegonne victorye, that yt maie take a perfect end assone as ye maie possablie; wherein we assure you as the tyme of the yere growe downwards towards wynter, being but a monthes matter, and all cyrconslances besyds do require, ther was never occasyon to dysyre yt at your hands then nowe, We be so occupied on every hand; And albeyt, god be thanked, the reast of the realme here is quiet save only Norffolke, being this informed frome Mr. Vicechamberlayne that the Suffolk men be pacyffid, yet to say the trough of things, that matter of Norffolk being hytherto evill governed is lyke to breade a charge before yt be endid; for where the marques of Northampton, having a power with him, was specially instructed tovoyde the fight, and being a number of horse should by speciall order have kept the feld and so have penned them from vitaill, and otherwyse so awaked them as to have made them sought theyr pardon; And therby to have preserved the kyngs subjects bothe of the marques parte and of thother corrupt mēbers who might have bene brought to the acknowledge of theyr dewties, yf it hade bene well handeled, he and suche advyse of counsiall as he had there lefte quite their Instruccõn and went to pynne them selfes within the towne of Norwich, which afterwards they were fayne to habandon, And but for the corage, the ranke Traytor Kett and his compayny had them upon the soden of theyr goying, which required [*sic*] ther was, God be thanked, no great losse saving the losse of the lord Sheffild, and otherwise ther was not D on bothe sydes slayne; for, though yt were bruted at the fyrst that Sr John Clere, Mr. Cornewalles, and others were slayne, yt hathe sythens appered unto us by them that saw therin, there was not a gentilman slayne, and gentilmen and serving men did as well acquit themselfs by corrage at the fight as ever did men.

And we trust by gods grace th'erle of Warwike shalbe able to bring yt shortlye to a full quiet, so as yf god be so mercyfull unto us as to end your things there, we shall the better attend forren doyings, and so satysfie your dyssyer to understand the state of our procedings; hetherto ye shall knowe that we have rather gayned then lost at the Frenchmens handes; for not longe before the turne of th'embassadors revocacõn from hence, which movyd us to staye the portes, And geve lybertie to arme agaynst them as hath bene signified unto you, we had assured word frome Gurnesey howe the Frenche men intending to have surprysed our shippes and th'isles with a certen nomber of theyr shippes and Gallees, were so hotlye saluted by oure shippes and th'island that by playne confession of them that sawe yt, thay lost at least m^l men, theyr shippes and gallees so spoyled as being forced to returne home, we knowe by this daie thay be not able to sett out agayne. Out of Fraunce we hard that one Towne and in one vessell there were brought at least three score gentlemen to be buryed, and an espiall inhibition is had in Fraunce not to speke of theyre successe in that Journey. Ye knowe they were wont yf theyre losse were but meane to brag of victorie. Thay toke a lytell Island called Serk and fortyfyed yt, but theyr meanyng was to have one of the Isles of Jersey, Gernesey, or Alderneye or all of them yf thay might. The next morning after the Imbassado^r being with us we had frome the lord Clynton suche newes as wherof ye shall word for word receyve the copie. A good entre and beginning we have, and trust yt will lyke god in whome we repose ourselfes cheyffly to graunt no lesse countennance of successe; for never was there so evill a chosen tyme for one prynce to thynke to do dyspleasure to other as this Frenche kyng thought to have had nowe.

Thus fare your good lordshipp right hartely well.

Frome Westm̃ the xxiiijth [a] of August, 1549.

Yo^r L. assured frends,

E. SOMERSET.

R. RICHE CANC^r. W. SANCT JOHN.

THOMAS SOUTHAMPTON.

WILL'M PAGET.

XXXII.—LETTER FROM THE COUNCIL TO LORD RUSSELL, AUTHORISING HIM TO BESTOW KNIGHTHOOD ON SUCH AS HE THOUGHT DESERVING OF THE HONOUR.

[Petyt MSS. No. 588, vol. 46, fol. 456.]

Frome the Counseill to my lord previe Seall.

After our ryght hartie c̃omendacons to yor good lordshipp.

The same shall understand that we have receyved your łres of the xith of this present with suche other łres and wrytings as ye sent with the same. And fyrst were ye declare to have lacke of monye and vitaill; as to monye we have sent all redie within these twoo dayes the som̃e of syxe thowsand poundes, which you must husband to th'uttermost, consyderinng as we have sayd monye was

[a] This must be a mistake of the copier for August 14th.

never so dere with us; and therefore as moche as ye maie devyse to dimynish your charges, and for vitaill, howe unhable we be to furnishe you therof by sea, ye, thorought we wold never so fayne, howe uncerteyne the wether is ye cane well consyder, And therfore we requyre you to provide the best ye maie to have things there which being not refused to the rebells, moche lesse ought to be denyed to you, being there in the service of the Kyngs Matie and the realme.

Ye require to have m^l men to land at the backs of the rebells; we have taken ordre that certen of the Kyngs Maties shippes and the two galees which be alredy dyspatched to put the vitiall into Alderney shall furwythe frome thence repayr to Plymmouth with that force thay cane muster; mary we thinke thay shall not be hable to land above twoo or iii^c men at most; and frome hence, what for th'uncertentie of theyr arryvall, yf we shuld sende any th'ymploment of some shippes otherwyse we cannot helpe you in tyme, and therfor yf for the better advñcement of your service there ye shalbe hable and thenke good to gette suche vesselles and botes as may be recovered there for the landing of men, And thinke ye maie of your own nombers spayre any to that purpose, we referre that to be done there by you which to your dyscrysion shall appere convenyent, lyke as understanding that Thompson the pyrit shuld be in Severn, we leve yt to your consyderacõn to practice with hym by hope of pardon to be an Instrument to admĩce yor enterpryses.

As to the ĩres of Sr Wylliam Goodolphyn; for so miche as toucheth the relyefe of the shepe upon the consyderacons expryssed in these ĩres, we be pleased ye cause to be signifid unto them that, though ye have no authorytie to dyspence with yt for the satysfaction of theyr suytes and peticions therein, yet ye will bothe traviall therein, and have no doubt to bryng yt to passe uppon theyre humble suytes; So as thay become agayne good subjects and leave imẽdiatly this theyr yvill lyef, which so moche dyspleasyth god and vayreth frome theyr dewties of alledgeance and subjectōn, and doing from hencefourth as becometh them, ye dare presume so farr of the Kings Ma^ts goodnes for them that ye will adventure so moche of yor owne lande as may pay the matier for them yf yt be not obteyned, And thay by theyre submission and good demeanour hensforth meryt yt at your hands.

Touchiug the comendacon ye make of the maior of Exeter and others who have or shall serve notably in this tyme of servis, whome ye wold be glad to advaunce to knighthood, having lycence to the same, we allow yor goodde termynacon therin, and referre yt to your dyscryssion to make suche of them knights as ye shall thynke to have meryted the same; for the suyte ye make that by dyscharge of the fee ferme Annuitie or otherwise The towne might be benefyted as for a memorie of the service, we be will inclyned to do them good. The thing may be consydered hereafter; in the meane tyme, ye may generally say that ye will upon your returne be a sutor that some remēbrance may be had of them.

We have presentlye addressed łres of thanks to Jermygn and pyerre Sainga because thay had no spiall recomendacōn by łres expressed to themselfs at the last tyme.

For Robt Paget, consydering his offences of the malefactors make mentyon, we thynke hym an evill instrument of this comon welth and to have deservid deathe with the worst, and therfore we have nowe resolved ye shall cause hym suffer as others in the lyke case offenders have alredye done the semblable.[a]

Thus we bid yor lordshipp right hartely ffayr well.

Frome Westm^r the xix^th of August, 1549.

Y^r L. assured frends,

E. SOMERSET.

T. CANT.   R. RICHE, CANC^r.

W. SANCT JOHN.

WILLM. PETRE, S^y.

[a] On the 16th of August, 1549, Lord Russell wrote to the Mayor and his brethren of the city of Exeter, to compel such citizens as had not contributed to the expense of defending the city to pay their share. Cotton and Woollcombe, p. 192.

XXXIII.—LETTER FROM THE COUNCIL TO LORD RUSSELL DESIRING HIM TO SEND UP THE RINGLEADERS FOR TRIAL.

[Petyt MSS. No. 538, vol. 46, fol. 458.]

Frome my l. protector and the Counsiall,

After our hartie comendacõns to yor lordshipp we have receyved your lres of the xixth of this Instant, and have heard with no small joye and pleasure your good procedings there ; for the which, as we have geven and owe to almightie god our most bounden thanks frome whome all victorie and good successe doth come, So we do render most hartie thanks unto you as to a chief mynister of so happie and so well achyved enterpryce ; And pray you to empart the lyke to others who under yowe have paynefully traveled in the kyng's ma^{ts} name and in ours, and chiefelye to those that have spiall lres sent frome us. Touching the twoo poynts of our former lres of dymynishing your nombers and pursuyng the rebells we do perceyve that ye have taken and do intend to take the best waye, The accomplyshment of them, and so pray yowe to do. The other parte of your lres concerning Sr Willm Harbetts and Sir Hugh Pauletts enterteignement and mony are all redie answered, the which we suppose before this tyme ye have receyved to your contẽtation. Ye do will to make the most diligent serche ye maie for Sr Thomas Pomeraie, and we pray you send upp hither, as ye can cõvenyently, Humfray Arondell, Maunder, the mayor of Bodmyn, and ij. or iij. of the most rankest Traytors and ringleders of them here to be examyned and after to be determyned of as shall apperteyn.

One thing we have thought yet good to admonyshe you, That for so moche as the pardon which ye have ys generall, Yf ye shuld gyve it sone, ye shuld peradventure quite at unwares some of the cheif authours of thes tumults, and peradventure of the most obstynate persones, and therfore ye shall do well to prolong the tyme, and with declaring that ye will sue hither for theyr pardon and some suche fayre wordes acquyting the rest while ye pyk out the most sturdie and obstynate rebells to make example of them by theyr ponyshment to the terror of all other. And then with exeception of those ye thynke mete to promulgate the kyngs ma^{ts} generall pardon to all others. When ye send upp the prysoners we do not doubt but ye will send them upp strongly enough and yf any attempt shuld be to delyver them out of theyr hands, ye will gyve them that shall bring the prysoners such charche that rather that shuld be inforsed to lose them than make them fyrst sure of escapyng that they may geve accompt of them to us quik or dead. We have provided books for Cornewall and Devshire as ye require, the which shall shortlie be sent downe. And so we bid you right hartely fayre well frome Westminst^r the xxi^{th} of August.[a]

Yo^r l. loving frends,

E. Somersett.
  T. Cant.   R. Riche Canc.
W. Sanct John. W. Paget. W. Petre S^y T. Smyth.

Post script.

An other occasyon is whie we wold require you in any wise not be hastie in geving the pardon, for upon th'examynacõn of these archtraytors which ye shall send upp, padventure some come to knowledge which els ye shall never have knowledge of; and therfore ye shall staie the geving of the pardon untill suche tyme as ye have efesones upon th'examynacõn had word from us.

Because we doubt tharryval with you of our former lres signifying th'allotment of the severall dyets of S^r Wiłłm Herbett and Sr Hugh Pallet, ye shall knowe we have allotted to S^r Wiłłm Herbet xl s by daie above by which ordynarye allowance we cannot convenyently passe, but shall otherwise consyder hym as one of whome we have a spiall care. And for Sr Hugh Pallet the same shall receyve four nobles by daye, bothe whose allowances we be pleased ye geve ordre to be defrayed towards them accordingly.

---

[a] A draft of this letter of Aug. 21 is in the Record Office, Domestic Papers of Edward VI. vol. viii. art. 47, one paragraph of which has been printed by Tytler.

XXXIV.—Letter from the Council to Lord Russell, requiring him to thank those who had contributed to the victory over the rebels.

[Petyt MSS. No 538, vol. 46, fol. 459^b.]

Frome my L. Prot^r and the Counsiall.

After my right hartie c̃omendac̃ons to yor good L.

Where as It hath pleased god to graunt yowe victorie uppon those rebells who have so lewdly agaynst theyr allegeance bene in open felde; We have thought good by these owr sp̃iall ł̃res to require yowe to geve hartie thanks in generall to all the gentilmen, serving men, and rest of the soldiors who have so valyantly acquyted themselfs in the servis of his ma^{tie}, which ye may assure them shalbe consydered to theyr comforts and benyfyts as occasyon maie require accordyngly.

Thus fare yor L. right hartely well.

Frome Westm̃ the xxijth of August, 1549.

Yo^r L. assured frends,

E. Somerset.

T. Cant.   W. Sanct John.

William Paget.

XXXV.—Letter from the Council to Lord Russell directing him how to act as regards pardoning the rebels.

[Petyt MSS. No. 538, vol. 46, fol. 460.]

From my l. protector and the Cõsiall.

After our right hartie c̃omendac̃ons unto yor good lordshipp. This shalbe to signifie unto the same our receipt of your ł̃res of the xxijth of this instant; for answere to the pryncipall poynts wherof which we think nedefullyest to be p̃ntly answered, your Lordshipp shall understand that whereas upon the examynac̃on of Humfrey Arundell and others by you apprehended which were the cheife doyers in that rebellyon we suppose verely that some others yet unknowne maie be dyscovered, eyther mete to be punished by the bodie or by the purse, towards the supplyn of the Kyngs Ma^{ts} charges that wayes susteyned; We have therfore thought good and also require yor lordshipp to geve order for the sure sendying uppon hyther unto us, not only of Humfrey Arundell but also of pomerey, wyse and young harrys whome we intend to examyne here to pyke out of them further matte^r. In respect whereof we think yt mete that your Lordshipp for a season longer do prolong the graunting of the generall pardon, which, being made as ye have yt as of sufficiency, yf ye ons do publyshe yt to geve pardon also to Arundell and other pryncipall offenders whome ye have in hold and to suche others as upon theyr desertion,[a] yt shuld in no wyse be expedyent to have pryvileged by suche generall words; never the les for a uoydaunce of the desperacōn which by deferrement your lordshipp dowtyth may engender worse inconvenyence, we wold ye shuld this forfourth proced as to pardon partycularly those whome upon theyr speciall sut ye shall thynk mete to be receyved. And for the generall sytysfaction of the people, to remayne in some hope and comfort your lordshipp may declayre that ye have alwaye wrytten hither for theyr generall pardone which shortly ye trust to receyve in ample forme. And in the meane while, what by the confessions of those ye have in hold, and by other knowledge gethered of suche persons as have lykewyse been notable mynestres a mongst the rebells, ye may cause the same lykewise apprehendid; So as by that tyme we shall think good to put furth the pardon the parsons most culpable maybe presentid by execution or detention.

We lyke verie well yor lordshipps ordre geven for the cassing of that parte of Sr Willm̄ Herbert's bande with the others ye have sent for the repressōn of the rebells lastly assemblid at Mynehed. Trusting the successe of the Jorney shalbe suche as both that parte of your nombre and the greatest part besydes maye also be shortlye

[a] This word is doubtful.

dysmyssed for the allevating of the charges, which beinge suche, and at suche a tyme, we doubt nothing bnt your lordshipp doth seke with us to have conted with the sonest.

Touching your Lordshippes advyse to us geven for staying of any graunts to be made for the releas of the relyefs of sheppe, consydering howe the extreme dealing of them abyding the uttermost tryall of the sword doth not meryte suche remyssion to the damage of the kyngs ma^te, we ar evin of the same opynion, that having this advantage his highnes shuld not for the presydents sake relent unto them, wheruppon other shyres not offending might eyther have cause to grudge or more bolducs to demand the lyke remyssion; which respecte doth also move us to be of contrary opynion to lordshipp in the Clothyers case, whome for examples sake we exteme mete to be held as shorte as thother and rather shorter, cõsydering howe generally big theyr malignimty at the relyefs pulling a waye of theyr workmen, ye and pryvie insencing and encouragment, this sparke of rebellyon toke the kyndling to come to so greate a flame; And therfore lyke as those sort of men must be specially loked unto seing afortymes were any graunt made to the kyngs Ma^ty seemyth to touche them thaye have bene so redie to repyne and procure incõvenyence to avoyde theyr owne burden, So we thinke mette at this tyme upon this oportunytie to procede in the establyshment and execution of that parte of the relyefe whereupon the thing being ones passed and brought into example we trust the next tyme lesse dyffyculte shall ensewe.

Thus we bid your Lordshipp most hertely well to fayre.

From West^r the xxvij^th of August 1549.

Yo^r L. most assured freuds,

E. SOMERSET.

T. CANT. WILLM SANCT JOHN.
WYLLM PAGET. JO. BAKERE.

Post Scrypt.—Yo^r lordshipp shall forther understand that at the receipt herof we had letters from Newe haven, wherby hath

appeared unto us that by reason of the captaynes or cowerdnes of
the soyldiors who strave to have yt delyvered the pece upon the
Almayne hill is in the po'ssyon of the Frenche kyng, who nowe in
psone is all in the feld there. We beleve it rather to have bene
delyvered by treason; the attempt the Frenche kyng hath not yet
made; but Bullenberg is also threatened; And therfore, consydering what we shuld have to do with them, we have thought good,
besydes the revocaçõn of the lord Gray, to require you to haste
the strangers horsemen, for this matter of newhaven may tempyt
to the world yf yt be spred over largelye. Also we be dyssyrus to
knowe what monye ye have at all hands receyved, what ye have
lefte, and what be yor nombers that we may charge the treasorer
hereafter.

XXXVI.—LETTER[a] FROM THE COUNCIL TO LORD RUSSELL COM-
PLAINING OF HIS HAVING EXCEEDED HIS INSTRUCTIONS.
[Petyt MSS. No. 538, vol. 46, fol. 462.]

Frome my protector and the Counsiall to my lord pryvie seall.

After our most hartie comendaçõns unto yor good lordshipe, we
have receyved yor letters of the vijth of September by the which
your lordshipe signifieth at good lengthe unto us bothe the maner of
yor procedings in the gyfte of the lands and goods of the rebells
in Devonshire and Cornewall, and also the consideraçõns movinge
you to use that maner of procedinge in the bestowinge of the same;
for aunswere wherunto we do pray and requiere yor lordshipe
not to thinke that we conceyved any ill opinyon other of cor-
ruption or of wronge doinge in you whome we all knowe to be
of moche honor and to have ever been voyde of those faultes.
Now we thinke not but that whiche haythe passed from you was in
your opinions best for the service of the kings Ma^{te}, to the furtherance wherof we veryly knowe you bent yor selfes hollye and

[a] This letter is in a different hand from the others, and spelt differently.

directed all yor doings accordinglie. We do not forgyt howe good and honorable service yor lordshipe and the rest in there places under you have done his Ma^{te} in this journey; all which soundeythe as moche to your honor and the comendacōns of the rest as maie be. And yet in this mater wher[e] we are most assured you meant all for the best, w[e] rest in the same opinion we weyre in at the writting of our former letters.

And to aunswere the parts of your letters where you seame to thinke the proclamacōn sent from hence and willed to be proclamed there to make so planlye with you in the bistowinge of those la[nds] and goods; we cannot agre therunto, for yf the proclamacion have that force, yt must be understanded to them onlye, and in that forme that is appoynted by the proclamacon: which forme and maner of seasure being by you altered as your selfe confessyethe, we se not that the proclamacōn is anny warraunt to your gyfts, whiche by the said proclamacōn beinge no parte warrantized;/and yf you consider th'end of the proclamacōn, yt maie manefestlye appere that consideracōn was even then had that no man shuld losse anny thinge otherwise nore in onye other sorte then the kings highnes by meanes and right of the forfatore ought and maie by his lawes dispose of the same. And by his lawes we doo not thinke that annye man sholde losse lands ore goods by fore he be atteynted of the crime which meryteythe that punyshment. And where yor lordshipe wisshethe that you had knowne that our meaninge had not bene to have that done whiche was proclamed, we must saie that if no more had byn done then that beareythe whiche was sent frome us to be proclamed, This matter wold be sone aunswered. Nowe yf yor L. besides the proclamacōn have taken other order, albeyt we knowe, as we said before, That you did yt for the best, yet where neither the proclamacōn bearethe yt, nore bie the lawes maye be justified, we se not howe we maie by anny meanes assent to that whiche the lawes beareythe not.

And touchinge the meanynge the vere _wo_{rd}e_s of the proclamacōn shewethe playnelye that it was onlye to drawe back and devide the force of the contrees which wer cumynge against you. For first it seameth to beare with all those which within six dayes after publicaĉon therof shulde withdrawe themselfs from the rebells and yelde themselfs to yor lordeshippe.

And for the greater terror of the rest, which after that tyme shuld contynewe ther rebellyon, it was pvided that ther lands, copieholds, farmes, and goods shuld be thers that shuld first have, take, or possesse the same, or shuld first enter into ther lands and farmes or tenements; if this order had bene executed, that one of them had entred uppon an other, or taken an others goods or cattalls, it must of necessitye have bredd such varyauns, strife, and contention amongs themselfs as yo^u shuld have had the lesse cause to have feared ther cūmynge forwarde. And this was our meaninge indede which, besides that the vere wordes of the proclamaĉon do well beare, shuld not (we thinke) be all togethers unknowen to you, yf you remember the tyme of sendinge that proclamacon, the small nombers then with you, and the difficultyes which wer made either to passe to Exceter or to make any greater nombers in these parties. And, seinge yor force was at that tyme vere small, we thought this the best pollicie to stay the multitude from cūmynge forwardes. And at that tyme yor lordshippe, lykinge well this o^r devise for Devonshere, required theruppon to have a like proclamaĉon for Cornwall, which was then sente, which things consydered, and wyainge withall that in th'ende of the proclamaĉon appeareth that graunte to be made none otherwise then his ma^{te} might lawfully dispose of the same, we think assuredlye ther can no advantage be taken by that proclamaĉon for the mayntenance of these gifts.

And where you seme to note, that yf order of the proclamaĉon had bene kept, ther must have ensued amonge the people greate sedicions, trouble, strife, and contention; Marye that was in dede the vere ende of the makinge the proclamaĉon, to set suche division and strife amongst themselfs, as for desire of revenge or feare of losse the cuntrey men shuld rather have tarryed at home and byn occupied that waye, then assembled togethers against the Kinge as they did.

And for the kepinge of proclamaçons in credit and execution of them when they be made, we be of the same opinion you be; though in the understandinge of this one proclamaçon we thincke otherwise ; and the matter was not altogether unconsidered before the sendinge of it to you, as may appeare by that we have before written. And yet as in the Kings Maties grants and letters patents, so in all proclamaçons where any doubte is, the lawes must declare and expownde.

As for your meaninge in theise gifts we assure you of our honour we have no mistruste, beinge assured you mente it for the best, and for th'encouragemente of yor soldiors and chastement of the disobedient subjects; we think also that you have used suche good moderaçon in the composiçons as reason wold, but yet whatsoever favorable moderaçon be used no man can be well satisfied where the lawes be not kepte.

And howsoever it seme to you nowe, it shall reste a grudge, not onlye in the heades of the sufferers, but in all other mens judgements of that shere and ells where that shall heare of this example of mens goods to be thus taken away without order of any law. We consider besides all this, that yor men, beinge in the Kings wages and under your government, might have bene well stayed from goinge to the spoyle, and that by these gifts the multitude of the c̃omon people, seinge ther lands and goods geven from them, wer therbye made the more desperate and moche the more stirred to followe ther develish enterprise.

As for yor orders devised for Cornewall, we have bothe sene them and returned th'articles unto your lordeshyppe, noted in the margente in suche sorte as we wolde wishe the same to be establisshed; pray you to gyve order accordinglye. And yf you have alredye gone throwgh with theis orders for Cornewall in suche sorte as you sade the same to us, you may as it were uppon a confidens of ther trowthes from hensfurthe, and for the better defens of the sea costes, the warres beinge open with Fraunce, cause there harnesse to be delivered agayne.

Fynallye towchinge monney we have consydered th'accompts wh[ich] you sente unto us, and by the same do understande that y[ou] chardge not the tresorer with so moche monney as was sent from us in such parts as be noted in a scedle herin closed, which we pray you cause to be examyned, and theruppon make us a perfect certification of the monney to be dewe, and order shalbe geven for payment either here to suche as will so require or there. And in the meane tyme for the diminisshing of the Kings m^{aties} chardges we wolde yor lordeshippe shulde dischardge yor horsemen, causinge suche men onlye to every bande to remayne for the receipte of the monney due as they shall think good.

And thus we byd yor good lordshippe most hartelye well to fare.

From $Westm^r$ the xth of September, 1549.

Yo^r lordeshipps assured,
lovinge frendes.

E. SOMERSETT.

T. CANT.

R. RYCHE, CANC.   W. SEINT JOHN.

J. WARWYCK.   WILLM PETRE.   R. SADLER.[a]

[a] Sir Ralph Sadler, or Sadleyr, is best known as the person appointed in the reign of Elizabeth to take charge of Mary, Queen of Scots. He first appears as a servant of Cromwell's, and afterwards in 1537 as a gentleman of the Privy Chamber, in which capacity he was in attendance at the reception of Anne of Cleves in 1539. He was knighted in April, 1540, at the same time with Wriothesley, afterwards Lord Chancellor, when they were both made secretaries to the King. He was one of the twelve appointed to assist the sixteen executors, and is also one of the twenty-six named as Councillors in Somerset's patent, where he is called Master of the Wardrobe. His name seldom appears in the Council books, though he was one of the forty in Edward's list of his Councillors, but he signed the warrant for Seymour's execution March 17, 1549, and the letter to the Princess Mary of July 7, printed above. He married a woman who had been a laundress in Cromwell's family, and was the wife of Matthew Barlow, an artisan, who was supposed to be dead, but when the first husband appeared she was adjudged according to the doctrine of the *Reformatio Legum Ecclesiasticarum* to Sadler. He joined the conspiracy against Somerset on Oct. 7. His name does not appear in any of the documents connected with the usurpation of Lady Jane Grey, or the accession of Mary to the crown, except amongst the 101 who testified to the Letters Patent for the limitation of the Crown June 21, 1563.

XXXVII.—LETTER FROM THE COUNCIL TO LORD RUSSELL, ORDERING HIM TO TAKE DOWN THE BELLS FROM THE CHURCHES.

[Petyt MSS. No. 538, vol. 46, fol. 465.]

From my lord protector and the counsell to my lord previe seall.

After our right hartie comendacons to your lordshipp, Where the rebells of the cuntrye of Devonshyre and Cornwall have used the belles in every parishe as an instrument to sturr the multytude and call them together, Thinkyng good to have this occasyon of attempting the lyke hereafter to be taken frome them, And remembryng with all that by taking downe of them the kyngs Matie maie have some comoditie towards his great charges that waye, we have thought good to pray yor good lordshipp to geve order[a] for taken downe the sayd bells in all the churches within those two counties, levyng in every churche one bell, the lest of the ryng that nowe is in the same, which maie serve to call the paryshoners togethers to the sermons and devyne servis; in the doyng hereof we require yor lordshipp to cause such moderacon to be used as the same may be done with as moche quietnes and as lytill force of the comon people as maie be.

And thus we bid yor lordshipp most hartely farewell.

From Westm^9 this xijth of September, 1549.

Yo^r good lordshipp assured loving frendes.

E. SOMERSET.
T. CANT.   W. SANCT JOHN.
   W. PAGET.   W. PETRE, Sy.
         E. NORTH.
      E. WOTTON.   R. SADLER.

---

[a] The order here was carried into effect, as appears by a letter of Russell to the Mayor of Exeter in Cotton and Woollcombe's Gleanings, p. 192, wrongly there dated Aug. 1549. The letter in the text was printed from this copy with several errors by Strype in his Memorials, vol. ii. p. 173. Between this letter and the following is a letter from Warwick to Cecil, of Sept. 14, 1549, asking for payment to be made to Captain Drury for his services against the rebels.

XXXVIII.—Letter from Somerset to Lord Russell, blaming him for not having executed Paget.

[Petyt MSS. No. 538, vol. 46, fol. 465.]

Frome my lord protector to my lord previe seall.

After our verie hartie comendacõns unto yor good L.

Where as we wth dyvers other of the Kyng's Maties Counsiall heretofore addressed our łres to you for dewe execucõn to be done and hade upon Pagett for his worthie deserts, which, as we be enformed, is not done but respected, uppon what occasyon we knowe not, where at we cannot a lytill marvell, the thyng so moche touching our honor; for, as we have been credably enformed, dyvers have not lefte unspoken that we shuld consent to the death of our owne brother, and nowe wold wynke at hym. Wherefore we hartely praye yowe, as yowe tender our honor, to se hym suffer that he hath deserved, accordyng to the tenor of our former łres, and that without delay.

Thus fare you well.

Frome Syon the xviijth of September,^{a} 1549.

Yo^r L. loving frend,

E. Somerset.

XXXIX.—The Protector's Letter to Lord Russell recommending merciful dealing with the Rebels.

[Petyt MSS. No. 538, vol. 46, fol. 466.]

From my L. protector to my L. previe Seall.

After our right hartie comendacõns unto your good lordshipp; the same shall understand we have receyved your łres of the xxijth

---

^{a} This letter appears in Strype's Memorials, ii. 180. There is a letter of the same date from Lord Chancellor Rich to Cecil, providing for the execution of the prisoners Essex and More, who are to be tried after they should have been sent to Brentwood.

of Sembr, by the wch ye fyrst require to knowe wether that those parties abowt you shall taste of the kyng's Ma^{ts} goodnes, lyke as others have, where no rebellon and upprors hath bene made, or not; as that for the relyefe of the sheppe none should paie but suche above the nomher of one hundreth; you shall understand for answere therof that the King's Matie, by our advyse, is pleased that thaie, beyng now sorie for theyr late dysorders, and theroppon receyved his highnes pdon, shall Inoye suche lyke part of his Matie goodnes in this behalfe as any other of his realme; for the execuçon of wch his Matie goodnes towards them these our lres shalbe your sufficyent dyscharge and warrant.

For the sendyng of anye Comyssions for the leaveyng of the relyef, we thynke it nedethe not; but do accompt the statute made in that behalf comyssion good anought for the same. And for the remembrance of yor former requests for Mr. Cov^{r}dall, Cholwell, and haynes,[a] we do you to wytt that for your devise for Coverdall and Cholwyn, we lyke the same verie well, and praie you to take suche order as the same maie be executed accordyngly. And yf there shall remayne in us any thyng for the fynyshing therof, we intend uppon the knowledge had therein to graunt to the same in suche sorte as you shall thinke covenyent. For the comyng of Mr. Haynes we have wrytten our lres to hym for that intent. Nevertheles, we thinke his presens at London nowe at the plament verie requesett; touching the comon prayer ye make mencyon of, We

[a] This was Simon Heynes, Dean of Exeter, who had been Master of Queen's College, Cambridge, from 1528 to 1537, and Canon of Windsor from 1535 to 1537, when he was appointed to the Deanery of Exeter, which he held till his death in October, 1552. He was employed in France in 1535 to ascertain the opinions of the learned as to the King's proceedings, and their attitude towards the Pope. His first service to the King was in 1529, when he was mainly instrumental in procuring the decision of the University of Cambridge in his favour in the matter of the divorce of Catharine of Aragon. He afterwards came under some suspicion, and was sent to the Fleet for lewd and seditious preaching (see the extract from the Council Book in Pocock's *Burnet*, vol. v. p. 269). In 1538 he was sent with Bonner to the Emperor's Court. He was one of the committee appointed in 1548 to examine the offices of the Church with a view to the projected alterations.

pray you that lyke as you were the author therof so the same may be sett forth according to our meanyng.

And so we bid yor lordshipp hartely fare well.

From Hampton Courte, the xxvth of September, 1549.

Your L. loving frend,
E. Somerset.

P^t script.—We do loke for you and Sr Willm̃ Herbert, at the furthest about the viijth daie of the next moneth, abouth which tyme we wold gladlye have you here for matters of importance.

XL.—The King's Letter summoning his subjects to defend him and his Uncle. Written Oct. 5th, 1549.

[Domestic Papers of Edward VI. vol. ix. art. 2.]

The kings ma^{tie} streyghtlie chargeth and c̃omaundeth all his loving subjects w^t all haste to repayre to his highnes at his m_a^{ties} honor of Hampton Court in most defensible waye w^t harnes and weapon, to defende his moste royall parson and his most interlie beloved uncle the lorde protecto^r, agenste whom c^rtayne hathe attempted a most daungerous conspiracye and this to doo in all c̃ovenient haste.

Gyven at Hampton Courte the fyfte^a day of October in the thirde yere of his moste royall rayne.

> To all Justices of p[eace], mayors, shrives, balives, Constables, [he]dbrowghes, and all other the Kynges Maties officers and subiects.

This is the verye copye of y^e kyngs m[a^{ties}] c̃omission sygned w^t his m_a^{ties} seale and hande and w^t my lorde protectors gracs singe.

---

^a This letter appears in Tytler's series of letters, with two or three variations, and with a wrong date of the 1st for the 5th of October assigned to it. It is wrongly entered in the Domestic Calendar of State Papers as of that date. The original,

XLI.—WARRANT OF THE KING TO SIR HARRY SEYMOUR TO RAISE MEN AND BRING THEM TO HAMPTON COURT TO DEFEND HIM FROM THE CONSPIRACY. AN ORIGINAL, SIGNED BY EDWARD AND SOMERSET.

[Domestic Papers of Edward VI. vol. ix. art. 3.]

EDWARD. By the King.

We grete you well.

Forasmoch as we be given to understande by insinuaĉon of rumors that a certen conspiracy is in acheving agenst us and our roiall personne, whiche we truste in god shall never prevaile, but come to that confusion that therto belongithe,

To the entent that we wold not be without the assistence and supportaĉon of oͬ trustie sarvaũtes and subjectes agenst all attempts, By the good advise of oͬ most dere uncle Edward the duke of Somerset governor of our personne and protectoͬ of oͬ realmes domiños and subjectes,

We have thought [good] it most necessary for the gret trust and confidence we repose in you, and so will and commaṇd you forthwith uppon the receipt hereof, to assemble such number of men armed as well as on horseback and that espially as on fote, as uppon this soddaine by vertue of anie our commission heretofore directed unto you, or by any other authoritie, Stewardshipp, office or libertye what so ever it be, or if ye have none suche then by authoritie and warraũte of theis our ſres, Ye maie possibly levye and gather and then with all expediĉon to bring hether to our Courte.

And at your coming ye shall for furder order therin understand by thadvise of our said derely beloved uncle the rest of our pleasure and determinaĉon.

which is in the Record Office, has a note appended to it in an unknown hand as follows :—" I received this letter the vi. day of October of George Tunstal, my lord of Canterbury's servant, between the hours of one and two before noon on the same day."

Geven under our signet at our honor of Hampton Courte the vth of October in the third yere of o^r reigne.

E. SOMERZET.

Endorsed :—

    To our trustie and well belo[ved]
    Sr Harry Seymour Kn[ight].

XLII.—LETTER FROM SOMERSET TO LORD RUSSELL AND SIR WILLIAM HERBERT, SUMMONING THEM TO HAMPTON COURT.

[Domestic Papers of Edward VI. vol. ix. art. 5.]

After o^r very hartie comendacõns to yor good L. and to yow good Mr Harbert, the same shall understand that for the suertie of the king's ma^{tie}, to whom how duetifull ye have both ever bene, the worlde speketh it to yor perpetuall comendacõn ; We be at this present very desyerouse to have yor presens here most assured of yor privat good affections towards us. Wherein ye have not a lytle bounde us and by cause Mr. Herbert may wth the more spede be here, if yt shall so content yo^u, by post, We hertely [desire] you so to doo, and to gyve ordre that yor servants may folowe. Wherin ye shall suerly be a great comforte to the king's ma^{tie}, whom god preserve, but also most hartely welcome unto us.

And so we bydd youe hertely well to fare.

Frō hampton court the vth of October,^{a} 1549.

Yo^r L. loving and assured frende,
E. SOMERSET.

Endorsed :—

    To o^r very good lorde
      the lord privie
      Seale and o^r loving
      frende Sr Will'm
      Herbert, Knight, and
      to either of them.

---

^{a} There are in the Record Office four other documents of this date in the Domestic Papers. The first two contain the Proclamation of October 5th in duplicate. The third is the letter to Sir Harry Seymour printed here. The fourth is with Somerset's autograph to his servant Golding to assemble the Earl of Oxford's servants for the King's service, printed by Tytler.

XLIII.—Another Letter from Somerset to Lord Russell and Sir William Herbert with Instructions to be given by the Bearer, Lord Edward Seymour.

[Domestic Papers of Edward VI. vol. ix. art. 7.]

After o^r ryght hertie cõmendacõns to yor good L., having sent this bearer, the lorde Edward, to declare and cõicate unto you certayne things touching thestate of the King's Matie, These shalbe to wyll and requyre yo^u on his highnes behalf to gyve fyrme credit unto him, and to do as he shall instructe you. So fare yor L. ryght hartely well. From Hampton courte, the vjth of Octobre, 1549.

Yo^r L. assured frend,
E. Somerset.

To o^r very good lorde
the lorde privie
Seale and o^r very
loving frende S^r
Wm Herbert, Knight.

XLIV.—Letter from the King to Lord Russell and Sir William Herbert begging them to come to him for his defence.

[Domestic Papers of Edward VI. vol. ix. art. 9.]

Edwarde.   By the king.

Right trustie and right well beloved we great you well. Lettinge yo^u understande that such a heneus and grevus conspiracye as never was seen is attempted agenst us, and o^r entierlye belovid uncle the lorde protector. The wiche thei are constrayinde to maynteine withe moost untrue and false surmyses. For they pretende and brute abroad that o^r said uncle hathe sould Bolloign, and deteineth wages, and suche untrue talles, the wiche we knowe of certaintie to be merelye false, and that by the reast of the Counsells confession nothing to have ben done by o^r said uncle but that reast of o^r Counsell did agrea unto; As we do not doubte but ye shall firmelie and suerly perceve at yor repaire to us. The wiche wee pray you to macke withe all spede for o{r} defence in this o{r} necessitye, whatsoever lres and from whom so ever 'ye shall receve to the contrarie. And we shall tacke the same moost thanckefully. Prayenge yo{u} in anye wisse not to faiell as ye tender our suertie.

Geven at o{r} honor of hampton Couert the vith of October[a] in the thirde yere of o{r} raigne.

    E. SOMERSETT.

To o{r} right trustie and
welbeloved Counsaillor
the L. Russell kep' of
o{r} previe seale and
Sr Will'm Herbert
knight.

XLV.—LETTER FROM THE COUNCIL AT LONDON SUMMONING THE PEOPLE TO THEIR ASSISTANCE AGAINST SOMERSET.

[Domestic Papers of Edward VI. vol. ix. art. 10.]

After o{r} right hartie cõmendacõns, for the savegarde and preservacion of the kings ma{ts} pson, whiche is in no small daunger by the falshoode and treasons of the duke of Somersett, who nev̈theles to cover the same nowe brutithe abrode that we of his ma{ts} counsaile, whiche seke only his highnes pres{r}vacion shoulde entende evill unto his highnes, whiche god forbydde; trustinge by that meane to abuse the people and so by theire helpes the rather to procede in his purpose; wee have thought good to requier youe not only as

[a] Of the five documents of this date amongst the Domestic Papers, the first, as calendared, is a letter from Somerset to Russell and Herbert, the original from which Secretary Petre copied, desiring them to hasten to the court. The second is a subsequent letter, telling them to take instructions from the bearer, Sir Edward Seymour. The third is another copy almost identical with this, and printed by Foxe, p. 1546, ed. 1570. The fourth is this letter from Somerset in the King's name to Russell and Herbert, which has also been printed by Tytler, vol. i. p. 214, with two unimportant mistakes; and the fifth is from the Council in London, summoning the people to their assistance, which is printed below.

muche as in youe is to let the people knowe the trouthe, but also, forasmuche as he doth alredy gather force, to putt your selfe in order, w'all the power ye maye make, presentlie to repaire unto us for the service and suertie of the kings ma^{tie} in this greate and weightie matter, as to good and lovinge subjects appteyneth. And so fare ye hartely well.

From London this vith of Octobre 1549°·

Yo^r very lovinge frinds

R. RYCHE CANC^r.   W. NORTHT.[a]
     W. SFINT JOHN.
J. WARWYK.   ARUNDELL.   F. SHREWESBURY.[b]
HENRY SUSSEX.
T. CHEYNE.
EDWARD NORTH.   J. GAGE.

[a] This was William Parr, first Baron Parr of Kendal, brother of Katherine, sixth wife of Henry VIII. He married Ann Bourchier, daughter of Henry, fifteenth Earl of Essex, with whose death in 1539 the title of Essex became extinct. Although his issue by her had been bastardised by Act of Parliament, entitled an Act for the Bastardy of the Lady Parr's children (34 Hen. VIII.), yet he was created Earl of Essex 23 Dec. 1543, after the death of Cromwell, who was the sixteenth person who had borne the title "with the same place and voice in Parliament as Henry Bourchier, late Earl of Essex, had." He was one of those appointed to assist the executors of Henry the Eighth's will, and was one of the first twenty-six Councillors of Somerset. He had illegally married Elizabeth, daughter of Lord Cobham, his wife being still alive, but the new marriage was decided to be good by Cranmer, Ridley, and others, and four years afterwards the marriage was declared legal by Act of Parliament, and annulled by a subsequent Act Nov. 28, 1553. He was created Marquis of Northampton Feb. 16, 1546. He joined the conspirators against Somerset Oct. 7, 1549, on whose trial he sat in 1551, having been rewarded for his services to Warwick by being made Lord Great Chamberlain of England Feb. 2, 1550, and also one of the six governors of the King's person after Somerset's removal. He seems to have abetted Northumberland throughout, and was tried and condemned Aug. 19, 1553, for treason, but was afterwards pardoned by the Queen. Upon Wyatt's rising in Kent he was apprehended on suspicion by the Lord Mayor Jan. 25, 1554, and sent to the Tower. He had been restored in blood but not in honours in 1553, and afterwards was created Marquis of Northampton Jan. 13, 1559, and presided at the trial of Lord Wentworth, deputy of Calais, for treason, April 22, 1559. The title became extinct at his death in 1571. His third wife, Helen, a daughter of a Swede, survived him.

[b] This was Francis Talbot, historically speaking, the eighth Earl of Shrewsbury,

XLVI.—LETTER FROM SOMERSET TO LORD RUSSELL URGING HIM TO COME TO WINDSOR AS SPEEDILY AS POSSIBLE. WRITTEN OCT. 6, 1549.

[Petyt MSS. No. 538, vol. 46, fol. 467.]

From my L. protector to my L. prevey Seall.

After o^r right hartye cōmendacōns to yor good lordshippe, here hathe of late rysen such a conspyracye against the kyngs Matie and us as never have bene sene, the which they can not maynteyne but wth suche vayne łres and fals tales surmysed as was never mente nor entended on us. They pretende and say that we have sold Bolonge to the Frenche, and that we do w^{t}hold wages from the soldyers and other suche tales and łres they do spreade abrode, of the which if any one thinge wer trewe we wold not wishe to lyve. The matter

but fifth earl in direct descent from John Talbot, created May 20, 1442. He succeeded his father, George, fourth earl, in 1541, and died in 1560. He had been the King's Lieutenant of the North in 1545, and was made Knight of the Garter April 23, 1546. He commanded the expedition into Scotland in 1548. He was one of the messengers sent to Lord Seymour to intimate the charges brought against him, and signed the warrant with Cranmer and others for his execution. He sided altogether with Somerset till Oct. 7, 1549, when with Rich, Northampton, Cheyney, Gage, Sadleyr, and Montague, he joined in Warwick's conspiracy against him. On the 10th of January, 1553, he attended on the Princess Mary when she paid a visit to the King at Westminster; and signed, with twenty-two others, the letter to the Princess Mary, declaring Lady Jane Grey queen. He was one of the principal mourners at the burial of Edward in Westminster Abbey, when the service was performed in surplice, on Tuesday, Aug. 8, according to the Prayer Book of 1552; though on the same day there was a Requiem Mass in the Tower at which Gardiner officiated and the Queen attended. He was one of those who signed Edward's limitation of the Crown, as well as the letter of July 12 to the Sheriffs of Notts and Derby, calling Mary a bastard, and also the letter in the name of Queen Jane of July 19 to Lord Rich, the lieutenant of the county of Essex, yet joined with Cranmer and others in proclaiming Mary, July 19, when Arundel and Paget were sent off to her with the great seal, and the next day signed the charge of the Council to Northumberland to disarm. He carried the crown at her coronation, and conducted Cardinal Pole to London, Nov. 24, 1554. He appears to have been in great favour with Philip and Mary, and was present at the proclamation of Elizabeth, Nov. 17, 1558, and was one of the first chosen to be of her Privy Council. He dissented from the Act of Supremacy March 18, 1559, and from the new Service Book April 18, yet afterwards was one of the commissioners appointed of the royal visitation for enforcing it in the Province of York, June 24, 1559.

now beinge browght to a marvelous extremytye such as we wold never have thowght it culd have come unto, especyallye of those men towards the king's Matie and us, of whome we have deserved no such thinge but rather moche favor and love. But the case beinge as it is, This is to require and pray you to hasten you hether to the defence of the king's Matie in suche force and poore as you may; To shew the parte of a trewe gentleman and of a verie frende, the whiche thinge we trust god shall rewarde and the king's m$_a$^{tie} in tyme to come; and we shall never be unmindefull of it to; We ar seure you shall have other lres from them, but as ye tender yor dewtye to the king's ma^{tie} we requyre you to make no staye but immedyatlye repayre wth such force as ye have to his highnes in his castle of Wyndesore, and cause the rest of such force as ye maie make followe you.

And so we byd you right hartelye fare well.

From Hampton courte the vjth of October.

Yo^r lordships assurid lovinge frende,

E. SOMERSETT.

Postscript.^{a}

They ar not ashamed to send posts abrode to tell that we ar alredye cōmytted to the towre and that we wold delyver the busshopps of Wynchester and London out of pryson and bringe in agayne tholde masse.

XLVII.—LETTER FROM THE COUNCIL AT LONDON TO THE KING DETAILING THEIR GRIEVANCE AGAINST SOMERSET. DRAFT PARTLY IN PETRE'S, PARTLY IN WRIOTHESLEY'S HAND.^{b}

[Domestic Papers of Edward VI. vol. ix. Art. 19.]

Most high and mightye prince, o^r most gracious sov^{r}aigne Lorde.

It may please your Ma^{te} to be advertysed that havinge harde suche message as it pleased your Ma^{tc} to sende unto us by your

---

^{a} This document was printed by Foxe, p. 1546, with tolerable correctness, but he omitted the postscript. It appears also in Holinshed from Foxe.

^{b} There are three copies of this document in the Record Office calendared as

highnes Secretarye Sir William Petre, Lyke as it was muche to yor grieve and discomfort to understande that upon untrue informations yor ma^{te} seemid to have some doubte of o^r fydelities ; So doo we upon o^r knees moste humblye beseche yor ma^{te} to thinke that we have alwayes servid the king's ma^{te} your moste noble father, and yor highnes likewyse, faithfullye and truelye; So do we mynde alwayes to continue yor ma^{ts} true servaũts to th'effusion of our bludds and losse of our lyves, And for the suretye of yor moste royall pson, savegarde and preservacion of your Realmes and dominions, have at this tyme consultid to gither, and for none other cause we take god to witnes.

We have hertofore by all good and gentle meanes attempted to have had your highnes uncle, the duke of Somerset, to have governid yor ma^{tes} affayres by th'advyse of us and the rest of yor counsaillours; but fyndinge hym so muche gyven to his owne will that he alwayes refusid to heere reason, and therwith doinge sundrye such things as wer and be most daungerous bothe to yor most royall pson and to your hole Realme, We thought yet agayne to have gentelye and quyetleye spoken with hym yn thies things, had he not gatherid force about hym in suche sorte as we might easelye pceyve hym earnestlye bent to the mayntenãce of his olde wilfull and troublous doings. For redressse wherof, and for none other cause, we do presentlye remayne heere, redye to lyve and dye your true servaũts. And th'assemble of almost all your Counsaill beinge now heere, we have for the better service of yor maieste, causid your Secretarye to remayne, herewith moste humbly besechinge yor grace to thinke in yor harte that th'onelye preservacion of yor pson and yor estate, for the discharge of o^r duetyes enforcith us to devyse how to delyver your grace from the pill your highnes standeth yn, and no other respecte. For what soever is or shalbe sayed to your highnes, no earthlye thinge coulde have movid us to

Nos. 17, 18, 19. There is a copy in the Council Book, p. 4, and it was printed from the original in the Cotton Library, by Burnet, vol. iv. p. 273. There are no variations of any importance. The signatures are here added as they exist in the original MS., but they do not exist in any of the copies.

have seemid to stande as a ptye but yor onelye preservacion, which yor ma^{te} shall herafter pceyve, and we doubte not repute us for your most faithful servaũts and Counsaillo^{rs} as o^r doings shall never deserve the contrarye; As god knowith, to whom we shall daylye praye for your ma^{tes} preservacion, and with our bodyes defende yor pson and estate, as long as lief shall endure.

[R. RYCHE, Canc. J. WARWYK.
    W. SEINT JOHN.
ARUNDELL. W. NORTHT.
F. SHREWESBURY. THOMAS SOUTHAMPTON.
T. CHEYNE.^a WILLIAM PETRE, Secretary. EDWARD NORTH.
JOHN GAGE. R. SADLEYR.
EDWARD MOUNTAGU. RICHARD SOUTHWELL.]

Endorsed on Art. 18:
 1549:
  Copie of the l^{re} from the
  Ll. assembled at London
  to the King.
  uppon the message sent to
  them by Sr William Pagett
  touching the duke of Som-
  mersett.

Art. 17 *has pasted on it:*
 This is a draft
  M. to the King's ma^{te}
  vij° Octobris, 1549.

---

^a Sir Thomas Cheyney first appears in 1520 at the Field of the Cloth of Gold, and afterwards as ambassador in France in 1522 He was afterwards Treasurer of the Household and Warden of the Cinque Ports from 1540 till his death in 1558. He was present at the Council, Aug. 10, 1540, when Paget was made secretary, and was one of the twelve appointed to assist the sixteen executors of the will of Henry VIII. He signed the patent for Somerset's protectorship and the order for committing Gardiner to the Tower, and was one of those sent to Lord Seymour to bring him to submission. On Oct. 7, 1549, he, with Northampton, Shrewsbury, Montague, Gage, and Sadler, joined the conspirators against Somerset. He signed Edward's limita-

XLVIII.—Original draft[a] of a Letter from the Lords of the Council in London to the Council at Windsor intimating their intention to remove Somerset from the office of Protector.

[Domestic Papers of Edward VI. vol. ix. Art. 22.]

My Lords,

After o^r right harty commendations.

Understanding whatt fals [*and*] ontrue and slandero[us] bills rumo^{rs} and reports bee [*bee*] spredd [*allmost in all*] in many places by meanes of the duke of Somersett and his adherents of the cause of o^r Assemblie, and being togethers wee have fyrst thought good to [*mak*] assure yor lordshipps of o^r honors, trothe and fidelites to god and the kings Ma^{te}, thatt wee mean nothing els butt the suertie of [*the Kings*] his m^{ates} [*honor*] pson o^r most gracious soveraigne lord, the preservation of his honor, and the good governaunce of his m^{ates} realmes and dominions, And for none other cause we tak god to wytnes.

---

tion of the Crown, and also the letter, dated July 9, of the Council to Mary announcing Lady Jane Grey as Queen, and also that of July 19 to Rich in her favour, but almost immediately declared for Mary, whom he on the same day joined with Arundel, Shrewsbury, Pembroke, Bedford, and Cobham in proclaiming Queen. He was of her Privy Council, and retained by Elizabeth as a councillor at her accession, but died immediately afterwards, Dec. 15, 1558. From a letter in Le Grand it appears that he had, in 1529, in some way offended Wolsey, and was dismissed from court, but was restored by the influence of Anne Boleyn.

[a] This letter, with the signatures of the Councillors, was printed from the original in Ellis's Letters, First Series, vol. ii. p. 166. It differs very little from this corrected draft. These two letters, written on the same day, are signed by the same Councillors, except that one has the name of Edward Montague, the other of Nicholas Wotton.

If the duke of Somersett wold att any tyme have hard o^r advises, if he wold have hard reason, and knowleged hymself a subject, o^r meaning was [w] to have quietly combined w^t hym for redresse of all things w^towt any disturbance of the realme; butt [he] knowing afterwards thatt the sayd duke goeth abowt to rayse greatt forces and numbers of men, to spredd abrod sclaunderous and ontrue reaports of us moch contrary to o^r [hn] hono^{rs} and reputations, we were forced for the meting them [wherw^t lyke as we be also forced] against o^r wills to assemble also some numbers about us, and now to charge the mater lyke as gryveth us to see whatt daungers and pill may ensue to the hole realme thorough division amongs o^r selfs, We have lykewise thought good to signefie unto you thatt if the sayd duke will, as becometh a good subject, absent hymself from hys mat^{te}, be contentyd to be ordred according [to reason] to justice and reason [and for] and disperse thatt force w^t is levied by hym, we will gladly comen w^t yow [for furthar order for] toching the suertie of his ^ma^{tes} pson and order of all [things] other things, wherin we nothing doubt, whatt so ever hath byn otherwyse ontruely reaported, yow shall fynd us [redye] both conformable and readye to doo as becometh good subjects and true counsaillors, nothing doubting to fynd the lyk conformitie also on yor behalfs.

Otherwise if we shall see that you mynde more the mayntenaunce of that one mans ill doings then th'execution of his ^ma^{tes} lawes and comen order, we must make other accompt of you then we trust we shall have cause.

Consider my lords for Godds sake, we hartely pray you, thatt we bee allmost the hole counsayl, men thatt have byn to [be] moch bounden by sondry benefites to forget o^r dueties to the kings Matie for whom we doo thatt we doo, and will gladly spend o^r lives for his suertie. If you forsake to come to this good and peaxell agreement, We must protest that the inconveniences w^h may ensue uppon this styrre must grow of you, the dawnger whereof we assurydly know is to none of you onknowen.

Thus praying God to send us and yow grace to doo that may

most conduce to his glorie and wealth of the Realme we bydd yow hartely fare well.

From London this vijth of October, 1549.

Yo^r assured loving freends,

R. RYCHE, Canc.   W. SAINT JOHN.   W. NORTHT.

J. WARWYK.   ARUNDELL.   F. SHREWESBURY.

THOMAS SOUTHAMPTON.

T. CHEYNE.   WILLIAM PETRE.   EDWARD NORTH.

JOHN GAGE.[a]   R. SADLEYR.

RIC. SOUTHWELL.   NICHOLAS WOTTON.

Endorsed:
M. to the lords at
Windsour vij° octobris,
1549.

XLIX.—LETTER FROM SOMERSET TO THE COUNCIL AT LONDON EXPRESSING WONDER AT THE DETENTION OF SECRETARY PETRE.

[Petyt MSS. No. 538, vol. 46, fol. 469.]

Frome my lord protector to the Counsell at London,

My lords we cõmend us moste hartelye unto you.

And whereas the kinges Matie was infourmed that you weyre assembled in suche sorte as you doo and nowe remayne there

---

[b] Sir John Gage appears first in 1523 as Comptroller of Calais and Captain of Guisnes. He was Vice-Chamberlain from 1528 to 1540, and then promoted, 9th Oct. to be Comptroller of the Household, which office he held till the death of the king. He was made Knight of the Garter in 1541, and was also Constable of the Tower. He was one of those who assisted Cranmer at the trial for the divorce of Catharine at Dunstable. He was also concerned in examination of evidence against Catharine Howard. He had been employed also during the reign of Henry VIII. in the visitation of the monasteries. He was one the twelve assistants to the executors of the king's will and one of Edward's Privy Council. He joined the conspiracy against Somerset, Oct. 7, 1549. He does not appear to have been

in as was advised, and such other of his counsell as weyre thene hereabout his person to send Mr. Secretarie Peters unto you with suche a message as no herme might have insued, the sewertie of his Maties pson wth preservasion of his realme and subjects and the quiet bothe of us and yor selfes as Mr. Secretarie cane well declare to youe; his Matie and we of his counsell heare doo not a lytle marvell that you staie still wth you the said Mr. Secretarie, and have not as weyre vouchsaved to send aunswer to his maj^{tie} nether by hime no^r yet any other.

And for our selfe we doo moche more marvell and are right sorie, as both we and you have good cause to be, to see the manno^r of yor doings, bent wth force of violence to bringe the kyng's m_a^{tie} and us to theis extremities, which as we doo intend, if you will take no other waie but violence to defend, as natoure and oure allegence dothe bynd us to extremytie of deathe ; And to put yt all to god's hand who gyveithe vectorie as yt pleasethe him, so if any reasonable condicõns and offers wold take place as hitherto none hathe bene signefyed unto us frome you, nore we doo not understand what you do requiere ore seake, ore what you doo mean, And that youe doo seake no hurte to the king's m^{atie} pson; As touchinge all other prevet matters to avode the effusion of Christien bloude, and to preserve the king's m^{aties} person, his realme and subjects, you shall fynd us agreable to any reasonable condicons that you will requiere; for we doe esteme the king's welthe and Tranquilytie of the realme more then all other worldlie things yea then oure owne lyfe.

Thus prainge youe to send us yor determynat aunswere hearin by Mr. Secretarie Peters, ore if you will not let him goe by this berer, We beseche god to gyve bothe [us] you and us grace to determyne this matter as maie be god's honor, the preservacion of the

---

implicated in Lady Jane Grey's usurpation, and received Mary at the Tower, August 3, 1553; was made Lord Chamberlain by Mary, and was Constable of the Tower when Somerset was sent there, and also when the Princess Elizabeth was imprisoned on suspicion of being implicated in Wyatt's rebellion. Upon the accession of Elizabeth he retired to the Continent.

kinge, and the quiet of us all, which maie be if the falte be not in youe.

And so we bid you moste hartelye faire well.

From the king's Maties castell of Wyndsor the vij^{th} of October, 1549.

Your lordshipps loving frends.

L.—Lord Russell's and Sir William Herbert's letter to the Duke of Somerset expressing disapproval of his line of action.

[Petyt MSS. No. 538, vol. 46, fol. 470.]

To the lord protector the vij^{th} of October.[a]

Pleasith yor grace we have receyvid your tres, not without our great lamentacōn and sorowe to perceyve the cyvill dyssencōn wch is happened betwene your grace and the nobilytie. A greater plage could not be sent unto this realme from god; being the next way to make us of conquerors slaves, and to induce upon us unyversall calamytie and thraldome, wch we pray god so to hold his holy hand over us, as we may never se yt. Yo^r graces last tres

---

[a] This is a mistake of the transcriber for October 8, as it is rightly dated at the end of the letter.

There are five distinct documents bearing this date (Oct. 7) in the Record Office. The first is in the handwriting of Sir Thomas Smith, from Somerset to the Council, printed in Holinshed 1058, and in Stow 598, and also in Tytler, vol. i. p. 214, wondering that they have kept Sir William Petre and returned no answer, and stating that every reasonable concession will be granted by the King. The second is from the Council to the King, here printed, stating that they have had his message sent by Petre, and that they are grieved that their fidelity should be doubted. The reason of their consulting together is to depose Somerset. This is a draft partly in Petre's and partly in Wriothesley's hand. There are also two copies of this. The third is from the Council to the Sheriff of ——, evidently a circular declaring the treason of Somerset, to compass which he had endeavoured to levy great numbers of men. None of the King's subjects are to be raised except by order of Council. The fourth is another to the Justices of the Peace to the same effect; and the fifth is to Cranmer and Paget at Windsor, protesting their loyalty, and offering to treat with Somerset if he will absent himself from the King, disperse his forces, and submit.

requireth us wth all deligence to repayre to the castell of Wyndso^{r}, and for answere this is to signiffie that so long as we thought that the nobelytie presently assembled had conspyred agãst the king's Matie parson so long we came forwards wth suche company as we have for suertie of his highnes as apperteyned.

And now having this daie receyved advertysement from the lords wherby yt is given to us to understand that no hurte nor dyspleasure is ment towards the king's Matie, and that yt doth playnly appear^{a} unto us

That this great extremytie procedeth only upon pryvate causes between your grace and them, we therefore thought most cõvenient in the heat of this broyle to levye as greate power as we may, as well for the suertie of the King's Maties person as also for the preservacõn of the state of the realme w^{ch} [*whilst*] this contentou enduring by factions between your grace and them may be in moche perell and daunger.

We are out of doubt the devil hath not so inchaunted nor abused theyr wyttes as thay wold cõsent to any thing prejudiciall and hurtfull to the kyngs most riall person, upon whose suertie and preservacon, as thay well knowe, the state of the realme doth depend.

And having cõsyderacõn of theyr honors' dyscryson and theyr contynuall trough unto the Crowne, we beleve the same so assuredly as no other argument may disswayde us for the cõntrayry. And for our owne partes we trust your grace doubteth not but that as we have and will and must have a spiall regarde and cõsyderacõn of our dewties of allegeaunce unto the king's ma^{tie}, so shall we not be necligent to do our partes lyke faythfull subjects for the suertie of his highnes accordingly; Besechinge your grace that his Matie in any wise be put in no feare and that your grace wold so conforme yo^{r}self as these pryvate causes redounde unto an unyversall dyspleasure of the whole realme.

---

^{a} Here the transcriber has omitted the words "that they are his highness' most true and loving subjects, meaning no otherwise than as to their duties of allegiance may appertain; so as in conclusion it doth also appear."

Wold god al maynes were used rather then any bludd shedde; wch yf be once attempted, And the case brought to that mesery that the handes of the nobelitie be once poluted eache wythe others bludde, the querell once begonne will never have ende tyll the realme be dyssendyd to that wofull Calamytie that all our posterytie shall lament the chaunce.

Your graces proclamacõns and billets put a brode for the rasyng of the Cõmons we myslike very moche. The wycked and evill dysposed persons shall sturre as well as the faythful subjects, and we and these other gentilmen who have served and others of worshipp in the countres where the same have been publyshed do incurre by this meanes muche infamie slander and dyscredyt.

Thus we end, beseching almightie god the matter may be so used as no effucion of bludde may flowe. And therw^th all a suertie of the king's m^atie and of the state of the realme.

From Andover, the viii^th of October, 1549.

Y^r graces loving frends,[a]

[JOHN RUSSELL.
WM. HERBERT.]

[To my lord Protectors Grace.]

LI.—CIRCULAR LETTER FROM THE COUNCIL AT LONDON TO SHERIFFS AND JUSTICES OF PEACE OF THE COUNTIES.

[Domestic Papers of Edward VI. vol. ix. art. 28.]

For as much as the duke of Somerset, abusing the kings m^ates hand, stamp, and signet, and w^tout th'advise of us of his highnes counsaill, hath sent furth divers and sundry writings to levye the kings m^ates subgets and disturb the commun peax of the Realme, for the maintenaunce of his own ill and oultragious doings only, to no small peril of the king's maiesties personne, and the disturbaunce of his m^ates good and loving subgets;

Thies be to will and requyre youe, and nevertheles on his highnes behalf straitly to charge and commaunde you, that you nor none of

---

[a] The signatures and address have been added from the copy in the Record Office.

you levye nor cause to be levyed any nombres of men by force of any such writting whatsoever, except thands of us of his ma^{tes} pryvy counsail or the more part of us shall be subscribed to the same. And further we requyre youe on his highnes behalf t'applie your labours and busines, every of you in your severall vocations, quietely and peaseably, as becometh good subgets, w^tout giving credit to any such rumours and bruits, as by the said duke be untruely and falsely spred abrode to the dishonour and slaunder of us his Ma^{tes} true and faithfull counsaillours, who be and ever shall be during our lyves redy to spende o^r bloode for the suretye of his most royal psonne, and the maintenaunce of the c̃omon welth of his m_a^{tes} most loving and obedyent subgets.

Geven at London the viii. of Octobre, the third yere of his highnes most noble reign.

To the shrief of ——
and to the Justices of peax of the said
countye and to all other the king's
Ma^{tes} constables, hedborowes,
and other his highnes ministers
and subgets of the same countye.

R. RYCHE, Canc^r.
   W. SEINT JOHN.   W. NORTHT.
J. WARWYK.   F. SHREWESBURY.
    ARUNDELL.
THOMS. SOUTHAMPTON.
WILLM. PETRE, Sy.   EDWARD MONTAGUE.[a]
   NICHOLAS WOTTON.
       JO. SADLEIR.

Endorsed:
Placarts graunted by
the Councill assembled
at London
to advise men not to obey
the precepts of the duke
of Somerset for levying
of forces.

---

[a] This was Sir Edward Montague, who had exchanged the office of Chief Justice

LII.—LETTER FROM LORD MORLEY TO THE COUNCIL IN LONDON TAKING PART WITH THEM.
[Domestic Papers of Edward VI. vol. ix. art. 30.]

Plese it yor good lordshyppes to be advertysyd that I have resayvyd yor most honorabill letters declaryng and expressyng un to me the dāgerous estate of the kyngs most Riall parson, hys dominiōs and realmes by the lord protectour; to that I make yor good lordshypps this true and faythefull subjects answer that like wyse as above all things next unto god I ā most bounden to defend the kyng, evyn so ā I most boūden to defend hys reame and my naturall and dere contrie. Wherfore so to do I shall accordyng to yor cōandments put my selfe in Redynes with that pore power I have wytheen one hours warning so other to lyve or to dy; and thus Crist Jesus preserve yor most honorabill lords all.

From mark hall this present day the viij day of October.

faytheful ora[t]our
HARRY MORLEY.[a]

Endorsed:
   To the most honorable
   lords of the co'sell
   in hast.

And again,
   The l. Morley
   to the counsell viij°
   Octobris 1549.

of the King's Bench for the inferior place of Chief Justice of the Common Pleas, Nov. 6, 1546. This office he held throughout the reign of Edward VI. He was one of the sixteen executors. He joined the party against Somerset Oct. 7, 1549, and on that day signed the letter to the King against the Protector, but not the letter from the Council in London to the Council at Windsor, which bears the same date. The Duke of Northumberland compelled him to draw Edward's will for the succession of Lady Jane Grey, but he was one of the first to desert her cause. His change of front did not save him from arrest. He was sent to the Tower July 27, 1553, deprived of the Chief Justiceship, fined 1,000*l.*, and forced to surrender the abbey lands that had been granted him by Somerset. He died in obscurity, Feb. 10, 1556.

[a] This was Henry Parker, ninth Baron Morley, son of Sir William Parker, by

LIII.—A Proclamacion[a] set forth by the state and bodie of the Kynge's Maiestes Counsayle now assembled at London, conteinyng the very trouth of the Duke of Somerset's evel Government, and false and detestable Procedinges.

The Kyngs Maiestes most honorable Counsail, calling to their remembraunce the quiet state, that this the Kynges maiestie's moost noble Realme of Englande and other his Maiesties Realmes and Dominions, stode in at the deceas of his highnes Father, of moost noble memorie Kyng Henry the eight, their late soveraigne Lorde and Maister, and studieng upon the causes of suche calamities, losses and displeasures, as of late have happened amonges us, not only by inward division whiche hath been already the death of thousandes of his Maiesties naturall subjectes, and oneles GOD of his mercie doo geve them that have been offendors grace to repente, and to determine to lyve hereafter in a due and Godly obedience, muste nedes brede to this Realme an utter desolation, But also by the losses of his Maiesties peices beyonde the Sees, the whiche his Highnes saied Father not many yeres before his deceasse wanne to the great honor of his Maiestie, and to the great commoditie of his realme, with the greate aventure of his most noble persone, and

Alice Lovel, sister and sole heir of Henry Lovel, eighth Baron Morley, who succeeded to the title in his mother's right, and was summoned to Parliament from the 15th of April, 14 Henry VIII. *i.e.* 1523, to the 28th of October, 2 and 3 Philip and Mary, 1555. He was one of the Commissioners sent in 1523 to present the insignia of the Garter to the Archduke Ferdinand, whose instructions are printed at length in Strype's *Ecclesiastical Memoirs*, vol. i. pp. 42-46. He signed the letter of the Lords to the Pope about Catharine's divorce, and afterwards sat on the trial of Anne Boleyn; his son, Henry Parker, having been made Knight of the Bath at her coronation. This son died before him, and was buried in December 1553, and is wrongly called Lord Morley in Machyn's *Diary*. He was one of the lords who dissented from the bill for the marriage of priests, Feb. 19, 1548, and in 1550 from the act for destroying the old office books and defacing of images. He died not, as is generally supposed, in 1555, but, as Machyn says, on Wednesday, Nov. 25, 1556, and was buried on the following Thursday, Dec. 3, and was succeeded by his grandson, Henry Parker, tenth baron.

[a] This proclamation is No. 48 (printed) in Coll. of Soc. Ant. mounted on three

the consumption of his inestimable treasure: they have founde and fully perceived that the only roote and chief cause of al these evils have growne by the malice and evil governement of Edward Duke of Somerset, lately called Protectour, whose pride, covetousnes, and extreme ambicion doth declare and shewe to all the worlde, that liste to beholde the same, that he hath ment nothing lesse than the preservacion of the Kynges moste Roiall maiestie, or the good ordre of his Realme and the safe keping of his grace's peeces beyonde the Sees, but rather that he hath sought the satisfactiō of his devilyshe and evill purposes, for the compassing whereof what wayes he and his have used to enryche hym, how he hath in all this tyme of the warres both with Fraunce and Scotlande buylded most sumptuously in a nombre of places, the Kynge's Maiesties poor Souldiors and others having sommes of money due to them unpayde of their wages and duties: how he hath laboured to make hymself strong in all Countreis: how he hath subverted all Lawes, Justice and good ordre of the Realme, whereby he hath fearfully shaken the Chayre of his Maiesties estate: how litle he hath esteamed the grave advise of all his Maiesties good and faithful Counsailors: howe litle he hath regarded th'order appoincted by our late sovereigne lorde Kyng Henry the eight, for the governement of his maiestie, his Realmes and dominions, now in his tender age: what devision he hath laboured to sowe in the Realme, if he

leaves. It is not in Grafton's little book. It is followed by another of Oct. 10, signed by the same nineteen, with the addition of the Lorde Wentworth and Sir Anthony Wingfeld, knyght of the ordre, the Kynges Maiesties vice Chamberlain, and capitain of the Garde, and Sir Edmund Peckham, knyght, high Threasaurer of all the Kynges Maiesties Myntes. It is No. 49, and is headed, "A Procl^n set furth by the body and state, &c. concernyng the devisers, writers, and casters abrode of certain vile, slaunderous, and moste trayterous letters, billes, scrowes, and papers tending to the seducement of the kynges maiesties good and lovyng subjectes." The draft of this in Record Office, vol. ix. It is remarkable that nearly all the proclamations of this period have disappeared. Grafton's collection contains none between August 23, 1549, and March 28, 1550, and the collection in the possession of the Society of Antiquaries has only one, dated Sept. 30, between August 15 and this one of October 8, against the Duke of Somerset.

myght have brought his purpose to passe betwene the Nobles, the Gentylmen, and the Comens, whiche muste nedes if it should continne destroye both parties, and at last be the destruction of the persone of our soveraigne Lorde the Kyng, whom God long preserve unto us, and of the hole Realme: Fynally what losse his maiestie and the Realme have of late suffered by his wilful negligence and lacke of provision and furniture of the peeces beyonde the Sees: And what damage his Maiestie is lyke more to susteine, onles God helpe it by his mightie hand, for that he wold not supply the lackes in time, albeit he was often moved to it, both by suche as had and have the charge of the peeces there, and by the hole Counsail, and by divers of them a part, every man that hath eyes maie see, and al good men doo in their hartes muche lament it.

Whiche thinges being so apparant as no man can deny them, the Lordes and others of the Kynge's Maiestie's counsaill, considering with themselfes, that if summe reformacion were not had, and summe better and more certaine order established, there must nedes ensue present daunger and perill to his maiestie's persone, and utter subvercion of the state of this noble Realme, with further losse of his Maiesties peeces in outwarde parties;

And mindyng, neverthelesse, to have had the same compassed in quiet ordre and without disturbans of the Realme, or trouble of the Kinges Maiesties good subiects, whiche have been lately much seduced, and by his craftie and subtil meanes under the color of the service of the Kynges maiestie and their reliefe deceived where in dede he ment nothing but to use them for his mischevous purpose, consulted at London together and fynally cocluded to have spoken with the said Duke of Somerset, and to have travailed by all the good meanes they could, to have brought hym to have been contented to have lyved within reasonable limites and to have put suche ordre for the surety of the Kinges Maiesties persone as appertayned: and yf that might so have been woon and obteigned, whatsoever his deservinges were, whiche bee in dede mooste unnaturall, ingrate and trayterous, yf he wolde have conformed himselfe to reason, for pities sake and the avoydyng of slaunder to have passed over all thinges without further extremitie. For if the Lordes and others of the Counsaill, whose duety it was principally to have regarde to hys Maiesties surety and to the preservacion and avauncement of the Commen wealth of this Realme had mente any further evell or displeasure to the sayde Duke, then is before specified they had tyme ynough and good oportunitie easely to have taken his body, and to have ordred it according to justice. But the sayde Duke of Somerset on the other syde, beyng burdened with a corrupte conscience, and yet so overcome with his moost detestable ambicion, as he could not tempre hys abhominable and moost wretched determinacion in aspiryng to his soveraigne Lordes and Masters place, as soone as he harde that certaine of the Lordes of the Counsail had met and cõsulted together, fearing as it plainly appeareth that it shuld be for his reformacion and knowing that he cannot answere to any part of his doinges, straight began to levy force and to spredde moost false brutes and rumors abrode against the counsail, blustering and blowyng by his owne mouthe, and by hys ministers in a nombre of places, that certaine Lordes had conspired a great treason against the Kynges Maiesties persone, and cryeng to the people to haste to the Courte in forcible maner for defence thereof: whereby many of them, beyng abused by his false reporte, both conceaved evell opinion of them that never deserved it and ranne thether in a disorder and uprour, whiche, neverthelesse, in the good people, for their zeale was not to be discommended: Albeit the treason in dede resteth in his harte, and in a few others combyned with hym, from the which almightie God defend his maiestie. For let all men most certainly perswade to themselfes, that there is no one counsailor nor other nobleman or others that have desyred thys moost necessary reformacion and ordre for the surety of hys Maiesties persone and the Commen wealth of the Realme, that hath been moved thereunto (as God shall helpe therin) upon any respecte but onely for discharge of their duties to hys hyghnes and to their naturall countrey. Neither is there one of them but so he myght lyve to see his Maiestie in suche estate as he myght commaunde his owne as appertaineth, and answere his enemies as hys moost noble progenitors have done, could not be content to be straight buryed. Which as the hole body of the counsail stãdyng in thys matter doubteth not but all good men that love the Kyng and the Realme wyll beleve and firmely credite whatsoever he or his complices have and shall brute and spreade abrode to the contrary: So, seyng he troubleth the hole Realme for the accomplyshment of his vyle treason, and useth the Kynges Maiestie, beyng now in hys tender age, for an instrument agaynst himselfe, causyng hym to putte hys hande to many of hys devises, and upon hys false informacions too speake wyth hys owne mouthe thynges tendynge in dede to hys owne destruccion, which is a pytifull case. The sayde Counsaill desireth, and in hys Maiesties name, and by his aucthoritie chargeth all his Maiesties good and faithfull Subiectes, as they love and desyre the preservacion of hys Maiesties lyfe, and the continuaunce of the noble state and cõmen wealth of this realme, not only to ayde and assiste them as they shalbe cõmaunded for the delyvery of his Maiestys persone from the handes of so greate a Traytour, which under the pretence of favour and help to be ministred to the good People and Commens, frameth him selfe as he thinketh a strength to destroy his Sovereyne Lord and al them that would his preservaciõ: which when they shal now understande, the counsayl doubteth not but they wil not only beware how thei be againe by false Rumours deceived but also in no wise to obey any preceptes, letters or Proclamacions whereunto his hande shalbe set (though he abuse his Maiesties most noble hande and Seale to them) but to reste and quyet themselves upon such Cõmaundementes, Proclamacions and Letters only as shall procede from the body of his Maiesties Counsayl, who seke only his highnes Preservacion as is aforesaid, and the good order of his grace's Realmes, Dominions and Subjectes and to have special regarde that Justice be ministred to evyll doers: Wherein, as they shal shew themselfes in dede good and most loving Subjectes, so the saide Counsayl intende both to see and provide oute of hande that they shalbe in all thinges reasonably considered, as shalbe for their benefite, accordyng to the Lawes and statutes of the Realme: And to recommende their Servyce hereafter when his Maiestie shall be of Age, and hable to direct his owne affayres, as shall undoubtedly be to the counfortes of them all and of their Posterites.

Dated at London the viij daie of October in the third yere of his maiesties moste prosperous reigne, published under his maiesties seale, and subscribed by the Lordes and others of his maiesties privey counsaill whose names foloweth.

 The LORDE RICHE, Lorde Chauncellor.
 The LORDE SAINCT IHON, Lorde greate Master and President of the Counsaill.
 The LORDE RUSSELL, Lorde privey Seale.
 The LORDE MARQUES OF NORTHHAMPTON.
 The ERLE OF WARWICKE, Lorde Greate Chamberlain.
 The ERLE OF ARUNDELL, Lorde Chamberlain.
 The ERLE OF SHREWSBERY.
 The ERLE OF SOUTHHAMPTON.
 SIR THOMAS CHEINEY, Knight of the order, and Threasaurer
  of the Kynges Maiesties house, and
  Lorde Warden of the Cinque Portes.
 SIR WILLYAM HERBERT, Knight, Master of the Kynges Maiesties horse.
 SIR IHON GAGE, Knight of the order, Constable of the Towre.
 SIR WILLYAM PETRE, Knight, Secretary.
 SIR EDWARD NORTH, Knight.
 SIR EDWARD MONTAGUE, Knight, Chief Justice of the Common place.
 SIR RAUFE SADLER, Knight.
 SIR IHON BAKER, Knight.

Sir Edward Wotton, Knight.
Master Doctor Wotton, Deane of Cantorbury.
Sir Richard Southwell, Knight.[a]

And God save the Kyng.

> Richardus Grafton,
> Regis impressor
> excudebat.

---

[a] This was Sir Richard Southwell, who is often confounded with his brother Sir Robert Southwell, the Master of the Rolls and a Privy Councillor, in the reign of Henry VIII. July, 1542. He resigned in 1550, under Edward VI. and died in Nov. 1559. They were both commissioned to visit the monasteries in 1535. Sir Richard was in attendance on the Duke of Norfolk at the reception of Anne of Cleves in 1539, and was one of those who informed against the Duke of Norfolk and the Earl of Surrey in 1546, when they were committed to the Tower. He was authorised, May 26, 1547, by Somerset, Rich, and others, to receive the surrender of the property of the Dean and Chapter of Norwich, on a false pretence that they should not be sufferers by the transaction. He was not one of the executors of the will of Henry VIII., but was appointed one of the twelve to assist them as councillors, and afterwards became one of the councillors appointed in Somerset's patent to be Protector. He was one of the chief contrivers of Somerset's fall, having been one of the conspirators on the first day, Oct. 6, and was in attendance Oct. 14, when Somerset was sent to the Tower; but when Southampton was driven away from the Council, and Arundel fined, he was put in the Fleet by Warwick for dispersing seditious bills. His name does not appear among the twenty-four councillors who signed Edward's limitation of the Crown, but his name as a Privy Councillor is amongst those who signed their consent on the 21st of June, as is that of his brother Sir Robert as sheriff of Kent. He was employed by Mary, after she came to the throne, and appointed Master-General of the Ordnance in 1554. He with Lord Hastings and Sir Thomas Cornwallis fetched Elizabeth to Court on suspicion of being concerned in Wyatt's conspiracy. He had been granted an annuity of 100*l.*, Dec. 4, 1553, for his services against the Duke of Suffolk.

LIV.—Letter from the King to the Council in London deprecating extreme measures against Somerset.[a]

[Domestic Papers of Edward VI. vol. ix. art. 25.]

Right trustie and right welbiloved Cosyns and right trustie and welbiloved we grete you well.

And have by your łres wch our trustie servaunt Willm Honnengs presented to us yesternight pceyved the causes which you alledge for your abode and assembles there, w^t yor excuse for the staying there of Sr Willm Petre, oon of our secretaries; And fynally what opinion you have conceyved of our derest uncle the lord protectour; for aunswar wherunto we let you wit that as farre as our age can understand, the rather moved by the visage that we see of our said uncle and counsell and others our servaunts p̄ntly w^t us, we do lament our p̄nt estate being in soch an im̄inent daunger, as unlesse god do put it into the hartes of you there to be as carefull to bring thies uprores unto a quiet, as we see our said uncle and counsell to be here, we shall have cause to thinke you forget yor dueties towards us, and the greate benefitts which the King our lord and father of most noble memorye hath employed upon every on of you. For howsoever you charge our said uncle w^t will fulnes in your łre, we and our counsell here have found him so tractable, as if you fall not in to the same fault wherew^t you bourden him, we trust that both you and he may contynew in such sorte and suertie w^tout suspition by a fryndely determinacōn and agrement amonge your selfs as may be to our savetie and the quiet of you and the rest of your good subjects.

Wherfore we pray you good cosyns and counsellours to consyder as in tymes past you have every of you in his degree [*served us every*] served us honestly at soundry tymes; So hath our said uncle,

[a] This is one of the four documents of this date printed by Tytler, vol. i. p. 220, the others being the letter from Russell and Herbert to the Protector, that from Paget, Cranmer, and Smith to the Council at London, and the private letter from Smith to Petre.

as you all know, And by goddes grace may by your good advises serve us full well hereafter; ech man hath his faults, he his, and you yours; And if we shall herafter as rigorously way yours as we here that you entend w^t crueltye to purge his, which of you all shalbe hable to stand before us?

To our pson, we verely beleve, and so doo you, we dare say, he myndeth no hurt. Yf governem^t he hath not so discretly used himself, as in your opinions he might have doune, we thinke thextremitie in such a case is not to be required at his hand; yet lieth it in us to remit it, for he is our uncle, whom you know we love; And therfore somewhat the more to be considered at your handes. And if he were another pson, yet though he had offended us, if thoffence tended not directly to our pson, as we be credibly enfourmed it doth not, ye woold we thinke in no wise counsell us to procede to extremities agaynst him, for feare of ony respect that might pticularly seme herafter to touche ony of you, whiche feare may be by wysedom on both parties provided for, and we the better preserved. Like as ptely by certayn articles exhibited unto us by our said uncle, which herw^t we send unto you, signed w^t our hand and ptely by our trustie and right welbeloved counsello^r Sr Philip Hobbye, Knight,[a] may appeare to you; unto whom we require you to

[a] This was Sir Philip Hoby or Hobby, son of William Hoby, of Leominster, who is spoken of by Wood as being a zealous Protestant—elder brother of Sir Thomas Hoby who translated into English Bucer's *Gratulation* and *Answer to Gardiner*, printed after the translator's death by Jugge: and uncle of Sir Edward, a writer of some eminence in the reign of Elizabeth and James I. His first appearance in history is in March, 1538, when he was sent by Cromwell with Hans Holbein to Brussels concerning the projected marriage of the King with the Duchess of Milan. As gentleman of the King's privy chamber he was appointed to receive Anne of Cleves in 1539. In 1543 he was imprisoned with Heynes, dean of Exeter, for his advanced Protestantism. He was one of Edward VI.'s first Council, but his name does not appear till the year 1549, when he returned from Flanders, and stood by the Protector. The state of affairs at the time of writing this letter is thus described by the King in his diary :—" Then began the Protector to treat by letters, sending Sir Philip Hobbey, lately come from his ambassad in Flaundres, to see to his family, who brought in his return a letter to the Protector, very gentle, which he delivered to him, another to me, another to my house, to declare his faults, ambition, vain-

gyve credit and to retourne him agayn w^t your aunswer accordingly w^tout fayling hereof, as you tender our preservaćon and the weale of our realme.

Yeven under our Signet at our Castell of Wyndsour the viij day of October in the third yere of our reign.

Endorsed:
 A copie of the kings
 m^{atie} l're from Windso^r
 to the counsell at London
 viij° octobris 1549 w^t the duke
 of Som'setts articles inclosed.

LV.—Letter of the Lords of the Council at London to the Council at Windsor.

[Domestic Papers of Edward VI. vol. ix. art. 38 and 39.]

From the counsell at West(m) to the lords at Windsour
ix° Octobris, 1549.

My Lordes,

After our most hartie comendaćons, we have receyved yor lres by Mr. Hobby, and hard such credence as he declared on the Kings Ma^{tes} and your behalfs unto us. The aunswars wherunto, by cause they may at more length appere to you both by our lres to the Kings Ma^{te} and by reaport also of the said Mr. Hobby, we forbeare to repet here agayn; Most hartely praying and requiring your lord-

---

glory, entering into rash wars in mine youth, negligent looking on New-Haven, enriching of himself of my treasure, following his own opinion, and doing all by his own authority, &c. Which letter was openly read, and immediately the lords came to Windsore, took him and brought him through Holborn to the Tower."— (Pocock's *Burnet*, vol. ii. pt. 2, p. 11.) In 1551 he was employed in France, and in the following year was sent to Flanders again, to mediate a peace between the Emperor and the French king. In this embassy he was continued by Queen Mary, July 12, 1553. Yet, July 15th, he wrote to the Council a letter, in conjunction with Sir Richard Morysine, in which Lord Guildford Dudley is spoken of as having been called king. Both of them were recalled Aug. 5, 1553.

ship and every of you and nevertheles charging and coṁaunding you in the Kings Ma^{tes} name to have a contynuall ernest watche, respect and care, to the suertie of the King's Maiestie our naturall and most gracious soverayn lordes pson. And that he be not removed from his Ma^{tes} Castell of Wyndsour as you tender your dueties to Almightie God and his Ma^{te}, and as you will aunswar for the contrary at your uttermost pills.

We ar moved to call ernestly upon you herin not w^tout greate cause; and amongs many others we cannot but remember unto you that it appeareth veary straunge unto us, and a greate wonder to all true subjects, that you will either assent or suffre his Ma^{tes} most roiall pson to remayn in the gard of the Duke of Somersetts men, sequestred from his own old sworne servaunts. It semeth straunge that in his Ma^{tes} own howse straungers shuld be armed w^t his Ma^{tes} own armure and be nerest about his highnes pson, and those to whom the ordinary charge is comitted sequestred a way, so as they may not attend according to their sworn dueties; if any ill come herof, you can consyder to whom it must be imputed ones thexample is veary straunge and pillous. And now my L. if you tender the preservaçõn of his Ma^{te} and the state, joyne w^t us to that end we have writen to the Kings Ma^{te}, by wch way things may sone be quietly and moderately compounded. In the doing wherof we mynd to doo no otherwise then we woold be don to; And that w^t as moche moderation and favor as we honorably may. We trust none of you hathe just cause to note any one of us and moche lesse all of such crueltie as you so many tymes make mençõn of. One thing in your łres we marvell moch at, wch is that you write that you know more then we know. Yf the matters come to your knowleage and hidden from us be of suche weight as you seame to pretend, or if they touche or may touche his Ma^{te} or the state, we thinke you do not as you ought in that you have not desclosed the same unto us being thole^a state of the counsaill. And thus pray-

---

^a On the 6th of October the conspirators were nine in number. On the 7th, 15 sign the letter to the King, and 14 that to the lords at Windsor, the name of

ing god to send youe the grace to do that may tend to the suertie of the Kings Ma^te and tranquillitie of the realme, We byd you hartely fare well.

From Westm̄ the ixth of October.

LVI.—Letter from Sir Thomas Smith to Secretary Petre stating his difficulties.[a]

[*Domestic Papers of Edward VI. vol. ix. art. 39.*]

Sir,—I most hartelie cōmend me unto you, and thank also most hartelie my lords of Warwicke, Arondell and you, that my brother George had leave to com and vysite me, which was both myn and his great comfort. For the love of God S^r help to bryng this tumult to som̄ moderate thyng, and yt wilbe straight candid to

---

Montague being omitted. On the 9th Warwick's name is omitted, but there is an addition of Montague and Baker, and on the 10th there is added the name of E. Wentworth.

[a] There is no date to this letter. That assigned to it conjecturally by the editor of the State Papers—viz. Oct. 9—is uncertain. It may have been written on Oct. 10th or 11th. How his application fared may be seen from the following extract from the Council Book :—

"At Wyndsour, Sunday, the 13th of October, the lords called before them Sir Thomas Smyth, Sir Michael Stanhop, Sir John Thyn, knight, Edward Wulf, one of his Majesty's privy Chamber, and William Gray, esquire, adherents of the said Duke, and the principal instruments and counsellors that he did use both at this time, and otherways also in the affairs of his ill government, whom when they had charged with their offenses they accorded to send to the tower of London, there to remain until further order were taken with them. The same day also Sir Thomas Smyth, for sundry his misdemeanours and undiscreet behaviour heretofore, being thought unmete to continue any longer of the privy Council, was both sequestered from the Council and also deprived from the office of one of his majesty's secretaries."

They were all sent the next day, Monday, October 14th (wrongly entered in the Council Book as the 13th), with the Duke to the Tower, conducted there by the Earls of Sussex and Huntingdon, the Lords Grey and Abergavenny, and Sir John Gage, the Constable of the Tower—and the next day Dr. Wotton, dean of Canterbury, was appointed secretary in the room of Sir Thomas Smith.

yor greatest hono^r that can be. I am sorie it is cōm so far, and to so mych an extremitie as it is. I am not able to judge of yor doengs, but I wold have wysshed that pclamacōn which I heare say is abrode had bene staied a while, and the thyng made for other mater then I here it is. The heats of both the pties at the furst, And the rumors hath done I se excedyng much hurt. But it is not yet so far I trust but it may take for composicōn or moderacōn at the least.

Yf ye can [*do it*] I pray you let me have knowledge by my brother in what state I stand in my self. For in thiese maters I cannot understand what I shuld thynk. I know nothyng wherof my conscience can accuse me. Yet thies thyngs will make a man to doute he can not tell what. I trust my tarieng here can not be prejudiciall unto me when I cannot go away. And I cannot tell what might be said though I might go away, if I shuld now leave the kyngs Ma^{te}. Well I cōmyt it all to god, and my lords and your judgments there. And I must and do repose mych in yor frendship to do and aunswer for me, if eny thyng be objected, and shew now such a part for me as ye wold wish I shuld for you in the like case, and I shall not forget it whiles I live. Thus I [*com*] most hartelie cōmit yow to god.

From Wyndesor castle.

Yo^r allwaies most
assurid,
T. SMITH.[a]

Endorsed:—
To the right honora-
ble and myne assured
frend Sr Will'm
Peter knight, cheif
Secretarie to the
Kinges Ma^{te}.

---

[a] This was Sir Thomas Smith, Secretary of State. He was one of the judges who deprived Bonner of the bishopric of London. He stuck by the Duke of Somerset and was sent with the rest of his adherents to the Tower, Oct. 14, 1549, and deprived

LVII.—Draft of a Proclamation[a] offering a Reward to any who shall give Information of Maintainers of the Duke of Somerset's Traitorous Proceedings.

[Domestic Papers of Edward VI. vol. ix. art. 40.]

Forasmoche as there be diverse lewd and sedicious [*folks*] personnes [*being so given to sedicoñ as they care not f*] whiche do labor nowe to mayntain the traitorous doings of the duke of Somerset, and for that purpose do divise the most vile false and traitorous bills, papers, and boks that ever were harde off, strawing the same in the stretes, aswel within the Citie of London [*and*] as in diverse [*other*] townes and other places in the cuntrey; wherein they do falsly and traitorously travail to slaunder the kings mat[s] Counsail, thinking therby to amase and abuse his Mat[es] good subgietts, which be in a redynes to joyne with the said counsail for the delyverey of the king our soveraign Lords most Royal person, remayning to his great peril and damage in the said dukes custody, and for the restoring of this noble Realme to some better order and quietnes, whiche shalbe the benefite [*of every man*] of us all universally; The kings Mat[ts] most honorable counsail, for avoiding of thinconvenience and extreme daunger that by such sedicious and slaunderous bills, papers and sorowes might ensue to his Mat[e], do in his highnes name and by his graces auctoritie require and nevertherles comande all and every [*the*] his [*highnes*] Mat[s] good subgietts whiche love his highnes and this Realme, to use all their wisedomes and pollicies and diligence to serche out the writers, divisers, casters and counsailors to such traitorous bills and papers, and the same to apprehende, and present

of his office of secretary, but was released on the following Feb. 22. He was afterwards appointed one of the eight civilians of the thirty-two commissioners for drawing up the *Reformatio Legum Ecclesiasticarum*, Oct. 6, 1551. At the beginning of Elizabeth's reign he was one of those appointed to review the Service Book, and the person in whose house the commissioners for that purpose met.

[a] The proclamation as finally written and issued is in the collection of the Society of Antiquaries. It is without date, but is marked in pencil there as having been issued on the 10th of October.

befor the said most honorable counsail, that they may receyve condigne punishment according to their demerites; wherin, as they shal do most acceptable service to his Mat^e and their natural cuntrey, So the said counsail dothe in his Mat^es name promise that whosoever shall attache and bring in any suche diviser, writer or caster abrode of suche, vile and traitorous bills, papers, strawes or letters, or give suche certain information to the said counsail of their names and doings as the same may be apprehended, and their offences proved against them, shal receyve for their travaills and paynes therin by waye of his Mat^s rewarde the summe of [*xl. crownes*] one hundrith crownes.

And God save the king.

And further the said counsail dothe in his Mat's name promise like rewarde to any man that shal apprehend or give knowledge of any person that by ringing of any bells, striking of dromme, proclam bill or letter or any other waye shal labor to styrre the people and to make them rise; wherby there might growe uprore and tumult to the daunger of his Mat^e and of the state [*of*] and comen wealth of this [*same*] Realme or to the slaunder of the kings Mat^s said counsail.

And god.

Endorsed:—
   M. of the proclamation
    for strawing abrode of
    sedicious bills.[a]

---

[a] One of the bills alluded to in this despatch has been printed by Tytler, vol. ii. p. 208, as also another entitled "The Copy of the Bill sowed amongst the Commons." He has also printed two letters from Somerset of the 5th of October, intimating that the conspiracy is against the King, and another of the 6th, signed by Somerset in the name of Edward, to the same effect. On the following day, October 7th, Somerset wrote to the Lords offering "reasonable conditions." This letter is in the handwriting of Sir Thomas Smith, and also appears in Tytler, vol. ii. p. 216.

LVIII.—Letter from Christopher Mount to the Duke of Somerset on the progress of Lutheranism, written from Strasburg, Oct. 10, 1549.

[Cotton MSS. Galba b. xi. fol. 43.]

Rariores modo ad excellentiam vestram, Illustrissime Dux, litteras mit[to], quandoquidem nihil in hisce partibus scriptu dignum vel hic fit [vel] aliunde auditur. Cæsarem intra hanc hyemem Spiram adven[turum] crebrior hic fama spargitur; cives enim Cæsaris jussu præmoniti sun[t ut] alimoniam tam pro jumentis pascendis quam hominibus excipien[dis] comparent. '

Ut illinc porro Argentinam adveniat, ut optimorum o[mnium] ingens formido est; ita contra, adventus ejus apud sacrificos et no[biles] in magnâ expectatione est; nobiles enim libertati civitatis infensi, [com]pressa, ad se solos regimen urbis transferendum sperant, perinde ut [alibi] factum videmus. Clerus nullâ aliâ ratione sentit veterem et abolitam su[persti]tionem restaurari posse, quam hujus solius adventu. Episcopi enim i[ra et] interminatio leniores sunt quam ut his civitas a verâ fide dejiciatur; aut modo pervincendum aut posthac omnino desperandum. Joachi[mus] et Mauritius Electores, convocatis theologis et primis concionatori[bus], deliberatione habitâ, moderationem quandam super quibusdam durior[ibus] in *Interim* articulis adhibuerunt, quam ad Imperatoriam Majestatem refer[ri] supplices rogârunt, ut ejus Majestas eam admittere velit; alias pop[ulum] induci non posse ad *Interim* recipiendum. Sed diserte oratoribus res[ponsum] est, Cæsarem omnino velle ut extra ullam quantulamcunque mutationem *Interim* ab omnibus observetur. Inter theologos quoque Saxonicos ape[rtæ dis]sensiones intercedunt. Nam concionator Magdenburgensis Amsd[orfius] contra Wittenbergenses scripsit, violatores et prophanatores ver[æ relig]ionis eas nuncupans, ut qui ignavis concessionibus et indignis [Christ]iana synceritate simulationibus, sub adiaphororum prætextu [religio]nem et fidem contaminent atque dissipent. Editæ quoque nuper-

[rime] epistolæ sunt in Melanthonis sugillationem, in quibus ipse [scribit] olim majorem constantiam et fortitudinem in Phylippo desydera[ndam], quanquam has opinionum conflictationes intermissas esse oportuit [quia] in doctrinæ summâ inter omnes consensio permanet. Imperat[or et] Rex qui ipse quoque nuper in Saxonia fuit jamdiu institerunt a . . . . . Saxonicum circulum pro Magdeburgensibus bannitis in ordinem . . . . qui modo consensisse dicuntur in contributionem (secundum ordi[narias] pensitationes ab Imperii circulis inferri solitas) sibi præscriptam Magdeburgen. bello adoriundis ; eadem quoque præstatio ab aliis . . . . ribus circulis in eundem usum exigetur. Cæsar prop[ediem] . . . . . mania habiturus creditur; sed de loco nondum constat; plurium [autem] divinatio Argentinam præsagit. Omnes Helvetici pagi præter [Bernenses] et Tigurinos fœdus cum Gallo inierunt, et modo oratores a singulis [pagis] ad Galliæ regem profecti sunt pro fœdere peragenda et sacrame[nto] confirmando. Rumor missionis illinc militum nuper a Gallo petitorum, quæ propediem futura putabatur, jam in silentium concedit. Helvetii enim non amant procul domo belligerari, in regione exhaustâ et depopulatâ.

Ego illustrissimæ Vestræ Celsitudinis patrocinio me, sub debitâ observantiâ, commendo; quam diutissime recte valere precor.

Datum Argentinæ 10 Octobris 1549.

Illustrissimæ vestræ celsitudinis famulus.

CHRISTOPHORUS MONT.[a]

---

[a] This name in full is written in Latin Christophorus Montaborinus; but he usually signs his name Mont and is sometimes called Mount. He was a native of Cologne who had a grant of denization in England, July 18, 1531. He first appears in history June 28, 1533, when he had a grant of 6*l*. 13*s*. 4*d*. "for translating of books." He was much employed by Cromwell; and at the end of July, 1533, was sent by the king with Vaughan to try to conciliate the German princes in the attitude he had assumed towards the Pope. He separated from Vaughan at Nuremburg, and went on to Augsburg, and was at the beginning of the next year joined by Heath. He was afterwards employed in Germany about the marriage with Anne of Cleves, and sent again to excuse the divorce of Anne, and again in

LIX.—Letter from Lord Russell and Sir William Herbert to Somerset, in answer to his letter of the 5th of October.

[Petyt MSS. No. 538, vol. 46, fol. 470.]

To the lord protector the xith of October.

Pleasyth yt your grace wth our humble cõmēdacoñs, we have receyved yor lres, and lyke as we moche reioise to understand the good confirmitie wch restethe in your grace, and the most reasonable offers wch the same haythe mad to the lords and the counsell nowe remayninge, request to doo what maie lie in th'uttermoste of our poweres to worke some honorable reconsilliacion betwene yor grace and them, so as, your said offers beinge accepted and satysfied, some good conclusions maie ensue of thiese miserable Tumults; the myschefe wherof we dobt and feare so moche as in all our lyves we have never beyn more trobled nor disquieted. And althoughe we have two daies paste adressed not onlye yor lres but also yor messages of speciall credid unto the said lords and counsell by Sir Rafe Hoptũ, the knight marshall, even to the same effecte and purpose wch yor grace requieryth of us, whiche shall we not remyt from tyme to tyme and from daie to daie so to plye [*in that*] our humblye servts in that behalf, as we hope in god some quietnes and tranquilitie shall followe according to oure good expectacon; We have geven order for the leaveing of some convenyent powere of men, w^{che} as the present state we have resolved to be for sewerty of the Kings m^{atie} and the preservacion of the realme, of all other things most necessarye to be done. Forren invasion is to he feared; yet moste of all the in convenyencis wch wthin the realme by this

1544 to the Duke of Saxony and the Landgrave of Hesse to cement an alliance with England. In a letter written from Frankfort, Dec. 27, 1546, he gives his address as Oxford and signs his name as Bergottus. He was of use on these embassies because of his knowledge of German and Latin, but was unable to correspond in English, his colleagues being imperfectly acquainted with German. In Seckendorff's history he is always called Montius.

inward devision maie ensue, we doo dobt and mystruste. And when this powere shalbe in arredynes, So as we maie be able for the comforthe and benefit of the wholle realme, withstand the worst at all occasyons, we shall drawe nere whereby we shall have the better oportunytie to be solysitors and a meanes for this good reformacōn on bothe parties. And most of all we wyshe that the same were at the present in suche towardnes as without mystrust of the myschief which is to be feared we might come a waie, nedyng no forther companye then those of our ordenarii famylies.

And thus we wysh agayne some spedye ende of this miserable dyssolacōn, and besech Almightie god to extend his mercifull hand for the suertie of the Kyngs m^{a}^{tie} and the comfort of the realme.

From Wilton, the xjth of October, 1549.

Your graces loving frends,
JOHN RUSSELL.
WYLLIAM HARBERT.

LX.—MINUTE OF THE DESPATCH TO THE AMBASSADORS DENOUNCING SOMERSET.

[Domestic Papers of Edward VI. vol. ix. art. 41.]

We commend us unto you.

[*After our most hartie commendacōns.*]

Whereas by the seditious and outragious doings, [*sedicious behaviour and detestable proceedings*] the corrupt government and detestable conspiracies of the duke of Somerset not only the most royal person of the kings ma^{tie}, our most gracious sovereign lord, was in [*some*] greatt daunger, but also the honor and estate of thole realme moche tossed and brought almost to the way of utter decay and ruyne [*for redresse wherof albeit*] we, thole body and estate of his m^{a}^{tes} privie counsell consulting together, have hitherto proceded therein without any great stirre or busines; and so trust with thelpe of Almighty God to go through to the delyverie of his highnes said person out of the daunger the same was in, and to restore the realme to his pristyn estate, as moche as in us lyeth; yet by cause the brute herof in forreyn realmes may be diverse and more vehement peraventure than it is in dede, we have thought good to signifie unto you thole trouth and ground of this mater as followeth:—

First, you shall understand that our late M^r the Kings $^{m_a tie}$ of most famous memory king henry theight having in his lief tyme obtayned by acte of parliament that it shuld be lefull for his highnes by his last will or otherwise as he shuld thinke good tappoincte and prescribe suche order for mayning of thaffaires of this realme and other his ma^{tes} realmes and dominions during the minoritie of our most gracious soveregñ lord the kings ma^{te} that now is as the said late king our m^r shuld thinke most mete and convenient, dyd according to the said acte by his last will under his great seale of England ordeyn and constitute certayn executors and other his counsillors (of whose wisedom fydelities and trouthes his ma^{te} in his lief tyme had sufficient prove not only to [*governe and mayñ thaffayres*] have the governaunce of [*our said*] the person of our said most gracious sovereign lord that now is during his tender yeres, but also to have the mayning and order of thole affaires and state of the realme during the same tyme. This will after o^r savd late m^{rs} [*accepte*] was accepted and sworn unto by thexecutors, [*wherupon immediately after his departing out of the world the said executors assembling themselfs to gethers in counsell resolved for the better answer tappoynt some one man to be as it war the mouth for the rest to hyre toching [?] of ambassadors and suche others as shuld be suters unto and aunswar as thaffayres of the realme should require the counsell*] who nevertheless considering that it should be [*necessary*] expedient to have one as it were a mouth for the rest, to whom all suche as had to do with thole body of the counsell might resort, [*for awnswer of such things, and to this rome they chose*] after some consultation chose by ther comen agreements the said duke of Somerset, then erle of Hertford, partely for that he was alredy one of thexecutors and a man also of service, but specially [*by*] for that he was uncle to the kings ma^te by the mothers side, [*by meanes of his sister he was joyned in blud to the kings ma^{te}*] with this condition notwithstanding, that he shuld do nothing touching the state of thaffaires of his highnes without thadvise and consent of us the rest of the counsell; which to perfourme he constantly promised and solemply sware in open counsell; and yet neverthelesse he had byn never so litle while in thoffice but he contrary to his said promise [*and othe*], he began to doo things of most weighte and importaunce by himself alone, without calling of any of us of the counsell many times therunto ; and if for the name sake he called any man he ordered the matiers as pleased himself, refusing to hear any mans reason but his own, and in short tyme became so hault and arrogant that he stucke not in open counsell to taunte suche of us of the counsell as frankely spake our opinions in matters so farre beyond the limitts of reason as it is wonder which thing perceyved, we [*thought our dueties. And here we began*] bothe all togithers openly and every one for the more parte of us aparte often times gentilly exhorted him to remember his promisse and othe and to stay himself within the bounds of reason ; but all hath not prevayled, for as we have devised with him for the preservacōn of the kings ma^ties person and honor, So hath he from tyme to tyme as he durst covertly laboured to bring his ma^tie, whom God long preserve, and his hole estate to suche confusion as he might of bothe dispose at his pleasure, declaring in his continuall procedings that he ment never taccompt with any superior; And [*that hat*] the successe of his governement hath byn suche as ther is no true herted Englisshe man that lamenteth not in his harte that ever he bare rule in the realme, not only for the losses of the kings ma^tes peces of Hambletue, Blacknes, Bullenbergh and other the small membres [*of B*] about Bulloyn, [*wherby*] as we have heretofore signified unto you, wherby also the chief peces of Bulloyn resteth at this present in most grete daunger ; all which things might easely have byn prevented if the gredy covetousnes and enriching of himself to finish his pompous buyldings which he had begon in iiij or v places most sumptuously, woold have suffered him to have sene to the furnisshing of the said peces with men municōn and money in tyme,[but also for the loss of Hadington in Scotland, which is presently given over to the grete dishonor of the kings ma^{te} and the realme, [*And yet of all th*] and all for want of necessaries and money for thencoraging of the poore souldiers whom he left unpayed of sundry notable somes of money, to the grete hinderaunce of his highnes service; and yet in the mean tyme hath he not spared to entertayne sundry of the notablest captayns and ringleaders of the cōmons which of late hath so troubled the realme, as heretofore we have more fully writen unto you, with no small gifts, and some of them with annuall lyvings, [*wherby may well appeare whosoever list to thoroughly to behold it that he*], and was in dede the very occasion of the said tumults himself as sithens hath most manifestly appered, meaning therby first to have destroyed the nobilitie and other honest personages of the realme [*and after w*] and after to have aspired to his m^{trys} place ; for nothing ells is to be conjectured of his mischevous and devellysshe enterprises ; what conferences discourses and practeses he hath had with sundry his complices to make himself strong [*lead*] how he hath exp[elled] suche honest men as were justices of peax in every shere, putting in their places others of his own broode, how he hath bestowed such offices as of the kings ^{ma}a^{tes} as fell dayly, upon his own men ; finally how he hath sought by all wayes and meanes to enriche himself and his, leaving the Kings mat^{es} as bare as might be it were to long to reherse. At length[a] when we saw

[a] From this place *when we saw* down to *oration* is almost word for word the same with the letter from the Council to Mary and Elizabeth of the 9th of October, as printed by Tytler, vol. i. p. 249, in which the letter continues as follows : " and, among many his untrue and idle sayings, declared that one special cause of our displeasure to him was that we would have him removed from his office, and that we minded to

that counsell could nott prevayll, and that his pride grewe so fast as doing what he listed, he woold here nothing spoken by the counsel for his mat es affaires, but either he woold contemptuously reject it or doing nothing passe it over in silence, we thought we could suffre no longer, well wayeng with ourselfs the state of thaffaires of the realme, and remembring therwith our duties unlesse we woold in effect consent with him in his naughtie doings, and so resolved frendly and quietly to treate the mater with him, and if we might by any meanes have brought him to reason, to have avoyded all trouble and slaunder, and to have appeased all things without extremitie, but we had not a fewe of us dyned above twyes to gither but immediatly he tooke the tower of london and raysed all the countrey about Hamptoncorte, where the Kings Ma tie then lay, bruting [*th*] and cryeing out that certayn lords had determined to repaire to the court to destroy his highnes, whom we pray to God on our knees to kepe and make as olde a king as ever was any of his progenitors ; and when he had gathered the people togither at hamptoncorte there he brought his ma te into the basse court and so to the gate to them that were without ; and after he had caused his highnes good prince to say, I pray you be good to us and our uncle, then began he his oration to moche untrue and slaunderous and folysshe to reherse, concluding in thende like an irreverent and unkinde subject that ere he woold be destroyed the kings ma tie shuld dye before him, which was to abhominable ; but when we understode thys his manier of his proceding, we thought it neither mete to go to the court, as we had resolved, neither to rest so unfurnisshed as he might use his will first upon us, and after the more easely procede in his purpose ; and so we have in quiet sort bothe

have your Grace to be Regent of the realm, and also to have the rule and government of the King's Majesty's person; dilating what danger it should be to his Majesty to have your Grace, next in succession and title to the crown, to be in that place ; and that therein was meant a great treason, which as God knoweth we never intended, considering all laws touching government to provide to the contrary ; neither any of us all at any time by word or writing hath opened any such matter to your Grace, as your honour knoweth." After this place it proceeds as in the text nearly.

gotten the tower for the king's ma^te from him, and furnisshed ourselfs of a sufficient nomber of hable men if nede be in suche sort as we trust in god very shortly to delyver our sovereign lord from his danger, and that without any bloodshed at all by the grace of god, and after establisshe a better order for his graces suertie then he hath used,[a] and by all wayes and meanes we can possibly traveyll to restore the realme to his former honor and reputaçon in the world as moche as in us lyeth.

Thus have we signified unto you thole discourse of this mater, to be by you declared over agayn to the senate, there and otherwise opened as you shall see occasion. And thus, etc.[b]

LXI.—LETTER FROM WARWICK AND THE OTHER LORDS ACTING WITH HIM COUNTERMANDING THE PREVIOUS ORDER TO REPAIR TO THEM.

[Domestic Papers of Edward VI. vol. ix. No. 44.]

After o^r most hartie comendaçons unto you.

Where by our former letters we have signified unto you the state of our doings, and uppon occasions of such assemblies of men as

---

[a] Here the letter to the princesses adds: "Beseeching your Grace not to conceive any lack to be in us that we have not advertised the same hitherto of our doings, for the matter was so much to us unlooked for and so quick that we were fain to travail almost night and day since the ruffle to keep him from advantage and put ourselves in order for him. He hath now carried his Majesty to Windsor late in the night, in such sort as may declare that he maketh no great store of him; but God we trust will help us to deliver his Majesty out of his cruel and greedy hands; wherein if it should come to an extremity, as we trust it shall not, and for our parte we shall do what we can to manage it so, if it can be possible, as no blood be shed on the occasion of it; we trust your Grace in our just and faithful quarrel will stand with us; and thus we shall pray to Almighty God for the preservation of your Grace's health."

[b] This is a rough draft very wetted and defaced, *endorsed*—
    M. of thole discourse
      of the duke of Somersetts
        doings to thambassadors,
        xi° Octobris, 1549.

were made by the Duke of Somerset, desired you to repayre towards us [with as m]any men as you might make to joyne with us for the suertie of the kings ma^{ts} person; you shall understand that nowe by the goodnes of god bothe the Kings ma^{ts} person is in helth and suertie and that without any tumult or great busynes the Duke is also in sure custodie; which thing, as we have thought good to signifie unto you, so do we praye you to staye your nombres at home without taking any furder traveile for this matter, geving you our most hartye thanks for your good readynes at this time; and so do byd you most hartely well to faire.

From London the xith of October, 1549.

Yo^r loving freends,

W. SEANT JOHN.

W. NORTHT. J. WARWYK.

F. SHREWESBURY. THOM^s SOUTHAMPTON.

T. WENTWORTH.[a] JOHN GAGE.

EDWARD MOUNTAGU.

JO. BAKERE. NICHOLAS WOTTON.

RIC. SOUTHWELL.

---

[a] This was Thomas Wentworth, knighted in 1523, and summoned to Parliament as Lord Wentworth, Dec. 2, 1529. He signed the letter of the lords to the Pope about the divorce of Catharine. He was in attendance on the King at his interview with Francis in 1532, and sat on the trial of Anne Boleyn and Lord Rochford. He was in the reign of Edward VI. Lord Chamberlain of the Household, and was with the Marquis of Northampton in the suppression of the rebellion in Norfolk. He was one of the six lords of the Council appointed to be in attendance on Edward after Somerset's deposition from the Protectorate, having joined the conspiracy against him on the 9th of October. In 1550 he was rewarded with the manors of Stepney and Hackney, and died March 3, 1551, being succeeded by his son Thomas, second lord, who was one of the earliest adherents of the Princess Mary at the time of Lady Jane Grey's usurpation. His funeral was on the 7th of March, and Miles Coverdale preached at it.

On the same day Cranmer, Paget, and Wingfield wrote from Windsor to the Council in London announcing the arrest of Somerset. This letter is printed in Tytler, vol. i. p. 241. Two copies of it exist in the Record Office, Domestic Papers of Edward VI. arts. 42 and 43.

LXII.—Draft of Letter from the Council to the Lieutenant of the Tower ordering the close confinement of the servants of the prisoners.

[Domestic Papers of Edward VI. vol. ix. No. 45.]

After our right harty commendations.

Albeit wee have heretofore by our letters specially admonished you to have good respect thatt none be suffered to speke with the duke of Somersett or any other prisoner by us committed, whereunto wee think veryly you and every of you have suche respect as thimportaunce of the mater requireth; yett considering thatt the sayd duke hath certayn of his servaunts appoynted t'attend uppon hym and some others of the rest of the prisoners have likewise our to wayte uppon them; Wee have thought good to require you to give such order that none of ther sayd servants licenced to wayte uppon any of the sayd prisonars as is aforsayd be suffred to go abrode, butt that they remayne contynually wher ther masters be for thadvoyding of such secret pratizes and intelligence as otherwise may be practized; wherunto we require you and every of you to have a speciall respect gyving commaundment on our behalfs to saunde and delenus the King's Ma^{tes} servants appoynted tattend the duke, to have also lyk consideration hereunto, as they tender the service of the Kings Ma^{te}; and thus we bydd you.

Endorsed:
    M. to the lieutenant, etc.
    of the tower xiij°
    Octobris, 1549.

LXIII.—Inventory of Goods conveyed away by the Duke of Somerset's Servants and others.

[Domestic Papers of Edward VI. vol. ix. art. 52.]

Account of the goods carried off by the duke of Somerset.

To the kings maiesties moost honorable Cownsayll.

Certaine informacions foloweth concerning the embeseling of certaine stuff and other goodes perteyninge of late to the late lord protectour by the servaunts of the same late protectour whose name foloweth, from Syon and Shyne as foloweth:—

In primis, conveyed to Mr. Whalys to his howse at Wymbleton upon the monday nexte after the duke of Somerset went to Hampton Courte to Wyndsoore in the night tyme, toow loode of Coffers and other stuff.

My lady of Somersett the monday aforesaid in the morning caryed with her openly in the sight of peple iiij square Casketts and lighted with the said Casketts at Mr. Whalys.

And further, the saide night afore rehersed was conveyed to Mr. Stanoppes house at Beddington too loode of Coffers and other Stuff.

And further, too loodes of Coffers weare conveyed to Croydon, to what place it is uncertayne, for suche skowt watches were at that presente that no man coulde perceyve thair receipte and unlading therof.

Item to Cavys howse, clerk comptroller with the said duke of Somerset at Rosshampton, was conveyed one loode of stuff the Wenesday nexte folowinge in the night.

Item Davy, porter with the said duke, in the saide weeke conveyed to his house at Richemounte a coffer with toow books with other Stuff, Dyvers and often tymes the same weeke.

Item Water Blackwell, one of his footemen dwelling in Richemount, hathe made muche conveyaunce every day and night home to his howse of muche stuff and goodes perteining to the said duke.

Item one halfeld, yeman of the skollary, conveyed to his howse at Rychemounte dyverse and many Coffers & Bedding and certayne other Stuff bothe day and night with a certayne bag with toow busshells of meale and a square Caskett in thother ende therof.

Item Ruttur in Rychemond, one of the carters, conveyed coffers and bedding and dyvers other stuff the weke aforesaid.

Item another Carter, one Willm Smyth, dwelling in Richamounte, conveyed night and day to hys howse Coffers and other Stuff.

Conveyed by boots in the night to Kewe certayne Stuff; but

where the same was laden it is uncertayne, saving the said duke hadd thre servaunts dwelling in the said towne named Sr Miles Partrige knight, Mr. Turnor his phisition, and one Sely, one of his yemen usshers, to which of them the same goodes was conveyed no man can certeynlie tell, because of suche scowtwatches as were present Sonday night in the weke aforesaid, which would suffer no man to loke owt at his doore but commaunded them yn agayne.

Item one huddy, surgeon to the said duke, conveyed in the saide weke on the Fryday before day after the said duke wente to Wynsore toow geldings owt of Shyne grownde and his boy rode away with them from one Turnors howse of Kewe before day.

Item the saide huddy the said weke brake open a doore at Syon and conveyed to the saide Turnors howse iij beddes with a coffer in the night tyme, and the belringer of the woorks at Syon which kept the water gate did let him bothe in and owt and he being examyned canne tell moore therof conveaunce in that behaulf donne.

Item Wetherhedd, called the surveyor of the workes, the weke aforesaid conveyed by carts out of Syon certayne bedding, carpetts and hanginge to his howse at Thislewoorth and dyverse other stuff.

Item the baylie of Syon called Springe souled all the weeke that the duke abode at Wynsoore as moche wood of the said dukes as he could possible and receyved moche money therfore.

Item James Lawrence of Hamme, warrener to the said duke, conveyed from the said dukes warren house toow beedes and dyverse other Stuff in the weeke aforesaide in the night.

Endorsed:

From the duke of Somersetts
Stuff and goods conveyd.

LXIV.—Account of the Kings Goods taken by the Duke of Somerset.

[Domestic Papers of Edward VI. vol. ix. art. 53.]

The plate belonging to the late Colledge of Seint Stephaunes in Westminster, delivered to his hands.

The riche copes, vestments, Alter clothes, and hangings belonging to the same colledge, whereof the duke had the best and Sr Rauf Ffane and Thynne the rest.

The duke of Norfolks Stuff and Jewelles delivered by Sr John Gate.

The best of Sharingtons Stuffe and Jewelles at London and Laycoke.

The Admiralles Stuffe at Bromham and Sudeley.

The leade, stone and stuffe of Sion, Reading, and Glastonbury, of great value.

The stallment of the Kings allaum, sold to certain merchaunts of London for xiiij of xv years day of paymt, for the which the duke, Smith, and Thynne had emong them xiiij ^{c} lb.

The m^l merks geven by the citie of London to the Kings Ma^{te} at his coronation.

The Customers offices within England in which he had by Thynnes practise notable somes.

The King's secreate houses in Westm^r and other places, wherin no man was previe but him self, half a yere aftre the King's death.

The giftes and exchaunges passed in h[is] name sithence the King's death.

It is thought that moche lande was conveyed for the duke in trust in the names of Thynne, Deleway, Seym^r, Berwike, Colthurst, and other his men, And that they have made assuraunce agayne of all to the duke and his heyres.

And it is thought that the said personnes know best where al the evidences of his lands and his speciallties doe rema[yn].

The dukes diet of viij ᵐ ⓜks by the year paide out of thaugm̃ court.

Endorsed:
> Informacons of certen
> stuff and plate of
> the Kings, which the
> duke of Somerset toke
> into his hands, given
> in by Sʳ Walter
> Myldemay.

LXV.—A LIST[a] OF PRISONERS IN THE TOWER AT THE END OF OCTOBER OR BEGINNING OF NOVEMBER, 1549.

[Cotton MSS. Titus B. II. fol. 67.]

The names of all the prisoners remaining in the Tower:

Thomas, late duke of Norfolke,
Edward Courteney,
Antony Foskewe,[b]
John Rybald, Knight,

Scottyshmen
{
Robart lord Maxfeld,
James earle of Moreton,
Robert Malle, lord of Palmure,
Davyd Douglas,
James Noble,
Patryke Barron,
}

[a] A corresponding list exists in the Record Office, from which extracts have been printed by Tytler, i. 268. It is headed "A Report of the Prisoners being in the Tower the 22nd of October, made by Serjeant Mullinax and the King's Attorney." Tytler omits several of the names in the earlier part of this catalogue, and it has the same separation between those who were there before October 14th and those lately committed, who are in both lists eleven, the last name of Edward Bowes not appearing, but having that of Hales substituted for it. The names are arranged apparently nearly in order of commitment, but there are some variations in the order in the two lists.

[b] This name is entered in Tytler's list as Anthony Foster, late Marshal of Ireland.

Symon Penbroke,
The byshop of Wynchester,
Julius, an Italyon,
William West,
John Harrington,
Sir William Sherrington, Knight,[a]

Frenchmen
{
Semaryall,
Moundere als le loyes,
Andrew Semere,
Lemonyall,
Peter Longer,
Levys Devall,
}

Rychard Colle,
William Hyckoke,
Robart Bell,[b]
John Fuller,
Robart Cappe,[b]
Thomas King,
John Stephenson,
Doctor Moreman,
Mr. Chryspine,
John Kokks, late servant to William Essex,
Mr. Feknam,
Rychard Tomson,
Thomas Richardson, clerk,
Unthanke, parson of Hedley,
Jaques Rouvett, Frencheman,
Robart Bell,

---

[a] From Wriothesley's *Chronicle* we learn that in the month of November "Sir William Shirington, knight, which was condempned the last yeare for high treason, had his pardon and was released out of prison in the Tower, and admitted to be one of the Comon House of the Parliament againe." This session began November 4, 1549.

[b] Bell and Fuller were committed to the Tower by Lord Wentworth on Whitsun even and Cappe on Wednesday in Whitsun week.

William Bell,
Humfrye Arrundell,[a]
John Wyndslow,
John Bury,
Thomas Holmes,
Captain Bartevile,
Peter Paulle, Italyon.

The names of those prisoners that be committed to the Tower of late by the Council:—

Edward duke of Somerset,[b]
Sir Michael Stannop, Knight,
Sir Thomas Smythe, Knight,
Sir John Thyne, Knight,
   Wolfe,
Willam Grey,
Sir Raffe Vane, Knight,
Thomas Fysher,
Rychard Palladen,
John Bowers,
Edward Bowers, stayed by Mr. Constable's commandment.

---

[a] Arundel and the three following were captains of the insurgents in Devonshire, and were tried Nov. 5, 1549, with Robert and William Kett. The four had been brought up by Lord Grey Sept. 8, and were executed at Tyburn Jan. 27, 1550.

[b] Wriothesley gives the names of Somerset and the five following as being delivered to Sir John Gage, the Constable of the Tower, on the 14th of October. The next four were perhaps not committed till later.

LXVI.—Edward's Letter to the Bishops ordering them to call in and destroy the old Books of the Church.

[Domestic Papers of Edw. VI. vol. ix. art. 57.]

EDWARD,

Edward, By the King

Right reverend Father in God, right trustie, and well beloved, we grete you well, and whereas the Booke entitled the Book of common prayers and administraçōn of the Sacraments and other rights and ceremonies of the Church after the use of the Church of England was agreed upon and sett forth by Acte of Parliam^t and by the same Acte commanded to be used of all Persones within this our Realm; yet nevertheless we are informed that divers unquiet and evill disposed Persons since the apprehension of the Duke of Somerset have noiced and bruted abroad that they should have again their old Laten service, their conjured bread and water, with such like vain and superstitious Ceremonies, as though the setting forth of the said book had been the onely act of the aforenamed Duke, we therefore, by the advice of the Body and State of our Privy Counsell, not onely considering the said Book to be our own Acte and thacte of the whole State of our Realm assembled together in Parliam^t, but also the same to be grounded upon holy Scripture agreeable to the Ordre of the Primitive Church, and much to the edifying of our Subjects, to putt away all such vain expectaçōn of having the publick Service, the Administraçōn of the Sacraments, and other rights and ceremonies again in the latin tongue, which were but a p̄ferring of Ignorance to knowledge and darknes to light, and a preparaçōn to bring in Papistry and superstition again: have thought good by thadvice afore said to require and neverthelesse straitly command and charge you that ye immediately upon the receipt hereof do command the Dean and Prebendaries of your Cathedrall Church, the Parson, Vicar, or Curate and Church wardens of every Parish within your Diocesses, to bring and deliver to you or your Deputy, every of them for their Church and Parish, at such convenient place as ye shall appoint, all Antiphoners, Missalles, grayles, Processionalls; manuells, Legends, pyes, porcastes, tournalls, and ordinalles after the use of Sarum, Lincoln, Yorke, Bangor, Herford, or any other private use, and all other Books of Service the keeping whereof should be a lett to the using of the said book of common prayers, and that ye take the same books into your hands or into the hands of your Deputy, and then so deface and abolish, that they never hereafter may serve either to any such use as they were first provided for, or be at any time a lett to that godly and uniforme order which by a common consent is now set forth. And if ye shall find any Person stubborn or disobedient, in not bringing in the said book, according to the tenure of these our Letters, that then you commit the same person to warde to such time as ye have certified us of his misbehavour; and we will and command you that ye also search or cause searche to be made from time to time whether any books be withdrawne or hid contrary to the tenure of these our Letters, and the same books to receive into your hands and to use as in these our letters we have appointed; and furthermore whereas it is come to our knowledge that divers froward and obstenate Persones do refuse to pay towards the finding of bread and wine for the holy Communion according to the ordre prescribed in the said book, by reason whereof the holy Communion is many times omitted upon the Sunday, These are to will and Command you to convent such obstinate Persons before you, and them to admonish and commaund to keepe the ordre prescribed in the said Booke, and if any shall refuse so to do to punish them by suspension, excommunication, or other censures of the Church. Fail ye not thus to do, as ye will avoid our Displeasure. Given under our signet at our Palace of Westminster, the xxv^{the} of December, the third year of our Reign.

T. CANT.^a   W. SEINT JOHN.   J. RUSSELL.
R. RYCHE, CANC.
H. DORSETT.   J. WARWYK.
ARRUNDELL.
THOMAS ELIEN.^b

---

^a In this document the signatures are an attempt to copy the autographs, but are really written by a scribe.

^b This was Thomas Goodrich, Bishop of Ely from 1534 to 1554, being the first bishop consecrated by Cranmer after the separation. He was a mere tool in the hands of Cromwell during the Vicar-General's administration, and amongst the first acts of his episcopate was the substitution of a new oath to be taken by those admitted to benefices, in which the abjuration of the Lutheran heresy enjoined by his predecessor, Nicolas West, was altered into a promise to renounce the Pope and all such his constitutions and decrees as had been or should hereafter be condemned by Parliament. His first appearance in history is as giving his sentence in favour of the divorce at Cambridge. Godwin significantly declines to say anything about his character, and Burnet gives him up as one of those who would make as much advantage of the Reformation as he could, "but would suffer nothing for it." He had succeeded Rich in the Chancellorship in Edward's reign, but was deprived by Mary, July 20, 1553, but managed to conform and keep his bishopric till his death, though he had signed the letter of July 9 as Chancellor, declaring Lady Jane Grey Queen. In the matter of the rebellion against Somerset his name does not appear, because he was not at that time of the Privy Council; the *Athenæ Cantabrigienses* erroneously states that he was made a Privy Councillor at the accession of Edward, but his name does not appear as a Councillor till after Somerset's déposition from the Protectorate, after which he appears to have followed the fortunes of Northumberland till his fall, to which he contributed by signing, July 20, 1553, the charge of the Council to Richard Rose, pursuivant, who was sent to Cambridge to procure that he should be disarmed. He had that morning joined with Suffolk, Cranmer, and the other Lords of the Council, who all dined with the Lord Mayor and adopted the side of the Princess Mary.

LXVII.—Cranmer's Letter to Parker ordering him to preach at Paul's Cross on March 16, 1550.
[British Museum, Add. MSS. 19400, fol. 7.]

After hearty commendations. These be to signify unto you that the King's Majesty's Council have appointed you to preach one sermon at Paules Cross on Sunday, the 16th day of March,[a] and not to fail thereof as you will answer unto them for the contrary. Wherefore I pray you purely and sincerely to set forth God's word there and to exhort your audience to their duties, obedience to his Majesties highness' laws, and statutes and to unity and charity among themselves as appertaineth. Th[us fa]re you heartily well. From my manor at Lambeth, the 8th of Januarii, Anno 1550.

Your loving friend,
T. Cant.

To my wellbeloved friend
  Mr. Doctor Parker
    at Cambridge.

LXVIII.—Cranmer's Letter to Bucer about the use of Vestments.[b]
[British Museum Add. MSS. 28571. Letters on the Reformation, 1547-1609, fol. 46, a copy.]

Doctissimo viro D. Martino Bucero, theologiæ in Academiâ Cantabrigiensi professori Regio.

Salve plurimum, D. Bucere clarissime, Legi libellum quem ad D. Petrum Alexandrum misisti de controversiâ inter D. Hoperum et D. Londinensem, in quo multa a te et docte explicata et pure disputata sunt. Quare nunc oro ut sententiam tuam quantâ poteris verborum brevitate constrictam de hiis quæstionibus ad me mittas.

---

[a] March 16 fell on a Sunday in 1550, so that Cranmer used the foreign commencement of the year.

[b] The answer to this is of Dec. 8, from Cambridge, in *Buceri Scripta*, p. 681.

An sine offensâ Dei liceat ministris ecclesiæ Anglicanæ illis uti vestibus quibus hodie utuntur atque a magistratu præscripta sunt. An is qui affirmaverit nefas esse aut recusaverit hiis vestibus uti peccet in Deum quia immundum esse dicit quod Deus sanctificavit et in magistratus qui violet ordinem politicum. Ad hæc, si brevissime responderis, et quid sentias primo quoque tempore ad me miseris, gratissimum mihi facturus es. Mei omnes tibi tuisque omnibus plurimam salutem et prospera omnia ex animo optant.

Vale. Lambethi 2° Decembris, 1550. Tuæ paternitatis studiosus.

T. Cant.

LXIX.—Letter from Dr. William Turner to Cecil, asking for the Presidentship of Magdalen College, Oxford.

[Domestic Papers of Edward VI. vol. x. art. 34.]

S. D. Iam tandem intelligo te hactenus me non amâsse tantum sed deamâsse, qui clam me, tot labores in dispiciendo mihi Eboraci victum exantlaveris. Faxit deus ut ad anuos octuagīta mea opera non egeas; hoc est ut ad supremum usque vitæ tuæ diem, perpetuâ mentis et corporis sanitate ad gloriam divini nōmis et reipub̄ salutem fruaris. Archiepiscopus Eboracensis valde se mihi benignum et humanum præbuit, et libenter Magni defuncti canonicatū, si quē habuisset, [*libēter*] mihi erat collaturus, verum id quod habuit muneris in tēplo eboracensi erat sacelli s. sepulchri præfectura, quæ per quosdam (uti audio) in hoc jam venit discrimen ut ad prophanos usus a sacris transferatur.

P̄ Christum mihi rogandus es ut nunc ubique aureis suppullulantibus ministris victum olim plumbeis destinatum cures, quantum unus possis, a pamphagis illis, ad sacros ministrorum usus conservari. Alioqui brevi futurum est, ut ne quid gravius efferam, ut ecclesia legitimis et eruditis ministris destituta in maximum ab hereticis et papistis furiosis veniat discrimen. Vacat jam archidiaconatûs functio p̄ Magni illins mortem quam utinam pietatis synceriori propugnatori quam Ogelthorpio qui nunc illam, promissionis cujusdam jure vendicat, propediem conferatur. Neque me istuc eo dixisse velim intelligas quod mihi collatum velim ([*sump'*] reditus enim multo pauciores quam qui ex ea redeunt abunde me meosque omnes alerent) sed quod si archidiaconatum illum Ogelthorpius consequatur, me ad Magdalenæi collegii præfecturam provehas. Porro is qui me horum certiorem reddidit, est hic meus gramatophorus Doctor Claybroucus[a] divi joannis collegii apud cantabrigienses olim alumnus [*fuit*] homo non vulgariter doctus et juxta pius, qui propugnandæ renascentis religionis causâ nervos et carceres in eodem collegio sustinuit et nunc solus (uti audio) in Eboracensi territorio torcular calcat. Is te coram omnia apertius docebit. Vale et me ut soles ama. Non est opus currenti equo calcar addere.

Londini.

Tuus GUILIELMUS TURNERUS.[b]

Septembris 27 et resurrectionis
meæ die secundo.

[a] This was Dr. William Clayburgh, who was made Prebendary of York, Sept. 22, 1549, and held his preferment till 1554.

[b] The archdeaconry which Turner wanted to get was vacant by the death of Dr. Thomas Magnus, which happened August 27, 1550, according to Wood, at Sessay, a parish near Thirsk, in Yorkshire. He was a foundling, first seen by some clothiers of Yorkshire travelling through Newark-upon-Trent, in Nottinghamshire, and had given him the surname of *Among us*, as being maintained *among* certain people there. He must have been an old man, having held the Archdeaconry of the East Riding since June, 1504. He held many preferments, having been made Canon of Windsor in 1520 ; he was also Rector of Bedall and of Sibthorp, and master of the hospital at St. Leonard's, York ; he was also sacrist of the Chapel of Our Lady and the Holy Angels at York, to which he was collated in Dec. 1504 ; he was incorporated at Oxford in 1520 ; he was chaplain to the King in 1513, in which year and the following years he appears to have been employed in the Scotch embassy. On the 14th of August, 1517, he had a grant of the deanery of the collegiate church of St. Mary Magdalene, Bridgenorth Castle. His name appears amongst the Councillors in 1520. The archbishop alluded to is the notorious Holgate. It appears that neither Turner nor Oglethorpe secured the archdeaconry, which was bestowed on Dr. John Dakyn, who was installed April 13, 1551. Ogelthorpe was afterwards Bishop of Carlisle, and in that capacity crowned Queen Elizabeth, and died soon after his deprivation.

LXX.—Letter from Dr. William Turner to Cecil about Preferment, Jan. 5, 1551.

[Domestic Papers of Edward VI. vol. xiii. art. 1.]

Syr i have bene w^t my lorde of Cantorberry to desyre hym to let me know what answer he had of the lawyers of the arches. And as far as I can perceyve, he can get no perfit answer of them. It were beste to desyre my lorde of Cantorberry to send in wrytyng suche answer as he hath receyved of them. He thynketh y^t the bisshop of bathe[a] had no autorite to put downe ye dene, notwithstandyng y^t he deserved the deposition, bicause he entred not in by ye bysshop, but by ye Kynges autorite, and therfore it were best y^t he myght be deposed by sum appoynted by ye Kyngis hyghnes and y^t sum learned men in the law shuld have ye examinatiō of hym, and acordyng to ye law depose hyme. I thynk that they will grant y^t if [he] y^t he had bene deposed by the Kynges autorite, y^t ye deposition had bene lawfull, because they grant y^t by takyng of ye second dignite he lost the first. The lawyers of the arches, knowyng y^t ye denery is labored for to be gotten for me, will hyndre ye mater as m[uch] as shall lye in them. But i trust y^t your wisdom shall pravale agaynst all theyr malice. I pray you do

[a] The Bishop of Bath and Wells alluded to in this letter was the notorious William Barlow, bishop successively of St. Asaph, St. David's, and Bath and Wells, who at the accession of Elizabeth, as Bishop-elect of Chichester, consecrated Matthew Parker to the archbishopric of Canterbury. The dean was John Goodman, who held the office from 1548 till 1550, when he was deprived and William Turner succeeded and held the office till the accession of Mary. Goodman brought a writ of præmunire against the bishop, who obtained a pardon. The judges proceeded with the case, and were summoned before the Privy Council, and Goodman was committed to the Fleet, Feb. 12, 1551. The deprivation was held to be valid, and he was discharged May 25, 1551. He was afterwards deprived again from the deanery to which he had been restored at the accession of Mary, and Turner succeeded to the deanery in 1560. A letter was written by the Council, dated July 5, 1550, to the fellows of Oriel College, Oxford, desiring them to accept Dr. Turner as master, *i.e.* provost, upon the King's appointment.

what ye shall thynk beste, and if thys can not be had i were very lothe to lose the other promotion of Oxforth also. Therfore when ye tyme shall cum, my trust is y^t ye will help to bryng me unto ye universite agayne. God kepe you. Amen.

fro Sūmerset place.
Januarii V^{to}.
WILL'M TURNER.

Endorsed:
    To the ryght worshipfull
    Master Cecill secretori unto
    the Kyngis hyghnes be
    this letter delyvered.

Vth Januarye, 1550, from Mr. Turner to my M^r.

LXXI.—LETTER FROM WARWICK TO PAGET, SUGGESTING THAT RUSSELL, NOW EARL OF BEDFORD, SHOULD BE MADE ACQUAINTED WITH WHAT WAS GOING ON.

[Cotton MSS. Titus B. II. fol. 57, art. 37. Original holograph.]

These may be to require your lordship to be vigilant and circumspect in the matter which now you have in hand. Per happes the Lord Chancellor and the Lord Treasurer[a] who thinketh may touch them lyte [*may*] can be content that it may be wrapped up in silence, and to say it is not expedient it should come in question. But God preserve our Master if he should fail. There is watchers enow that would bring it in question, and would burden you and others (who now will not understand the danger) to be deceivers of the whole body of the realm with an instrument forged to execute your malicious meanings. Mark well the words that Baker yesterday spake in the king's presence concerning the fault, if any now must be imputed to the lords. Well I would wish, as well for the surety

[a] St. John, lately created Earl of Wiltshire.

of the King's majesty as for the truth of the matter, that men should not be against the perfect reforming of it now, specially seeing it hath been thus far debated, which I reckon even a happy thing: praying you to participate this unto my lord privy seal. And so I commit you both to the tuision of the Lord.

At Greenwich the 22th day of January, 1550 [1551].

Your loving friend,
J. WARWYK.

Endorsed:
    To my very good
      lord my lord Paget
      these be delivered
      with speed at
      London.

LXXII.—EXTRACTS FROM THE COUNCIL BOOK OF EDWARD VI. RELATING TO CHURCH MATTERS.

Monday, Jany. 3, 1549-50.

The said Councillors[a] accompanied with Justice Hales, Doctours Olyver and Leyson and Mr. Gosnalde did peruse the process of

[a] The lords present were the Lord Chancellor, the Earls of Wiltshire and Dorset, the Bishop of Ely, Wentworth, Wotton, Montague, and Baker. Dr. Nicholas Wotton was made the first Dean of Canterbury in 1542, and was installed Dean of York Dec. 4, 1544, and held both these offices till his death, Jan. 26, 1567, through all the changes of the reigns of Henry, Edward, Mary, and Elizabeth. He was one of the sixteen executors of the will of Henry, and of Edward's Privy Council, and at the beginning of Edward's reign was ambassador in France. He was one of the nine conspirators against Somerset who met Oct. 6, and upon Somerset's deposition he was made secretary in place of Sir Thomas Smith, who was imprisoned with Somerset, but resigned Sept. 6 of the following year in favour of Cecil. In 1551 he was sent to the Emperor to remonstrate with him for interfering with the Princess Mary's hearing mass, April 10. But neither he nor his brother Sir Edward were concerned in the usurpation of Lady Jane Grey, he being at the time ambassador in France. His brother, Sir Edward Wotton, first appears in a public capacity in 1540 as Treasurer of Calais, but is mentioned in the retinue of the Duke of Suffolk at the reception of Anne of Cleves at Dover. He too was one of the earliest conspirators against Somerset.

the matter for the which the bishop of London was imprisoned and deprived.

Sunday, Feby. 2, 1549-50.

Letters several to the Bishop of Duresme [a] and Ely to appoint in their several dioceses their chaplains and such parsons and curates within the same dioceses to preach as by their discretions they shall think meet; the Proclamations and restraints notwithstanding.

Letters several to the bishop of Chester [b] and John Gibbs, archdeacon of the same, to appear before the lords immediately after the receipt of their letters.

[a] This was Cuthbert Tunstall, Bishop of London 1522, translated to Durham in 1530. He was at first on the King's side in the matter of the divorce, but afterwards recanted and condemned the book he had written in favour of it, but afterwards supported the King in most of his actions, especially in the matter of the divorce of Anne of Cleves. He preached at Paul's Cross on Quinquagesima Sunday, February 27, 1536, in defence of the royal supremacy, and was the only bishop except Cranmer who was amongst the executors of Henry VIII.'s will, and was one of the twenty-six first councillors of Edward VI. He resisted all the changes inaugurated by Edward VI. and his Council. He was sent to the Tower Dec. 30, 1551 and deprived of his bishopric in October, 1552, when the bishopric was dissolved. He was released from the King's Bench Aug. 5, 1553, and reinstated, and the bishopric restored at the beginning of the reign of Mary. And on the accession of Elizabeth he refused to take the oath of supremacy and was deprived, though no bishop was appointed till after his death Nov. 18, 1559. He assisted in the consecration of the six bishops at St. Mary Overy's church in Southwark, Gardiner and Bonner being the other consecrators.

[b] This was John Bird, who appears to have been educated partly at Cambridge and partly at Oxford, where he took his degree of D.D. in 1513. He was afterwards provincial of the order of Carmelites. He was a great supporter of the King's supremacy, and after having served as suffragan bishop of Penrith, and abetted all the proceedings of the King in the divorce of Catharine of Aragon, and afterwards in that of Anne of Cleves, he was appointed to the bishopric of Bangor, and thence translated to the newly-created see of Chester, which he held from 1541 to 1554, when he was deprived for heresy and because he had married. He soon afterwards recanted and acted as suffragan to Bonner, Bishop of London. He gave the Council, Jan. 12, 1548, an account of the sale of church ornaments and jewels within the diocese of Chester, and of the appropriation thereof. He did not live long enough to have the sincerity of this last change tested, as he died in the year 1558.

One Lermouth, a Scot, being sent for by the lords upon that he was accused to have preached seditiously and against noblemen, bishops, and magistrates, and likewise against the Book of Service, appeared this day before the lords, whose further examination was remitted to the archbishop of Canterbury, the bishop of Ely, and Sir John Baker, to be by them declared to the lords.

The bishop and learned whose names be underwritten appointed by the lords to devise Orders for the creation of bishops and priests.[a]

Friday, Feby. 7.

Doctor Bonner, late bishop of London, being sent for to appear before the lords in the dining-chamber next to the star-chamber; It was by the lord Chancellor declared unto him that the King's majesty having appointed eight of his highness' privy Council, four of the lawyers of the realm, and four civilians to consider whether his appeal should be allowed, did, after long and mature debating of the same, conclude that that might not be received; whereupon his highness willed them to declare to the said Dr. Bonner that the sentence pronounced against him by the Archbishop of Canterbury and the rest of the commissioners stood in force, and thereby he deprived of his bishopric.

Feby. 21.

Letter to the bishop of Rochester [b] to repair to the lords for purposes to be declared to him at his arrival.

Monday, Feby. 23.

The bishop of Rochester to be bishop of London and Westminster, and to have lands of M^l p. ann. to be appointed by the King's majesty.

---

[a] No names are inserted.
[b] This was the notorious Dr. John Poynet, afterwards translated to Winchester.

Friday, the last of February, 1549.

It is thought convenient by the lords that seeing the rest appointed to devise the form for consecrating of priests have agreed upon the book and set their hands to the same that the bishop of Worcester shall also do the like, specially for that he cannot deny but all that is contained in the book is good and godly.

Tuesday, 4 *March,* 1549.

The bishop of Worcester[a] committed to the Fleet for that he obstinately denied to subscribe to the book devised for the consecration of bishops and priests.

Monday, March 17, 1549-50.

Letter to Mr. York,[b] Sheriff of London, to stay from felling the bishop of London's woods.

Letters of thanks to the inhabitants of the isle of Jersey for the embracing of his Majesty's laws and proceedings in the order of the Divine service, wherein if any scruple should arise amongst them, to refer it to the Council to bear to Sir Hugh Pawlet now

[a] This was Nicholas Heath, afterwards Archbishop of York. He had in the late reign gone some lengths in the King's service, and was made Bishop of Rochester in 1540, and removed to Worcester in 1543. He appears to have disapproved of all the measures of the Privy Council in this reign, and was deprived Oct. 10, 1551, for refusing to take down the altars in his diocese. After Mary's accession he was translated to York, and made Lord High Chancellor 1556, and consecrated Cardinal Pole to Canterbury. Upon refusing the oath of supremacy he was deprived of his archbishopric and committed to the Tower, but was soon afterwards released and lived in retirement till his death, which took place in 1579.

[b] This was Sir John Yorke, treasurer of the Mint in Southwark, at whose house the conspirators against Somerset dined on Tuesday, Oct. 8, 1549, just before they proclaimed him a traitor. He was rewarded for the part he had taken by being knighted Oct. 17. At his house also Somerset met Warwick and the rest of the Council Feb. 6, 1550, when he was liberated from the Tower. Sir John was afterwards sent to the Tower July 31, 1553, according to Wriothesley, or July 27 as Machyn gives it, and was released in October. He conformed in the reign of Mary, and kept his place under Elizabeth.

appointed Captain and to his deputy all due obedience and to be conformable to such orders as they shall prescribe unto them for the order of Justice, &c.

Saturday, March 29, 1550.

Letters to the Mayor of Bristol upon receipt of their letters inclosing two seditious bills to enquire the authors of the said bills by comparison of writings and the examination of idle and suspect persons and to look to the surety of the city and be ready and able in all events to resist the lewd attemptats of the seditious.

Tuesday, April 8.

Letters to the Chancellor of the Augmentations to make a book to the lord John Gray and to his heirs for ever of the parsonage of Kirkby Bellews in the county of Leicester of the yearly value of 14l. 15s. 6d.

27 April, 1550.

A warrant to the lord Chancellor to make out a writ to the sheriffs of London for the execution of John of Kent condemned to be burned for certain detestable opinions of heresy. It was agreed by the whole Council that the King's Majesty should be moved for the restitution of the duke of Somerset unto all his goods, his debts and his leases yet ungiven.

UDALL'S ANSWER

TO THE

COMMONERS OF DEVONSHIRE AND CORNWALL.

[Royal MS. 18 B. xi. fol. 1.]

An answer to the articles of the commoners of Devonshire and Cornwall, declaring to the same how they have been seduced by evil persons, and how their consciences may be satisfied and stayed concerning the said articles, set forth by a countryman of theirs, much tendering the wealth both of their bodies and souls.

Having of late perused (good countrymen of Devonsheir and Cornwall) certain articles of demands proposed by you in divers camps by east and west of Exeter (as it is there termed), and not only smelling thereby but sensibly also perceiving all this uproar a mongyou my simple and plain-meaning countrymen (for I speak to the ignorant that have been deceived, and not to the malicious that are all desperate) to have been stirred up by the sinister persuasion of certain sedicious papysts and traitors, whelps of the Romish litter, abusing your simplicity and lightness of credit to the accomplishment and execution of such malicious purposes as that generation have now a long season gone with child to bring to pass (for

Antichrist and all his brood hath evermore of their natural property and custom from time to time been sowers of tumults, of discord, of sedition, of rebellion, and of conspiring against all good and godly princes, and against all good Christian orders in any realm) I have thought it my bounden part and duty by answering to every of your said articles, and satisfying you in them, to call you home again to a due remembrance and consideration of yourselves, as it were to set up a glass before your eyes wherein ye may see not only your folly and errors in which ye are yet drowned but also the subtle and crafty train of them that have seduced you to make you instruments of their mischievous intents, and finally that ye may evidently perceive how far simple people may be brought to go astray if they will, upon a good zeal and pretence give credit to every light blast of error and vain doctrine. We be all subjects of one realm, born under one king, and governed, fostered, and nourished in the lap of one common weal, brought up under one law, and by reason thereof are as members of one body, which of very nature must (as much as in us lieth) one be sorry for another's grief, one lament another's sickness, and one help another's sore.

The due consideration whereof will not suffer me to be slack at this present in admonishing and warning you because that as S. Paule saith, *If one member be evil at ease, all the members do suffer with the same.*[a] And most true it is, good countrymen, that many thousands which were never in Devonsheir, never had to do with any of you, nor never saw any of you, do lament this your folly, do bewail your fall, and with weeping eyes do hourly pray to God to reform your hearts and to give his light into your eyes that ye may have grace to see how far ye have swerved from your duty, and how far ye have by devilish persuasions of certain desperate and malicious persons been seduced to incur the indignation of your natural liege lord, and by transgressing his laws to fall into the danger of utterly perishing, yea and that for matters not worth the loss of the

---

[a] 1 Cor. xii. 26. The translation is probably Udall's own.

least hair of one of your heads, for all your matters are in appearance trifles, and at this present of very slender substance or pith; but in the end your utter confusion both of body and soul impossible to be avoided. So far may simple ignorant people under the name and color of God's true worshipping be entrapped and by the subtle and wily lymmes of Antichrist entangled in the devil's snare. And that simple folk may so be beguiled, abused, and seduced is manifest in the example of Adam and Eve, who by eating the forbidden apple of the tree of knowing good and ill encurred God's high indignation, deserved to be expulsed Paradise, deprived of the natural innocency and justice in which they were created, to be made subject and thrall to sin and all the miseries of this wretched world, and consequently to become subject to death not only of body but also of soul, both their selves and all their posterity, for their transgression, and yet would some simple ignorant silly souls at the first sight think Adam's offence a small matter to be in such extreme manner avenged that his punishment should be extended to all us also, that are his seed after him. So when the oxen that drew the ark of God stumbled, and a certain man being named Oza [a] of a good zeal, and of a good intent (because he would not have had so holy a thing as the ark of God to fall to the ground), did put up his hand to stay the ark. And yet God struck him even there presently to death, that he never went foot further. A man would think [Fol. 4 that Oza had been rather worthy of thank at God's hand than of so sudden death, because he did the thing of a good mind and devotion. But the matter was that God had commanded no person should presume to touch the ark except of the tribe of Levye the sons of Caath, whom he had specially deputed and assigned to that office, and God will have his word obeyed and followed, as he doth bid and appoint, straitly commanding and charging that nothing be either added thereunto of our own devices nor anything taken from it. Neither shall ye do (saith he) every one that seemeth good in

---

[a] 2 Sam. vi. 3-8.

your own eyes. But whatsoever I command you that shall ye do and neither more nor less. Thus ye see that simple folks may by ill persuasion of such as they take for good men (and yet be indeed seducers and deceivers) be led a wrong way, as the simple people of the Jews were by their false priests and ministers of Baall whom they trusted. And no doubt there is, but many of them were good simple and true meaning folks, and thought they did all for the best and would full fain have done better if they had known better or been better taught. Now, your fault, good countrymen, though it be very hainous, yet is it not utterly uncurable if ye will in season reform yourselves. Your blindness is miserable but yet possible to be brought again to light, if yourselves shall not love the darkness of wicked popery more than the clear light of God's most holy word and gospel. Your disease, hath not yet, I trust, taken so deep root but that it may be cured, if ye can be content to follow the good advice of such as would your health. Your evil is not yet so far gone but that ye may, by good counsel, be recovered if ye will not wilfully refuse all remedies. Your wound, though very sore festered, is not yet so desperate and past all cure but that some hope of amendment doth remain in case yourselves will be conformable and put your own good wills to us. Wherefore, having yet some hope and trust of you (as charity cannot despair) though ye have by sinister counsel and teaching been perverted, yet ye have not so hardened yourselves against God and your king, nor so shaken off the yoke of loyal obedience to your natural sovereign lord and prince, but that, being better informed, ye will repent your folly and take better ways, leave error and follow the truth, forsake pernicious doctrine and cleve to the sincere word of God set forth by the king's majesty and his most godly council, not only with long study and travail of the best learned bishops and doctors of the realm but also with the assent and consent of the universal clergy and the whole parliament; I shall particularly in order recite all your articles and so discuss every of them as ye may evidently see how unreasonable they be for any subjects so undiscretely and presumptuously to require of their sovereign lord and king contrary to his laws; how dangerous to yourselves if the king's majesty and the realm did not better forsee the thing than ye do. And of how small substance they be, that ye should for respect of them run headlong after two or three obstinate papists into wilful contempt and rebellion against your natural liege lord in such sort as the like example hath never yet been seen or known since the beginning of the world in any realm, either christen or heathen.

THE ENTITLING OF THE ARTICLES. [Fol.

The articles of us the commoners of Devonsheir and Cornwall in dyvers camps by est and west of Exeter.

See even in the very first entering how hainous an offence, and how grievous a crime that Englishmen which in their own country finding themselves grieved they cannot tell wherewith, theirselves will seek redress, not by complaint as is the part of subjects, but by encamping themselves and rebelling against their natural prince. What other fruit or end may hereof ensue unto you but devouring one another and an universal desolation of your own selves, besides the extreme peril of God's high wrath and indignation, besides the undoubted plague of mortality which (unless ye call for mercy in season) must needs light upon you by the severe rod of princely justice in our realm. Ye do in the meantime neglect your husbandry, whereby ye must live: your substance and catall is not only spoiled and spent upon unthriftes, who but for this your outrage [Fol. know no mean nor way to be fedde: your houses falle in ruin, your wives are ravished, your daughters defloured before your own faces, your goods that ye have many long years laboured for lost in an hour and spent upon vagabonds and idle loiterers. Your meat is unpleasant, your drink unsavory, your sleep never sound, never quiet, never in any safety. What must befal to your children hereafter when your own living is thus through your own folly brought to penury and famine? What shall ye leave to them when ye have wastefully consumed all your substance upon vagabonds that could not live but on your spoil and ravine? For wete ye well (good countrymen) that two sorts of beasts there be (for I should name them wrong to call them men) that are the chief causes of this tumultuous business. The one idle, loitering ruffians that will not labour ne can by any other ways get anything to maintain them withal but by an open and common spoil, which thing such other parts of the realme as upon the like occasion have attempted the like outrage, an[y] of them, you only excepted, have well espied and accordingly acknowledged their faults and with most humble submission betaken themselves to the king's mercie. The other sort is of rank Papists, which could none other ways work their malicious and devilish disturbing of God's glory but by the mean of sedition, which could not have had any entrye except it were by them craftily and subtilly conveyed. These under the colour and name of the commonwealth first reysed the simple people, persuading them to be for a good and godly purpose. But their meaning among the others was and among you yet still is none other but when the people be well up then they to work their feactes, the one against the king and the magistrates, and the other against the commonwealth in robbing and sacking; and you in the meantime never to know what they went about. And though I doubt not but every of you (if ye will soberly and wisely examine your state and substance since your first beginning of this tragedy) shall full well espy and (alac for pietie) find over true in your purses and in your houses; for otherwise be it in case that some great enormities there were which required speedy reformation, to whom appertaineth of reason and congruence the redress of such evils? to the subjects or to the prince? to the laws or to the heady wilfulness of

b.]

those who lust? by an order of a policy or by tumult and rebellion? by the way of humble complaint and petition or else by the folly and outrage of a confuse uprore? Were there never so many griefs and matters of querell and the same never so great, never so just, never so unreasonable, yet if every private person should be officer for himself in his own cause and upon his own private authority at all times and by such means as himself lusteth: then where is a king without whose power no common weal can long prosper? Where is the force of laws without which no policy can flourish?. Where is the authority of magistrates without whom the public peace and tranquillity cannot be conserved? Where is order without which no realm can long continue? Where is the due administration [Fol. 7. of justice without which no kingdom may endure or stand? but must of necessity fall to decay and utter ruin as in this disordered tumult all things do amongst you? Take these things away and what surety or safety may any man be in? If men shall be robbed and their houses spoiled who shall redress it? If travellers be slain by the highway who shall see justice ministered?

Oh my countrymen, if ye knew how ill a way ye take for your own safeguard, how ill a way ye take for the redress of your griefs, for the surety of your goods, catalles, houses, wives, daughters, heirs and all your succession, yea, and for your very own persons too, ye would abide great wrongs, grievous oppression, yea, and extreme tyranny, ere ye would thus unnaturally move a tumult against your prince and sovereign. If this then may not be done in just causes and worthy griefs, but princes rather must be obeyed then any perturbation of the common weale attempted, how great then is this your offence to do the same for two or three points of popery put into your heads by such as care not for your destruction so they may have a piece of their wills. Be your own judges, good countrymen (I speak always to the innocent that have been seduced under the colour and seame of good). What shall be said of you an hundred years hereafter when cronycles shall report that a certain portion of the English people called Devonsheir men and Cornish b.] men, did for popery (which if God be God will long ere that day be utterly confounded and defaced and the name thereof throughout all the Christen world abhorred and detested) did rebel against their natural sovereign lord and king, most earnestly travailing to set forth and publish the true word of God and the true religion of Christ unto them. Leave off, therefore, good countrymen, your camping at your own doors and bestow that your stoutness of courage and force of martial prowess in serving your natural prince and country against their enemies [a] and the same your enemies and mortal subverters. Bestow your force I say on the king's enemies in this most necessary time as becometh true, loving, and obedient subjects to do. So shall ye please God where now ye do nothing but provoke his vengeance. So shall ye get laud and praise where now ye purchase to yourselves slander and reproach both afore God and men for ever to endure. But now let us come to your articles and see what things they be for which ye make all this murmuring and all this great business.

The First Article.

First we will have all the general Councils and holy decrees of our forefathers observed, kept and performed. And whosoever shall again say them we hold them as heretics.

Here can I not forbear to say unto you as Paule saith to the Galathians (who, when they had been brought to the right faith of

[a] In the King's answer to the rebels, dated July 8, these enemies are thus specified: "What greater evill could ye commit, than even now, when our forren enimie

Christ, and had been brought to a good frame and staygh therein, were by such like seducers as have now perverted you, and even of a much like sort turned clean away from the right faith, and brought to desire the bondage of Moses' lawe and the observing thereof). *O, foolish Galathians* [a] (saith he) *Who hath bewitched you that ye should not give credit unto the truth. Are ye so unwise that after ye have begun in the spirit ye would now end in the flesh, for ye once took a good course,* saith Paul to the Galathyans, *and did run well. Who hath been a lett unto you that ye should not obey the truth?* [b] *Even that counsel that is not of him that called you. A little leven doth soure all the whole lumpe of dowe. I have trust in your behalfes in the Lorde that ye will not be of such a wrong and perverse mind: he that troubleth you shall bear his judgment whatsoever he be. I would to God they were separated from among you, which troubleth you.* He saith also to the same Galathians in the first chapter: [c] *I marvel that ye are so soon turned from him that called you in the grace of Christ unto another gospel, which is nothing else but that there be some which trouble you, and intend to pervert the gospel of Christ,* etc. For speak to me in reason (good countrymen), and tell me : Have we any forefathers more ancient than Moses and the prophets were? And, being Christen men, can [Fol. 8 we have any better master than Christ, or any better doctrine than his? Can we have any General Councils comparable to the Councils of the Apostles, or any decrees better than were made by them? These forefathers doth the king's Majesty, with the advice of his most dear uncle Edwarde duke of Somerset and the rest of his council, most tenderly exhort you to follow. Such a

in Scotlandd and upon the sea seeketh to invade us to doo our realme dishonour, than to arise in this maner against our law, to provoke our wrath, to ask our vengeance, and to give us an occasion to spend that force upon you which we meant to bestow upon our euimies, to begin to slaie you with that sword that we drew forth against Scots and other enimies, to make a conquest of our owne people, which otherwise should have beene of the whole realme of Scotland."—Holinshead, p. 1006.

[a] Gal. iii. 1-3.   [b] Gal. v. 7.   [c] Gal. i. 6.

master he provideth for you, and his most sincere and pure doctrine he most earnestly travaileth to set forth unto you. Such decrees doth he uncessauntly wish and desire you to observe, keep, and perform to the uttermost that may be. And where ye hold all persons as heretics whosoever shall gainsay them, Beware, good Devonsheir men, that ye do not unawares give sentence on yourselves, for if by your words of General Councils, of holy decrees, and of forefathers ye mean those that I have here above mentioned, then truly these forefathers ye openly gainsay and violently resist, their counsels ye hold not, their decrees ye observe not. In case ye mean any other General Councils, forefathers, and decrees than are above specified, then truly ye keep not them neither (for how can ye observe decrees that ye know not), much less do ye perform them, that is, keep them thoroughly to the uttermost iote of them. Which if ye should go about to do, ye should find to be a yoke importable as well to our forefathers in these latter times as to us. God gave but Ten Commandments as a law to his people. And yet was there never any (saving only Christ) that either did or was of himself hable perfectly to perform and fulfil them. How can ye then observe, keep, and perform the pope's traditions and unsavory commandments, being (I suppose) above so many thousand more than God himself gave. And what a folly is it in you so unadvisedly and rashly to pronounce any men heretics, which neither know what heresy is, nor know the Councils and decrees for which ye call them heretics. Ye may by this matter see, good people, how ye are seduced by certain perverse persons that make you the instruments of their wickedness, and incense you in your gross ignorance of the right and true doctrine of God, and in your blindness to uphold and maintain their devilish errors and most pestilent poperye. What good Christen heart seeing and perceiving how that same wicked generation hath bewitched you can any less than even bleed for very pity and sorrow to see so great a number of people, which might in great welth, quiet, and safety have lived at home in their owne houses serving God, their king, and their country, guiding their wives, children and families, providing for their posterity after them, now to go wandering and roving in unlawful and rebellious manner, suffering themselves to be abused and made a cloke and (as it were) a covert and defense for a few wicked persons that seek their own destruction both of body and soul for ever.

The Second Article.

Item, we will have the laws of our sovereign lord King Henry the Eighth concerning the Six Articles to be in use again, as in his time they were.

Oh, lord of heaven, what deceitful spirit of vanity is it that doth possess your minds. Would Christ ye were of knowledge to see and to ponder the bottom of your own demand in this behalf (as I am well assured the most part of you are not). But because ye were in the late message from the king's majesty sent unto you (which would Christ ye had had the grace to regard, as your duty was, and to be ruled by it) ye are sufficiently answered, I would here utterly let it pass, saying that I cannot but advertise and warn you that full little the simple and plain meaning sort of you do know what those persons meant or intended which first put this into your heads. The Popish priests and the young wanton priests made it unto you a querele of religion for their sacrament of the altare, they made it a matter of devocion for their confession auricular by which hath more mischief been wrought in the church and true faith of Christ than by any one thing that ever hath reigned among us. What hath been wrought and practised thereby in high affairs of princes and commonweales, how many princes' and emperours' deaths have thereby been conspired with other like matters, neither is this an apt place to declare nor briefness which I must at this time use will suffer me. But to speak that toucheth you and us all by auricular confession the priests knew what was every where done. By the lack thereof is cut from them all opportunity of moving men's wives to folly, of enticing men's daughters to lewdness and vice, for now they cannot so conveniently take their pleasure and secrets with your wives and daughters as they would do and had been accustomed; for ye be wonderfull sore deceived if ye think that they were the best priests or most chaste livers that most cry out against the marriage of priests. But whosoever among them is most lascivious lest can be content to be bound to one wife, according to the law of Christ and of matrimony. And why should that matter stick so sore in your stomachs since it is manifest that all the priests of the old law, yea, even to Zacharie, father of Seynt John the Baptiste, were married? If godly wedlock had been a thing unlawful or unpure, neither should the priests of the old law have been permitted to marry: nor Christ or his Apostles would have leaft it unforbidden. And, I beseech you, were it not better and more standing with the laws of God that a priest should live in Christen matrimony with a wife of his own than to keep another man's wife in advouterye, or to live in fornication, as it cannot be denied but that they commonly did? We read in the Scriptures that wedlock is holy and honorable afore God. We read not anywhere that chaste matrimony is sin. But we read in many places that advouterers and fornicators shall not inherit the kingdom of heaven. These and such other things they be that ye would have now. But why or wherefore ye have nothing to allege, but because ye will. Good people, let no such opinions trouble you, ne any such bloody persuasions lead you out of the right way. Consider that laws are made as the state and cases of times require. The law of the Six Articles came in but of very late years, and indeed was over-sore and violent to continue any long time. It was perchance at that season necessary, yea, and perchance violently wrong and wrested in by the hotte labour of certain papists. And now is it by the whole parliament thought meet to be abrogated, as many other laws from time to time have been and in all realms under the sun daily are. Persuade yourselves, as indeed true it is, that the king's Majesty and his Council better knoweth what they have to do than ye or we all can devise, and our parts to be that without grutche or murmuring we stand to such order in things as they do take. What brute beast is so insensate and wide of reason that he can allow that ye should now go about to establish that the whole realm (of which yourselves are a part) did then think mete, for the extreme bloudiness thereof, to be abolished. But this article also is at large answered in the king's majesty's late message unto you.[a] And therefore I say here no more thereof, but refer you to the said message.

The Third Article.

Item, we will have the mass in Latin as was before and celebrated by the priest without any man or woman communicating with him.

Good people, if the question should be asked why ye thus will, I daresay ye could not make any good or sufficient reason thereto. And God forbid that you should in this point have your will which is neither good nor godly and yet directly repugnant to the law. [And what (except your wilful and unbridled will) should move you to deny that any man or woman should communicate with the priest, since in every mass that they said of the old fashion, though they received the sacraments all alone without any person but themselves communicating with them, yet they evermore said, *hæc nos communio Domine purget a crimine, etc.*, they called it a communion (which is a common participation of more than one together),] so that it may evidently appear that in the beginning it was used as the king's majesty hath now most godly set forth the use thereof,

---

[a] There is no notice of this point in the King's answer of July 8, 1549.

to the inestimable comfort of all good Christen hearts and consciences. This article to you that have not as yet the full knowledge of things requireth a larger discourse and circumstance than I may now use in this little answer and exhortation. But because that over and beside the king's majesty's book of divine service there be so many godly and learned treatises made of the Lord's supper, I remit you unto them, beseeching Almighty God to endue you with his grace that ye may quiet yourselves while God and the king's most merciful sufferance giveth you time thereto, and that ye may with greedy desires rather employ your studies and labour to geat true knowledge of God and his most sacred word, so much as for every Christen is requisite. And when ye shall (in this matter in especial) know that as yet ye know not, right well assured I am that ye will then say and do in this matter otherwise than ye now do. In the meantime ye shall better discharge your duty of obedience to God and to your king, rather to regard what his majesty with the advice of his said dearest uncle and council setteth forth for you to follow, than at the light motion or information of such lewd persons as being themselves trespacers against the king and his laws would fain have their offence escape under the cloke of a multitude taking part with them to make yourselves guilty of murmuring and disobedience against your sovereign, which sin never yet in any nation escaped without grievous punishment by the scourge of God.

The Fourth Article.

Item, we will have the sacrament hang over the high altar and there to be worshipped as it was wont to be, and they which will not thereto consent we will have them die like heretics against the holy Catholic faith.

Here is well verified in you that Christ saith in the gospel. If the blind lead the blind both fall in the ditch. For your blind guides have in this matter fondly and superstitiously moved you to will that from the beginning was used nothing so: for first as touching the use of the sacrament and the reservation of it, ye shall understand that because the Communion is a spiritual receiving, which consisteth in the spiritual participation of the sacrament, of Christ's most blessed body and bloude to be received of the Christian congregation in the remembrance of Christ's death suffered for the redemption of mankind and for the remission of our sins; and forasmuch as the said sacrament was ordained to that spiritual use only, for the flesh (saith Christ) profiteth nothing; the spirit it is that giveth life; for the Jewes and Pharasyes had Christ daily conversant among them, they daily saw heard and touched him and yet were never the better for it; for these causes (I say) the sacrament of Christ's most blessed body at the first, [Fol. 1 and by the continuance of many hundred years was no more reserved after the communion than the sacrament of his blood now is. At last, as superstition began to creep in and to grow, it was thought mete to have the sacrament reserved for the use of sick persons, which many times fell suddenly diseased and many times died without communion. But yet all this while was neither reservation of the sacrament in the other kind (because it could not so conveniently be kept as the other) nor any worshipping of the sacrament was ever either used or meant. Then did it oftentimes chance that the sacrament thus standing abroad was sometimes by the wantonness of children or by the unreverent handling of parish clerks and other lay people, either taken away or broken, or otherwise abused. Then was it at last provided by a decree that for to avoid the unreverent handling and abusing of the sacrament it should be set up in some secret place nigh unto the altar where it might be ready when need were to use it. Then were there devised (as is well found, both in the decrees and other writers of stories) almeries, some all close, and some with preatie cancelles or grates, where it might be safe from the unreverent touching and handling (as [Fol. 1 the decree termeth it) of the lay people. After this it came to pass that by negligence of the curates and parsons, sometimes it moulded and putrified, sometimes it was eaten up with myce or other vermin, or had some other mischance. Wherefore at length some priests that were wiser than others devised a way both how to keep it safe from handelyng and from myce or other vermin, and yet to have it in a readiness too. For when they kept it in almeries sometime they lost their keys, and could not come to it when they would, nor without some charges of making new locks and keys. Thus came in first the hanging of the sacrament over the altar, which is not nor never was any point of necessity, nor decreed by any constitution of the Church. And in a great number of places, even here within this realm, both abbeys and other churches, the sacrament was never yet unto this day hanged over the high altar; so that this is a very fond and vain article to be made a matter for subjects to encamp themselfes against their king's proceedings upon the lewd and [a] incensyng of three or four obstinate papistical priests and their adherents, being wicked and devilish disturbers of the common weale. To whom (so long as they shall continue in this traitorous disobedience and rebellion, not having in them the spirit of Christ which is author of all truth, peace, and condign obedience) the sacrament cannot be anything beneficial or available, no, though it honge at their breasts in their own bosoms. It is *totoe ferre* out of square that men should make so much pretence of devocion to the sacrament, and do so far contrary to the doctrine and example of Christ whom the sacrament representeth. And as for a worshipping in such wise as in some places hath been accustomed, was never ordained in the Catholic Church, but did upon the reservation hereof creep in as pilgrimages and superstitious worshipping of images with other like abuses did. Wherefore that ye would all persons to die as heretics that will not consent to your unadvised and unskilful determination is an uncharitable and a bloody sentence to proceed from Christen men and far from the

---

[a] Either some word as been omitted here, or the word *and* is superfluous.

devotion or charity that ought to be in them which make so earnest a pretence and title to have Christ carnally present amongst them. If ye shall like charitable and good Christen men weigh no more but even this one point, ye shall well find that those blood-suckers that first moved you to this uproar had not Christ in them but are of Satan and have his spirit reigning in them, by whom they seduce and pervert you to your destruction except ye soon repent, and cry to God and your king his minister for grace and mercy ere God's extreme vengeance light upon you, who undoubtedly will not long suffer this your outrageous enormity and rebellion unpunished.

THE FIFTH ARTICLE. [Fol. 1

Item, we will have the sacrament of the Altar but at Estur delivered to the lai people, and then but in one kind.

In this also shall ye evidently see (good Devonsheir men and Cornishemen) how your simplicity and lightness of credence is abused by your pestilent seducers and disturbers. For the devil their master, being even from the beginning a liar and the father of lies, hath this property, that he is evermore contrary to himself, and that his sayings never agree, ne hang together. Therefore give them over, good countrymen, as pernicious counsellors and crafty deceivers of you that make you upon their sinister inducing to say and enarticle ye wot not what. For in your first article ye hold them all as heretics that will in anywise gainsay the counsels or decrees of our forefathers, and now ye will have the sacrament of the altar but at Estur onely delivered to the lai people, etc. Gratianus that gathereth and setteth forth the decrees in the second distinction entitled *de consecratione* (that is, of consecration), treating of the sacrament, allegeth a decree of Fabianus, bishop of Rome, in these [Fol. 1

words : [a] *Etsi non frequentius saltem ter in anno homines communicent (nisi forte quis majoribus quibuslibet criminibus impediatur) in Pascha videlicet, et Pentecosten et Natale Domini.* That is to say, though they will not oftener, yet at leastwise let men thrice in the year receive the communion (except peradventure if any person be letted with any great sins) that is to wete, at Esture and at Pentecoste which we call Witsontyde and at Christmas. And it foloweth immediately out of a solemn decree of Soter Bishop of Rome that besides the three times afore limited men should also receive the communion on the daie of the Lord's Supper, which is the Thursday next before Estere daye. It foloweth also immediately out of a decree made in the Council of Martin bishop of Rome: *Si quis intrat Ecclesiam Dei, et sacras Scripturas audit, et pro luxuria sua avertit se a communione sacramenti, et in observandis mysteriis declinat constitutam regulam disciplinæ, istum talem projiciendum de Ecclesia Catholica esse decernimus,* &c., that is to say: If any person doth enter into the Church of God and heareth the holy Scriptures and for his own sensuality or lasciviousness or superstition (for so doth the glose there expound it, *pro luxuria, id est superstitione sua, credens forte non esse communicandum,* that is, if he leave it of a superstition, believing peradventure that he should not do well to receive it at that present), if such an one do

[l. 15.] turn his back away from the communion of the sacrament, and in observing the mysteries swerveth from the appointed rule of the discipline and order of the Church; this fellow being such an one we decree to be a person worthy to be cast out of the Catholic Church. It followeth also out of a decree made in the Council that was called Concilium Agathense in these words: *Sæculares qui in Natali Domini, pascha et pentecoste non communicaverint, catholici non credantur nec inter catholicos habeantur,* that is to say. The seculars or lai people which shall not at Christmas, at Esturtide

---

[a] Esti non frequentius, saltem in anno ter laici homines communicent (nisi forte, quis majoribus quibuslibet criminibus impediatur) in Pascha videlicet et Pentecoste et Natali Domini.—De Consecr. Distinct. II. cap. 16.

and at Witsontyde receive the communion let them not be thought catholic nor let them be reputed in the number of persons catholic. This is now an order of the Church to receive the communion oftener than at Estur onely: and an earnest decree it is, which to gainsay, yourselves by your own sentence do hold for heresy. See now, good people, how ye are led by the evill doctrine of perverse and wicked guides which goe about for maintenance of their obstinacy to bring you into the devil's bands. But let us see more of the decrees which yourselves so earnestly seek unto. The said Gratianus in the distinction afore alleged bringeth in a sentence of Sainct Ambrose, one of the four doctors of the Church, by which sentence he willeth that such as from time to time do commit sin should from time to time take the medicine of the holy Sacrament against sin. The words of Ambrose are these: *Si quotiescunque effunditur sanguis Christi, in remissionem pecca-* [Fol. 1 *torum effunditur; debeo merito semper accipere: qui semper pecco debeo semper accipere medicinam:* that is to say—If Christ's blood as often as it is shed it is shed for the remission of sins I ought of good cause from time to time to receive it. I that am from time to time a sinner ought from time to time to receive that is the medicine for sin. Chryssame then is more than thrice a-year and as it may seem by this place of St Ambrose we are bound also to receive the Sacrament of Christ's blood and so consequently to receive the Sacrament in both kinds. It is furthermore alleged by the same distinction out of Sainct Austen, whose words are these: *Quotidie Eucharistiam accipere nec laudo nec vitupero: omnibus tamen Dominicis diebus communicandum hortor, si tamen mens in affectu peccandi non sit;* that is to say, Every day to receive the communion, I neither commend nor dispraise. Yet I exhort men to receive the communion every Sunday, at leastwise if our mind be not in will to sin. Whereby manifestly appeareth both that some did in St. Austen's time use to receive the communion every day, and also that S. Austen would all well-disposed persons to receive it every Sunday. And this Austen also I am sure is one of our holy forefathers whom whosoever will gainsay ye hold them for heretics. But if some of your seducers will say that Austen then speaketh only of priests, that point is nothing so; for the plain words (whosoever shall read and understand the place) do evidently declare that he meaneth of all faithful and devout Christen people; for besides the placēs above cited, it foloweth there out of the same Austen in this manner: *Dixerit quispiam non quotidie accipiendam Eucharistiam: alius affirmet quotidie. Faciat unusquisque quod secundum fidem suam pie credit esse faciendum.*[a] *Neque enim litigaverunt inter se aut quispiam eorum se alteri præposuit, Zachæus et ille Centurio, cum alter eorum gaudens in domo sua susceperit Dominum, alter dixerit, Domine non sum dignus ut intres sub tectum meum, ambo salvatorem honorificantes, quamvis non uno modo; ambo peccatis miseri, ambo misericordiam sunt consecuti, etc.* that is to say: Some will peradventure say that the communion is not to be received every day: another affirmeth that it should be taken every day. Let every body do the thing that according to his faith he of his devocion believeth ought to be done. For Zacheus and that same Centurio did not strive between themselves, nor either prefer himself to the other, when the one of them rejoicing did receive the lord into his house, and the other said—Lord, I am not worthy that thou shouldest come under the roof of my house, both of them honouring our Saviour albeit not after one way, both of them miserable and wretched through sin, did both of them obtain mercy, etc.

Where note that he saith every body, and also that both Zacheus

---

[a] There is here an apparently accidental omission of a sentence, viz. :

Neuter enim eorum exhonorat corpus et sanguinem Domini, si saluberrimum sacramentum certatim honorare contendunt.

The rest of the sentence is as follows :

Ambo honorificantes Salvatorem diverso et quasi contrario modo, ambo peccatis miseri, ambo misericordiam consecuti. Ad hoc valet quod manna secundum propriam voluntatem in ore cujusque sapiebat.

and Centurio were laimen and not priests. What can they now allege for themselves that have by sinister persuasion put into your heads that the sacrament of the altar is not to be received but at [Fol. 16 Estur only? Do not your own wives (in case they be with child) receive the sacrament more than once a-year, and at all other times as well as at Estur? But ye go further and will receive it but in one kind, which point cannot mene anything else but that ye will of a perverse frowardness and obstinacy resist the King's Majestys most godly proceedings; for since that all the royalme besides you have willingly joyfully and with thanksgiving embraced it, what other construction may be made of separating and (as it were) cutting yourselves off from the rest of the Royalme but that ye will wilfully withstand the King's proceedings; not of a judgment but of a stomach; not of reason but of wilfulness; not by an order but by most stubborn headiness. I dare say ye cannot allege any one, no not so much as a slender reason why, but that ye are so persuaded by your blind and malicious leaders, ye can not tell why. For if the sacrament of Christ's body be so high and so holy a thing as undoubtedly it is, and the sacrament of the most blessed blood of Christ no less to be esteemed than the sacrament of his body (for they be both one in effect, and one thing they contain and were both of them equally ministered of Christ unto his disciples as things of equal food, of equal fruit, of equal profit and of equal comfort to the soul of every good Christen man) how can it be but that ye (if ye were rightly minded or instructed and not misenfourmed, ne by the malicious maintainers of popery and superstition wrong borne in [Fol. 1 hande,) should by receiving both kinds, receive also double comfort to your souls? Alac for pietie that ever the Devil should have so much dominion in any wicked persons as that they might be able so miserably to beguile and seduce so many good simple folks at once. But weigh ye the thing every of you in his own conscience. If the sacrament of Christ's blood be of the same effect and of the same dignity as the sacrament of his body is, do not ye in refusing the one, despise also the other? Do ye not in contemning the one declare yourselves not to have such right and godly estimation of the other as ye ought to have? Can any man believe or think of you that ye have a good opinion of the sacrament of Christ's body if ye refuse the sacrament of his blood? There were never any silly poor men so far bewitched that their senses, their wits, their judgments, and their reason have been so grossly blinded and perverted. I cannot without tears write of this your miserable case; nor any good man (I think) read or hear it without sorrowful lamentation. Awake therefore, good countrymen, and consider yourselves how and by what persons ye be deceived. Full little know ye what mischief they intend (yea even against yourselves) that have by their sinister counsel brought you to this outrage of open rebellion for those things for which ye have great cause daily on your knees to thank God and the King's majesty

l. 17 b.] and his council and most heartily to pray for them. Neither doth his Majesty enforce or compel any of you to receive the communion any oftener than once a year except the parties devocion be such that he will himself. But forasmuch as if ye be Christen men ye cannot avoid ne deny but that the receiving of the sacrament is the most special good and consolation that a Christen man's soul may have, how can ye deny but that the oftener ye receive it the more ghostly comfort and joy ye shall receive. And therefore in the Acts of the Apostles it is in very many places declared, that such as daily increased and gathered to the number of the faithful believers did continue daily in one mind and in breaking of bread, that is to say, in receiving the most sacred communion in commemoration and remembrance of Christ's death and passion. Ye see then, O ye Devonsheir men and Cornishemen, that, whether ye will stick to the holy scriptures only or else to the decrees of general Councils or else to the constitutions of the old fathers, Christen men ought to go very often to the most holy communion, and that they are not to be accounted for members of Christ's Church that will either refuse or be slack so to do. And in case ye first repenting and emending this your folly with all other your misdeeds and then asking mercy of God and the King with reconciling yourselves to his Majesty's favor and protection (for otherwise ye cannot receive the sacrament but to your per- [Fol. 1 petual damnation); but if thus doing ye would use the communion according to the institution thereof first observed and exercised by the Apostles and now lately restored by the whole parliament of the royalme, I doubt not but ye should receive such grace thereby that your eyes should be opened to see Goddes truth; your judgments should be rectified to know the difference between the loyal obedience to your sovereign and the unlawful following of three or four desperate traitors that care neither for God nor devil; your hearts would be mortified and suppled for ever to return to the due obeisaunce of your sovereign lord and governour by God's ordinaunce appointed unto you and consequently to abhor and detest all such as would attempt to persuade any of you to the contrary.

THE SIXTH ARTICLE. [Fol. 1

Item, we will that our Curates shall minister the Sacrament of Baptism at all times, as well in the week-days as on the holyday.

This Article also is in the late message of the King our sovereign lord to you so well and fully answered that I can nothing hereat this present but wonder that ye should hold it still. What should it mean that having received from the King's most excellent majesty's own person and from his Council so large a declaration of his most godly mind therein as might satisfy Turks and Saracens, ye cannot content yourselves? Yet if ye will ponder the cause and meaning of Baptysme on the Sondaies in the presence and hearing of the whole parish, it cannot be avoided but that (unless ye have hardened your hearts against all that is good and godly) ye must needs like it wonderfully well. For can I well avouch myself to be a Christen man and not know Christen laws? At our baptism we promise to keep God's commandments. Can I keep them and know not what they be? We promise to continue all days of our life in the true belief of Christ. Can I keep this promise and know not the articles of Christ's faith? Christ himself prescribed unto us a godly form of praying, which we call the Lord's Prayer, and some call it the Paternoster. Is it possible for me, with heart and mind and true devotion to make this prayer to God and know neither the meaning nor the contents thereof? Forasmuch therefore as these [l.19b.] are things necessary for every Christen man, woman, and child to knowe, and forasmuch as they may not, without peril of damnation, be unknown of any person, either young or old, what better or more convenient way might be devised how to emprint the premisses in everybody's heart, or what better way admonish all folks once a week of their promise and covenant that they made with Christ at the fountestone? And yet is there not any one word to the contrary, but that at all times of nede the infants may at any day or hour be baptized as oft as any case of necessity requireth. So that this is on your parts a querell picking and not seeking of a redress. It is a repining at good things, and not a desire to have the ill amended. But woe be to the authors of this your murmuring when they shall make answer afore their judge, from whom no secret thoughts, imaginations, ne practices of such as are workers of iniquity shall be hidden.

The Seventh Article.

Item, we will have holy bread and holy water made every Sunday, palms and ashes at the times appointed and accustomed, images to be set up again in every church, and all other ancient old ceremonies used heretofore by our mother the holy Church.

Can ye have any holier bread made than the Sacrament of Christ's body? Can ye have any water so holy as the sacrament of his blood? What good shall ye take of your old accustomed holy bread and holy water if ye despise these? If the most holy sacraments be utter damnation to the unworthy receivers and to the unreverent handlers of them, what benefit may grow to you of this ceremonial holy bread and holy water, containing in it no [Fol. 2 mystery but itself? What reasonable creature (yea though he were but a Turke or a Pagan) but he will abhor to hear that any subjects will for any such things make any commotion against their prince, and by plain words profess encamping of themselves? But besides this ye will have also palms and ashes at the days accustomed. How many of you simple unlettered folks (if the question should be asked), yea, or rather how few of you, can tell what palms and ashes did mene, wherefore they were given, or what they did signify? Alas for petie that ever men should be so drowned in folie as for things of no substance or utility to be so earnest against their King and governour, and so hottely to resist against the sacrament of Christ's most blessed body and blood, and against his most sacred and lively word, godly, sincerely, and diligently ministered unto them, in place of vain and dumb ceremonies. Ye refuse the Bible, which is God's word, and holy Scripture, and require palms and ashes, that are men's traditions fondly instituted and much more fondly used among the people. Ye refuse the communion and participation of Christ's most precious and blessed Body and Blood, and make a quarrel for holy bread and holy water, the signification whereof I dare of my conscience depose the most part of you never knew ne heard of. Ye do now even much like as if ye should pretend a wonderful eager and fervent desire to have a thing, and when it was brought unto you ye would quite put back the thing itself and embrace the shadow of it. Ye play now like as the Jews, when they murmured against God and against their governour Moses in the wilderness, they being a stiff-necked and rebellious people, notwithstanding that God had delivered them out of the servitude and bondage of Egipt, had preserved them from the most cruel tyranny of Pharao, had conveyed them by making them a dry path for them through the mydde depths of the Red Sea, and had there by miracle drowned Pharao and his host that pursued after them, had safely led them through a great pece of wilderness by the mark and guiding of a pillar of a cloud in the day time and of a pillar of fire by night, had in a time of their thirstiness made the bitter waters sweet for them by miracle; yet were not contented with all these, but murmured against Moses, their governor, and Aaron, his brother, and said unto him (Exodus 16), Would God we had died by the hand of the Lord in the land of Egipte, when we sat by the flesh pots and did eat bread our beally full, for ye have brought us out into this wilderness to kill this whole multitude for hunger. God seeing their intractable nature and importunity rained down Manna unto them, which needed none other dressing but putting of it into their mouths and there to have the taste and savor of such meats as every of them severally did most phansie. Yet could not Moses please the hardhearted and froward Jews with all this; no nor God neither, but that they said, Our stomach is ready to overcast at this most light meat. We will therefore back again into Egipt, &c. Even so play you Devonshere men now. Ye contemn and refuse the communion of Christ's body and blood, given you according to the very true institution of Christ and his Apostles by the rule of the Scriptures, and in place thereof return again to your old holy bread and holy water. Either ye do not esteme ne take the [Fol. 2 sacrament for such a thing as it is, or else ye openly condemn yourselves of a Judaical stiffness to despise that is the best and most comfortable pledge that we have on earth of God's assured reconciliation and favor towards us, and instead thereof choose to have that never was any sacrament, nor never had any promise of God's favour annexed unto it. And scarcely were the Jews so hard hearted as ye be. For they felt always some kind of lack ere they would repine. Ye have more goodness provided for you than your own hearts could imagine to wish, and in better wise than yourselves can desire, and yet are ye not satisfied, when ye are not hable to find or espy any reasonable fault. Neither do ye think it enough to require such things only as among the ignorant multitude not being well instructed might seem to have any colour and appearance of good, but also require such things as are known to have been manifestly abused to the manifold provoking of God's most grievous vengeance if he were not a God of infinite mercy and patience. Ye would have images to be set up again. So would the children of Israel in the desert needs have a golden calf to be set up that they might worship it and do sacrifice unto it Because they would have a God that they might sensibly see with their bodily and carnal eyes. Which thing God had by express commandment and not without grievous threatenings forbidden. So ye renounce the true and lively sacraments of Christ's most sacred body and blood by him in express words commanded and call for images of your own handy work to be set up in the house of God which he plainly forbad. Ye will against the word of God have images set up which if ye should worship ye cannot truly deny but ye should do manifest idolatry, and in case ye mean not to worship them why would ye have them set up in the holy places of worshipping? And ye will have them set up in [Fol. 2 every church as if ye should say, We will not only do open idolatry ourselves but also we will at our pleasure have all the whole realm follow us and do idolatry as we also do. No (thanks to Almighty God) neither be the other parts of the roialme so infect and drowned with so gross blindness that they will follow such devilish alluring: nor ye shall have power to bring your wicked will in this point to effect. No—God shall rather confound you and your images too (if ye do not the sooner repent) and send you such plages as he hath always done to wilful Idolatrers. If time would suffer me I would here bring into you a number of places out of the holy bible which declareth the most grievous vengeance and stroke of God that he hath always sent upon Idolatrers and worshippers of images, as if ye shall read the Scriptures ye shall find almost no leaf void of some warning to beware of worshipping images—nor void of God's threatening for that most grievous wickedness; which cannot be unknown to any man that knoweth the second commandment, which saith: Thou shalt not make unto thyself (Exod. 20) any graven image neither any similitude that is in heaven above, either in the earth beneath or in the water that is beneath the earth. See that thou neither bow down thyself unto them, neither serve them. For I the Lord thy God am a jealous God and visit the sin of the fathers upon the children unto the third and fourth generation of them that hate me, etc. And see how ye are carried with this devilish doctrine of these Papists that have bewitched you. Ye cry to have in use the laws of King Henry the 8th concerning the six articles, by force whereof ye might be brought in danger of many mortal perils and in this puinct ye disallow and reject the doings of King Henry the 8, who commanded and caused such images in all places to be plucked down, as one that full-well knew the vengeance of God to hang over their heads that wilfully will be wilful Idolatrers. But this is the religion that ye are now trained in by meane of your seducers that have thus troubled your wits, whom God shall visit when he seeth his time. Thus have these wicked limbs of the devil subverted all true religion in you and have brought you to deserve God's wrath instead of his mercy and grace, have made you desire gall instead of honey, and have made you incur the danger of utter destruction instead of quiet wealth and tranquillity, which but for them ye might have lived in.

THE EIGHTH ARTICLE.

Item, we will not receive the new service because it is but like a Christmas game, but we will have our old service of matins, mass, evensong, and procession in Latin, not in English, as it was before. And so we Cornishmen (whereof certen of us understand no English) utterly refuse this new English.

When did ever any subjects before this time, or what subjects in any realm saving only you, make such a stubborn and presumptuous answer to their King, ministering unto them most wholesome laws and most godly doctrine? Forsooth ye may all the days of your lives be sorry in your hearts that the world should see either [Fol. 2 such indurate blindness, or else such obstinate stubbornness to reign in you that ye neither can choose the good from the evil, and yet will resist your prince with most prudent advice of all estates and degrees, and with the perfect consent of the whole realm providing for you and offering you the best. Ye allege for a cloke of your wilful disobedience that the new service is but like a Christmas game. Call ye the word of God but a Christmas game? Call ye the Holy Bible a Christmas game? Call ye the holy sacraments of the body and blood of Christ and the sincere administration thereof a Christmas game? Hath the King's Majesty's Council, the wisest men the best learned bishops and doctors of the realme, so long sitten together in conferring, writing, and framing it. Hath the whole Convocation and parliament upon mature examination thereof allowed it for service most godly and most mete to be uniformly used throughout all the King's dominions and so admitted it by a law; and make ye thereof a Christmas game? Consider, good countrymen, for God's sake how undiscreetly this hath been said of you, and how far you have overshot yourselves. The only word, though there were none other point of wilful disobedience, contempt, and rebellion joined with it, were a right heinous word in subjects to the derogation of their prince's proceedings, yea though the fault might in some part be true. But in this case what excuse may it have, how may it deserve pardon being bolstered and bragged out with open encamping in the field? It is not, good countrymen, a Christmas game but your Christmas men, those traitorous seducers of you whom ye have cause (and your children's children shall feel more cause) to curse, have abused the most holy things and to the great peril of their souls have made a mockery of it among you. For your parts, good people (for my conscience geveth me that a great number of you be simple and innocent and do not know neither how far nor wherein ye have offended), but for your parts, I say, if it shall please God to give you grace in season to reconcile yourselves after ye shall once have made a devout Christmas game of this new service, that is to say, after ye shall have well used it one Christmas, ye shall find such sweetness and ghostly comfort in it, that all days of your life after ye will curse, abhor, detest, and defy all such pernicious ringleaders of mischief as will attempt or entice you to make any more such midsummer games as ye have now at this present time played. And doubt ye not but ye shall find the right using of the new service a better Christmas game than this is a midsomer game. But (to proceed a little further) ye will have your old service of mattens, mass, and evensong and procession in Latin as it was before. And what a vauntage have ye then wonne? For sooth none, but that when ye may now, being it in Englishe, understand something to your edifying, ye shall then be sure to understand nothing, ne to receive by it any good at all. And in calling it old service ye are foull deceived. This service that is appointed out of the bible, whereof no part was unwritten these fifteen hundred years that is your old service. The other that ye call old is new and some of it made within one hundred years, little scripture in it saving here and there a patch, and the rest partly out of some freres bosom, a piece out of some monk's cloister, another portion out of some book of false feigned lives and miracles. And are ye so unwise, so rash, and so gross that, seeing and knowing the same your so deep blindness and ignorance, ye will yet take upon you that ye can better see what is good for you than all the king's counsel, than all the prelates, than all the doctors, than all the clergy, than all the lords and commons of the whole universal realm. Or be ye so stubborn and stiffnecked that where all the royalme besides you have received and embraced it ye alone will, contrary to your king's will and contrary to his laws, have a several way by your own selves. The King's Majesty might have been in such hope of your good love and affection towards him, of your homage and loyal obedience, of your good zeles and minds towards his royal dignity and proceedings, that in case he had but with a slender by-word willed you to receive it for his sake, and so use it until ye had taken due proof and trial whether it were good and godly or no, ye would promptly and willingly (as becometh natural loving subjects) have received it at his commandment, yea though the same commandment had been directed but to you and no more. And have ye now so little fear of God and so evil consciences that ye dare with such rebellious mouths openly repel that [Fol. 2 all the royalme besides do judge good and godly? And yet if there was any colour of reason, any spice of religion, or any spark of godly zeal in this your will, I would rather excuse your good minds than accuse your fault. I would rather judge you worthy pardon than great rebuke, because that naughty persons have abused your ignorance and have deceived you. But now have I no defence for you, nor cannot choose but condemn your wilfulness, which (except ye call yourselves home in time) must of force be broken, nor such a pernicious example suffered in a Christen common-weale. The book of your articles doeth further say: Also we the Cornishmen (whereof certain of us understand no English) utterly refuse this new English. Good neighbours, ye Cornishmen, do ye not understand English as well as Latin? Yes (I dare say) both more of you in number and also better do ye understand the English than the Latin. And though ye did not, yet in such presumptuous manner utterly to refuse it, doth make your cause wurse and not better. If ye had understand no English and for that consideration had by the way of petition made humble request to the King's Majesty and his Council in this or some other like fourme. Where it hath pleased your most excellent Majesty by the authority of your high court of Parliament to sette forth unto your most loving and obedient subjects in the English tongue one uniform way of divine service to be used in all churches within this your highness' realme of Englande, So it is, most gracious sovereign, that we the Cornishmen, being a portion of your most loving faithful and true obedient subjects, being also as much desirous to take thereby such ghostly consolation and edifying as others of your majesty's subjects do, and being no less hungry, prompt, glad, and ready to receive the light and truth of God's most holy word and ghospel than any other part of your Majesty's realm, most humbly beseech your Majesty that with such convenient speed as to your most excellent highness shall seem good we may by your grace's provision have the same fourme of divine service and communion derived and turned into our Cornish speech that goeth abroad among the rest of your most loving and obedient subjects in the other parts of this your realm of England, etc. If ye had (I say) made such an humble and godly request as this I doubt not but the King, our sovereign lord's Majesty, would have tendered your request, and provided for the accomplishment of your desires. But, We Cornishmen utterly refuse this new English, is an high word and a full, unfit to proceed from subjects to their prince and sovereign liege lorde. It were too much for a parishioner to say to his curate, or a neighbour to his constable; much more too much it is for subjects so to say to any rulers or governors. And in this your saying, good Cornishmen, besides your folly in following such lewd deceivers as have moved you to this uproar, ye wilfully detect and notify yourselves to be partakers of the rebellion by the Devonsheir men attempted. Repent ye therefore in season and leave your presumptuous folly, making speedy refuge to the King's mercy, who I trust (though he have over great cause so to do) hath not yet shut up all his mercy from you, nor hath yet cast off his princely love, affection, and tenderness towards you his subjects, if ye will suffer him to use his natural goodness and clemency.

The Ninth Article.

Item, we will have every preacher in his sermon and every priest at his mass pray specially by name for the souls in purgatory as our forefathers did.

Alac for petie that ever such language and trumpery should trouble so many simple ignorant souls. And even in this point ye gainsay no man more than our late sovereign lord King Henry the 8th, to whose laws ye pretend an earnest zeal. But full little thought they of purgatory (and less I think cared they for it) that for such slight surmises and querells as these brought you to be rebels against your King. But put the case it were granted that the priests should so pray in their masses (as I doubt not but the Popish sort did while they raigned), What would you have them pray? If the souls that ye would have prayed for be not yet come out of purgatory and gone to heaven I fear they have lost their way thitherward and will never come there. The souls of them that die in the state of grace, that is in the true faith of our Lord Jesus Christ, are sure to be glorified in heaven, together with their bodies at the general resurrection, and in the mean time they sleep in Abraham's lap (saith Scripture) in rest and peace, in hope and expectation of the joys to come. The souls of them that depart in wickedness or infidelity go straight to hell by the very sentence of God in the Scriptures which cannot be changed nor altered, for in hell (saith the prophet David) there is no redemption. Where is then the purgatory that ye would have? Christ in the gospel, preaching of the rich wicked man and of the poor Lazarus, saith that the soul of the rich man, for all his gay, solemn, and sumptuous burial, went straight to hell. He telleth also of Lazarus that at his dying hour the Angels came and fet his soul and immediately placed it in Abraham's lap. Christ speaketh not any one word of purgatory, no nor any place of all the Scriptures from the first word of Genesis to the last of St. Johan's revelation called the Apocalypse. But ye are persuaded by certain Popish merchaunts among you that a purgatory there is, for God (say they) will needs have a third place—Scriptures have they none; authority of the true ancient doctors of the Church have they none; reason have they not but that God will needs have a third place. Then if in so tragical a matter as this I may for the plainer and further informing and instructing of your ignorance use a myry reason, if God as they affirm will needs have a third place, why may not the Devil contrariwise for his kingdom claim to have a fourth place? for if God will not suffer any soul to come into heaven, before it be thoroughly purged of all his wickedness, Why may not the Devil on the contrary part say that he will not suffer any soul to enter into hell till he be so clene scoured of all his honesty that he shall not bring any drop of goodness or virtue thither with him. But I would advise you, good people, so to live here and so to die in Christ that your souls may not so long dreame in purgatory as you are taught to imagine of others, lest peradventure ye find not that ye are borne in hande for purgatory as no Trental matter nor no money matter, as ye have been persuaded. These are but dreams, good people, that ye are by the sinister means of certain papists deluded withal; which papists mean another thing than purgatory. They mean a kingdom and a reign over your simple consciences here in this world, which they are sorry to see in such sort go from them. But as touching purgatory, good people, the blood of our Lord and Saviour Jesus Christ is as hable to wash away, to cleanse, to remit, and to cover all the sins of as many as live and die in his faith as he was by the same faith to purge and wash all our sins clean away at our baptism before we had reason or knowledge in our own selves to seek or take refuge to his mercy or to make any claim to his most bitter passion. As for change of God's sentence and judgment there can none be after this life. But (as the scripture saith) where every tree falleth there shall it bee.

The Tenth Article.

[Fol. 2

Item, we will have the Bible and all other books of Scripture in English to be called in again; for we be informed that otherwise the clergy shall not of long time confound the heretics.

Yea, but I trust in God's mercy the King's Majesty will not have it so. And of two great evils, better it were that the Devonsheir men and the Cornishmen also should speed and fare full ill than the souls of all Englishmen with our posterity should lack the food and ghostly consolation of God's most holy word. I trust God is not yet for the respect of your malicious and wicked practising so angry with all the whole royalme that he will for your sake forsake us all and give us up to our old blindness and errors again. I have rather a sure hope and shall earnestly pray that he will one day, as he is all merciful and Almighty and turneth the hearts of whom he will, vouchsafe to illumine your hearts and to open your eyes that ye may see this your folye, repent your error, acknowledge your blindness, and embrace the true faith and grace of his gospel. Which if it shall please him of his botomless mercy and infinite goodness to do, I doubt not but ye shall be as loving and obedient subjects to your sovereign lord the King as ye are now stubborn rebels, and shall be good and profitable members of the commonweale as ye are now cumbrous [Fol. 27 sores and byles to the same. There be no better men than such as from folly return to better grace; and the farther ye have waded in this wilfulness, the more obedience will ye from henceforth come to if ye call for grace and well consider what ye have done. The deeper that ye have been drowned in this outrage the more profitable members I hope ye may be made. This fall may be an occasion of a more strong standing in your loyal obeisance hereafter if God give you his grace to arise again. David was the better after he had fallen. But then ye must not lie still in the puddle of traitorous disobedience, ye may not still lie wallowing in the foul myre of stubborn wilfulness, but at once see your own folly, emende your offence, and acknowledge your duties of obedience to God and to your King. Which that ye may have grace to do, many that never were in your country with teres wish and pray for, lest by the wrath of God he be forced to destroy you with all your sede, which as much as he may laboureth to save you—lest he be constrained to be your scourge that of a most princely tenderness seeketh to be your physician, lest he be driven to play the master which would fain shew himself, as he is, a tender father. But what is your reason why ye would have all English books of Scripture called in again; for we be informed (say ye) that otherwise the clergy shall not of long time confound the heretics I do not so much marvel that there should be some among you that have travailed in Antychriste their father's behalf so to persuade you, as I do marvel that among so many heads as be in your camps there should not be found at leastwise some one that could smell and espy out what such a wicked information might mean or tend unto. Ye shall not nede to seek examples of this practice any ferther than your own selves, when[a] the papistical sort keeping the scriptures from you have kept hitherto in such blindness and gross ignorance that ye know not what pertaineth to your souls' health or damnation, but embrace darkness for light, vain and dumb ceremonies for the law and true commandments, superstition and idolatry for true worship of God, shadows of evil things for the true substance of good, popery for godlines, the chafe of foolish vanities for the good corn of substantial Christian knowledge, the dregs of the old Pharisaical dreams instede of the new must of Christ's lively doctrine, the puddleway and suddes of mennes tradicions for the pure and clere fountain of the Apostles' ordinances, putting affiance in masses, in trentals, in man's merit, in purgatory, instead of the holy communion of the sincere faith in Jesus Christe and of heaven. This blindness have they hitherto kept you in by shutting up the scripture from you. That if they might likewise have

[a] Probably a mistake of copying for *whom*.

[l. 28.]

the scriptures plucked out of all Englishmen's hands indeed it would be easy for them to reign as they lust, for otherwise ye see already that the public knowledge of the bible and holy scriptures hath confounded their trumpery and hath opened to the eyes of the world all their deceitful doctrine. And in case ye among you had been readers and folowers of the scriptures (as these articles evidently declare that ye have not been) ye should not at this day have been so blind to put your consents to such trumpery and [Fol. 2 rifraf as this, and much less to have forsaken your obedience towards your sovereign to follow the damnable leading of three or four traitorous rebels which seek their own destruction and care for no more but to have some company to perish with them.

The Eleventh Article. [Fol.

Item, we will have doctour Mooreman and doctour Crispyn, which hold our opinions, to be safely sent unto us, and to them we require the King's Majesty to give some certain livings to preach amongst us our Catholic faith.

This only demand doth sufficiently declare of what spirit ye are and whence all your other articles of request doth proceed. But if Mooreman and Crispyn be of your opinions (as ye openly testify) then doth the King's Majesty, like a most worthy sovereign and like a most loving father, to keep from you that cannot but hurt you. And ye on your behalf do partly like men which not being in their right minds doth require to have given them a sword wherewith to slay themselves, or like men in a sore sickness, which of their corrupt appetite desire things hurtful and contrary to their diseases; and partly like wanton children, with over much favour and cockering of their parents more than half marred, who of an inordinate lust proceeding of nothing but of a fond wilfulness do crave they wotte not what

themselves. They will cry, as the common proverb of Englande saith, to have the calf with the white face, they will cry to have a piece of the moon, etc.; for they will have things nothing to purpose and without any reason why. And in this behalf methinketh
l. 29 b.] ye do plainly declare that all your attemptates procede only of a wilful stubbornness, of a presumptuous disobedience, and of a malicious cancardeness, so stoutly to require such as ye know to be in the King's Majesty's hands and whom his Majesty upon just causes and princely considerations hath thought persons unmete (as yet) to be emong you. But what other thing is this in effect but to say, We will have nothing ordered as the King and his Council do order it, but the King shall be ordered by us, and we will have all things contrary to his ordering, not because we will have it better, but because we will have it otherwise. We will not be ruled by our prince but we will have him be ruled by us. I remit to your own hearts, to your own consciences, and to your own judgments whether these sayings be reasonable; whether such enterprises be subject like; whether these doings be to be suffered. And now tell me, good countrymen, in case the same that ye now do were done by some other country than your own, whether ye would allow them in such trifles and for such baguage and rifraf as ye are blinded withal to resist their prince. For put in case that Mooreman and Crispine were in deed such doctors as had no pieres; add thereto that they were men of such price and such wortheness that their like could not be found for their knowledge and learning; put that they were of such blood that even for their birth they were to be esteemed as precious jewels; yea and, besides all this, put that they were wrongfully misordered and had had all kinde of rigour shewed towards
l. 30.] them, where indeed they have had nothing ministered unto them but clemency, mercy, favour, good counsel, and reason; leat all the premisses be true; yet put the King's majesty, your sovereign lord, your natural prince, a most right inheritor to the crown, a most innocent babe, and one whom God hath sent and doth protect to be your safeguard, one who travaileth incessately to redress all enormi-

ties and all griefs of his most dearly beloved subjects, a prince of such towardness as for his years we have never had the like and for the likelihood never shall have the match hereafter; put the King's Majesty (I say) in one balance and in the other balance put Mooreman and Crispin. Are these two so much worth that ye should for the respect or affectionate favour of them despise your governor appointed by God's ordinance, resist your prince, insourge against your king, contemn your loyal obeisance to your ruler? Where hath the like example ever been seen in any royalme? Full little do ye know, good people, how the rank papists that have thus bewitched you do abuse your simplicity, and do make you innocent folks instruments of their mischief; by which they intend in the end to devour and destroy you too. For as touching the thing self; What if Mooreman and Crispine had never been borne? What if they had, many years gone, died their natural death in their beds? Are they such men as all religion, true faith, and sincere knowledge of God must have died with them; or hath God given his spirit and knowledge of his word with the gift of preaching and expounding the same to them only and to no more? Or be ye better able to see and to determine what and [Fol. ? who be meet preachers for you than the King and his council are? See yourselves, good countrymen, and weigh how little reason is in this your fond demand and give yourselves over in season to the King's goodness and mercy, who, having as it were lost part of his sheep and having now found where they renne strayghyng, would fain bring you home again safe on his shoulders, and recovering you would more rejoice than in the ninety and nine that never straighed. As the widow in the gospel that had lost her groat turned up all the house to find it again and to save it from perishing, so the King hath made and still maketh all means possible to find you again and would set more by you so recovered than by the rest of the grotes that were never lost. But in case ye will not, then will there be no remedy nor grace but to sift the chaff from the good corn and cast the chaff into the fire, rather to cut off the rotten members than to suffer that they may corrupt all the whole body, rather to pluck up by the roots the unfruitful weeds than they should have power to choke the good flowers. Wherefore rather reconcile yourselves in season. Mercy might have been ready for you if ye might have been worthy to receive it. Be not so stiff in requiring them that ye ought not, but rather follow the council of St Paul and cut off from among you that do in like manner disturb you, for if ye have no better ground or reason of this your demand but because ye will, then must ye (as wanton gotes that are unruly) be broken of your wilful wills, ye must be bridled of your unreasonable requests. And if ye will not of your own good minds, ye must be forced to take that is by the King and his Council thought good and mete for you. Such as shall play too much the wanton must be ordered like wantons. And in case they be found utterly incorrigible or untractable, then must the rodde not be spared, yea and the putrified members rather be cut off (as is aforesaid) than the whole body to be corrupt or infect with their poison.

The Twelfth Article.

Item, we think it very meet, because the Lord Cardinal Poole is of the King's blood, that he should not only have his free pardon, but also sent for to Rome, and promoted to be first or second of the King's Council.

Ye think on this article as ye have thought on all the rest, that is to say, never a word right, but do in your saying as uncunning musicians, who, to play a thing upon their instruments, take a wrong time and begin on a wrong key, and, so doing, the more they play, the further still and further out of tune; or like a wayfaring man who, being on his journey towards any place, strayeth out of his way and taketh a wrong path, and then the farther that he goeth the ferther still and ferther out of the way. As touching

Cardinal Poole, let his facts and our king's laws weigh all his cause as it is worthy. And evident it is that though he were once of the King's blood he was made and of likelihood borne of some drop of staigned blood, of corrupt blood and putrified blood. He could else never have found in his heart wilfully to forsake his native country and practise so much treason and war as he hath done against this realm and against King Henry, whom he had found so good and so beneficial a prince and a cousin unto him, as a long book could not suffice to declare. As concerning his pardon, though his deserts have appeared to be such as no true English heart can think worthy any pardon, though his ingratitude hath been not only towards his own blood and kinsfolk, but also against his prince and country, so odious and detestable that scarcely any honest ear may abide to hear it reported, much less may vouchsafe to have it forgiven, though his attemptates against the King's crown and royal dignity hath ap- [Fol. 3 peared such as any English heart cannot but abhor to hear spoken, yet if he would (as becometh him) sue for his pardon, coming hither, behave himself as should appertain to a true, a loving, a faithful, and an obedient subject, I cannot despair of the King's mercifulness to him (whom I see so slack to use his royal sword in avenging himself on you) but he might obtain it. But as for being first or second of the King's council, it were too high a leap of conscience (though he would be an honest man) at the first day to be made of a King's Council, and without trial of his fidelity to be suddenly made of the father's mortal enemy the son's chief councillor, and at the first choppe to be placed so near the crowne which he hath so long years afore laboured to subvert, and may worthily be suspected to prick at for himself. But take ye no care for the matter. Partly King Henry the 8 did provide, and partly the King's majesty and his Council shall well enough without your counsel espy and find out mete Counsellors to be about his royal person. Your parts shall be to learn and exercise the duties of obedient subjects ere ye take upon you the authority to appoint and furnish the King of counsellors. If Poole be so mete a man for such a room, the King and his

Council, when they shall see their time, will determine that matter. Once in the mean time the matter is so much the more to be suspected and mistrusted that ye think it mete. If yourselves had been of such fidelity and obedience to the King's Majesty that when other countries begun to stir ye would have been quiet and have kept you in your local[a] obedience to your prince, there might some ear and credit have been given to your good and lawful motions. But having used yourselves as ye now have, what person may think it mete that any part of your counsel or opinion shal take place, whom the King's Majesty as yet hath more cause to take for enemies than for subjects; much less for friends and well-willers.

The Thirteenth Article.

Item, we will that no gentleman shall have any more servants than one to wait upon him except he may dispend one hundred marke lande: and for every hundred marke we think it reasonable he should have a man and no more.

Although I doubt not but ye shall beare in this matier as much stroke as in any of the rest, yet are not my slender wits hable to construe your meaning herein except your minds be to have more vagabonds and idle ruffians to come and cleave unto you and to be of your campes; for otherwise sure I am that there be already more people in the royalme than can tell where to inhabit and more persons by many hundreds than do well know how and where honestly to get their livings. Lette gentlemen of their benevolence to keep servants, and where or how shall the rest live? Ye have already in all parts of the realm found yourselves grieved with gentlemen, and among all other matters especially for that having so great lands and possessions they retain so few servants and keep so small

[a] Probably a mistake of copying for *loyal*.

houses. And now like politic redressers of evils ye appoint a gentleman that may dispend two thousand marks to keep twenty [Fol.3] servants. I could espy another hole in your meaning but it needeth not at this time. I will rather that that pass, and exhort you that can so well devise remedies in other men's affairs to look first upon yourselves and first reduce yourselves into the worthy name of the King's true subjects and cure your own families well at home; and then shall ye better see what is mete to be done in others, and your good advertisements be more tenderly regarded. For otherwise neither this article nor any of the others is such wherefore ye should encamp yourselves and ask a peticion of your sovereign with naked sword in hand. If this matter of gentlemen or any other had seemed mete to be reformed, it is lawful for every man to put up his bill to the King's Majesty's high court of parliament for anything that he thinketh expedient for a common weale.

The Fourteenth Article.

Item, we woll that the half part of the abbey lands and chauntry landes in every man's possessions howsoever he came by them be given again to two places where two of the chief abbeys was in every county, where such half part shall be taken out, and there to be established a place for devout persons who shall pray for the King and the commonwealthe, and to the same we will have the alms of the church boxe given for these seven years; and for this article we desire that we may name half of the Commissioners.

To this article I can nothing say more than I have to the article next afore going. Neither can I give you any better advice [Fol. than to suspend your hasty will therein till the next parliament. I dare say ye shall that way sooner obtain a lofe than by this meane that ye now use ye shall get a crumme. Seeking a reformation or asking a benefit by lawful meanes ye may have the favor, the voice and the furtherance of every good body, but in the rebellion that ye now attempt upon so slender causes I dare say not the most eager enemies that this realm of Englonde hath will allow you. And what king will grant any petition to proud and obstinate rebels as long he hath by God's ordinance the sword in his hand to subdue them, and the iron rod of severe justice to beat them? And in this case, though the King's Majesty would let you alone to synke in your own folye, yet the vengeance of God cannot long be from you if ye thus continue, but that ye shall perish by pestilence, by famine, by the sword, or by God's sudden stroke from heaven otherwise.

The Fifteenth Article.

Item, for the particular griefs of our country we will have them so ordered as Humfrey Arrundell and Henry Braie the King's Mayor of Bodman shall enforme the King's Majesty, if they may have save conduct under the King's great seal to pass and repass with an harrolde at Armes.

[l. 34 b.]

I have already shewed you your best remedy. And now mete it were and more standing with your duties to declare your griefs to the King and his Council and at their hands to receive such order and direction as should appertain than to appoint to your King and sovereign lord how and by whom ye will at your own will and pleasures emende your injuries. And ye may already see what great distress ye have wilfully brought yourselves unto, that ye must now be fain to have your advocates and spokesmen to be safe conducted by an harolde at armes under the King's brode seal, where tarrying every man at home quietly in his own house ye might safely and with favour have sent either these or any others to make presentment of your lawful causes and pursuits, yea and perchance long ere this day have had the most part of your griefs remedied with the hundred part of the loss and charge that ye now sustain besides the peril and danger of your goods and lives, if the King of his gracious goodness and tender compassion should not upon your humble submissions extend his mercy towards you, as I trust in God he will, and I emonge a great number more shall most constantly pray to Almighty God so to mollify his heart that he may do.

The Sixteenth Article.[a] [Fol. 3

Item, for the performance of these Articles we will have four lords, eight knights, twelve esquires, twenty yeomen pledges with us until the King's Majesty have granted all these by parliament.

Even of a very conscience is this reasonable or a mete demand for subjects to require of their King? Had it not been a great deal more reason that ye, having by this your seditious uproar most worthily lost the King's favor together with your trust and credit, should quietly have departed every man to his own house and with humble petition for such relief concerning the particular griefs of your country as might seem most expedient for you, to have picked out so many of the best of you and to have offered them for pledges to the King's Majesty that ye would from henceforth live quietly and be his loving and faithful obedient subjects, and to the uttermost of your powers defend him and his right against all enemies whatsoever. Seke all the Chronicles since the first creation of Adam unto this day and ye shall not in any realm either Christen, of Jews or of Gentiles find the like example of this your attemptate. Wherefore great cause ye have, good countrymen, to be sorry for this your

[a] This last is an article additional to the fifteen which were answered by Cranmer.

most wilful transgression, if ye have grace to see it. Is it not enough to have so obstinately disobeyed, to have encamped yourselves (as ye call it) to have sett against his towns and cities, to have spoiled and slain his subjects, your own flesh and blood, but that your presumption must proceed to so high a vilanie that ye will for your misdemeanour require pledge of your king, to whom (if ye should be used as ye are most worthy) all your heads were too slender and too basse a pledge for his assurance of quiet? If ye were under a cruel tyranny ye would obey. Are ye so stiffnecked, are ye of so Jewishe an obstinacy, are ye of so servile a nature that ye will sooner obey for fear than for love? rather be ruled by severity and rigour than by mercy and tender favour? It is a servile pertinacie and induracion not to obey the prince rather than the swerde. A devilish rancour it is which words cannot appeace till violence and force subdue it. An unnatural currishness it is to swell without cause and murmur against the prince and magistrates so earnestly endeavouring themselves to provide for the wealth and good state of the realm. Is there any man that can complain of the due execution of true justice except in shewing over much favour and mercy towards malefactors since our most noble king Edward the VIth hath reigned? And now, will ye, being by three or four light papists misinformed, attempt the subversion of all good order and reformation by his godly industry brought to so good pass? See your ingratitude and unnaturallness against a most benign prince and your own enoincted Sovereign. Where no heathen people have ever been so wicked to resist their King and to stand in their wickedness, ye, contrariwise, while his majesty and his most prudent Council do study, devise, labour, travail, and go about to set all things in such staighe for the honour, wealth, and commodity of England as it was never in yet; ye (I say) in the mean time go about to hinder and let your own benefit with sturdy rebellion for matters to be laughed at more than to be fought for, if ye were good Christen men. The King's Majesty with the advice of his Council espied the evils and griefs of the realm ere ye minded them yourselves; they studied how to redress the same, and set forth proclamations for that purpose ere any of you opened your lips to complain; and now will not ye tarry the time till it may be accomplished and executed? Wherein ye do much like as if a man being put in mind to drink a draught of drink which he afore did not much pass on, should find himself grieved that he hath it not before it can be drawn, or as if a man who having a privy malady which he did not afore espy or well consider, and having a physician or surgeon that of his own good mind would offer to make him perfectly whole, should fall in a rage with the same and be ready to sleagh him because it were not done already. And what tender love the King's Majesty with his most dere uncle Edward Duke [Fol. 36 of Somerset, and the rest of his Privy Council beareth to his Common weal and subjects of England, though other examples there were none, might even of this very one thing sufficiently appear and be judged, that being thus sore provoked to extend his royal power against your rebellion, he rather travaileth (like as the hen doeth her chickens) to gather you home to goodness again, or rather like a most mild father hath sought means how to spare the sharpness of his rodde rather than to put the same in ure. The King hath offered you mercy, he hath shewed himself to tender your wealth, to seek your safeguard, to consider what may folowe of your folye. He hath like a most prudent and politic prince considered and weighed your folly, he hath like a most tender father advertised you of your offences, he hath like a most puissante King declared his pleasure, he hath like a prince of justice put you in remembrance of his terrible and dreadful sweorde; he hath on the contrary part offered his most gracious mercy and pardon, and can your hearts be so perverse that ye will rather be ruled by a slave or two than by your own King? Are ye so far gone that nothing may emende you but the iron rodde? It hath never until these present days either in heathenesse or in Christendom been seen that ever any King so wynked or held his regal sweorde of justice in so hainous a contumely and cause of indingnacion; for what other thing hath [ol. 37.] now made you to move sedicion but because ye were like with all speed and possible expedition to have a present and perfect redress and easement of all your griefs? So ill can some men's natures abide wealth, and such happe some people have wilfully to bring confusion upon their own heads, when they will be their own officers to do the things themselves of their own private authority, which ought to be done by the magistrates, or when they will upon devilish instigations of wicked seducers shake off the yoke of their due allegiance.

Now to come to an end, your articles are subscribed with these names here following in this manner.

By us,
HUMFREY ARUNDELL,
BERRY,
THOMAS UNDERHILL,
JHON SLOEMAN,
WILLIAM SEGAR,
Chiefe Capitanes.

The subscripcion of the Articles.

JHON TOMPSON, prieste.
HENRY BRAYE, maior of Bodman.
HENRY LEE, maior of Toreiton,
ROGER BARET, priest.
   The four governors of the camp.

Doubtless a worthy and meet subscription for such capitaines and such camps. But, good people, my countrymen of Devonsheir and Cornewall, if those capitaines and governours of your camps, especially the priests (whose duty and charge it was so to do), instead of this rank popery wherewith they have nouzled and
[l. 37 b.] infected you, had fed you with the sincere doctrine of the Bible and of Christ's true gospel, ye would have suffered many injuries, yea and deaths also, ere ye would have camped for the mater. In the Bible ye should have learned that obedience is more pleasing to

God than sacrifice. In the Bible ye should have learned that Christ's obedience and subjection (yea even to the death) was for our example, that we should do the like. In the Bible ye should have learned that princes and magistrates are the ministers of God, and therefore throughly to be obeyed, and that no man ought to speak evil of them, much less to resist them or arise against them. The doctrine of God's word is that every man diligently beware that he provoke not his prince's indignation, and that the yoke of our prince's subjection must be willingly taken upon us, yea though they be naughty men and corrupt. The doctrine of the gospel is not to dishonour their prince but to serve him, and pray duly for him. God's most holy word pronounceth a plain sentence of eternal damnation upon all such as be seditious rebels against their kings or magistrates. And truly, good countrymen, if ye knew or would call to your considerations what a thing it is to murmur, to swell, and to insourge against your prince, how grievous an offence it is afore God to move any tumult or rebellion against your governour by God's providence and ordinance appointed unto you: if ye had due information and teaching out of the most sacred Bible what wrath and vengeance of God hangeth over the heads of all such as so [Fol. 3 do, and over their posterity for their sakes, ye would much sooner have been persuaded to die than thus to disturb your sovereign lord and King. Rather would you have been brought to sustain any other kind of most extreme misery than to move this rebellion, except the devil had so full mastery and possession of you that ye would profess an open contempt of God himself, and would wilfully lift up your hearts to provoke God's indignation and vengeance upon you. It is to be read in the 16th chapter of Exodi, when Moses was by God's ordinance and appointment chief ruler and governor [Exod. of the children of Israel: Chore, Dathan and Abiron, with two xvi.] hundred and fifty complices, lift up their hearts to swell, murmur, and insourge against him. Then Moses exhorted them to take better ways with them. But (they stubbornly persisting in their proud and wilful obstinacy) as soon as ever Moses had ended his talk of exhortation unto them, God stroke them suddenly in the sight of all the children of Israell by miracle. The ground clove asunder that was under them, and the earth opened her mouth and swallowed them and their tents also, and all the persons that had joined in rebellion with Chore, and their tentes and goodes with them. And they and all that pertained unto them (saith the Bible) went down alive to hell, and the earth closed upon them, and they

[l. 38b.] perished from among the congregation. And then came out a fire from the lord and consumed the two hundred and fifty men that offered incense. Beware of this terrible and dreadful example, ye Devonsheir men and Cornish men, both captains and campers. Consider that the same God that punished rebellion then seeth your doings now. Your fault is much more odious afore God than the fault of Chore and his complices was, because we [are] christen men and ought to know our dutys. God beareth as much hatred to sin now as he did then. Nevertheless God is merciful to such as repent and amend; this his long suffering (as Seynt Paull saith) is to provoke sinners to repentance and amendment if it may be. If not, the longer that God of his mercy and patience holdeth his hand, the sorer will the stroke and the plague be when it cometh. If he spared not his elect people of Israel when they murmured against their ruler, what will he do to you except ye revoke and amend in season? If ever King might complain of the ingratitude and unkindness of his subjects, now it is. For what persons are they by whom ye are induced thus to rebel? Three or four traitorous ruffians who seek to devour you when they shall have spoiled others, and as many popish priests void of all learning, virtue, or civil honesty. And wherefore is it that ye move all this tumult. For the filthy suddes and dragges of stynkyng poperie, being directly repugnant to Christ's doctrine and to the holy bible, and for a sort of dumb ceremonies which do nothing advance or further true religion, but hinder it. And yet if ye read the prophet Esai in the first and in the sixty sixth chapter, the prophet Michias in the 6th chapter Amos in the 5th chapter, and Paule in the 9th to the Hebrewes, [Fol. ye shall find that God himself did abrogate the ceremonies of Moses' Law, much less then doth he pass on such as have in them no religion at all. Your King hath clean delivered you from the tyranny of the Romish Antichriste, and yet are ye so unthankful towards him that ye will needs back again into Egypte to be bond and worse than bond under Pharao. But perchance some of you yet unto this day be of such gross ignorance that ye cannot consider; And some of Antichrist's whelps there be among you which keep you still in such blindness that ye cannot see what a benefit it is to be rid and despatched of the most insupportable yoke of the tyranny of Rome which in dede far passed the bondage of Egypt under cruel King Pharao. For Pharao held no more but the bodies captive. The Romish Antichrist held also the souls and consciences of all men in most wretched thraldom. Wherefore if ye had knowledge to perceive and weigh how much ye are bound to the King our sovereign lords majestie for this most heavenly benefit, ye would think and confess yourselves the most bounden people of the world all days of your life to lie prostrate unto him at his feet, and continually to pray for the prosperous estate and reign of his majesty long years to continue over you. But some perchance will say, We resist not our king. We mean nothing against his Majesty's royal person, crown, or dignity. Forsooth I can full well believe that a great part of you are good simple people, and are persuaded that ye do well, and that ye have not directly meant any harm agst the King's person, his crown, or his dignity. But good people, these harlottes and these wicked limbs of the devil, that by false colours and persuasions of religion have enticed and [Fol. 39 brought you to this rebellion, they mean no less than treason and mischief, as much as in them lieth to all these. But God's protection useth not to forsake and give over good princes, that he may prosper sedicious rebels. And in the meantime ye resist your king if ye resist his proceedings; ye withstand your king when ye withstand his Councillors or Magistrates; ye contemn the king when ye disobey his laws. Neither can your ignorance in this behalf make you unculpable. There is no head so grosse, there is no wit so dull, but that it may easily perceive that it is an offence to resist the proceedings of a King, at the motion or enticement of a vile fellow or twain, not worthy the name of subjects in a commonweal. Another sort allege for their defence that the King is not yet of age, as though King Henry the 6th, who being yet a sucking infant and babe was crowned King of Fraunce in Parise in his cradle, was not even then as verily a King as in any time of all his life after. But because this puinct is most pithily declared unto you in the King's Majestys late message, I remit you to better reading and weighing of the said message. Some wranglers allege that the proceedings came not from the King but from his council; as though any King, though he be forty years old, will do in manier any thing at all of himself without the advice of his council, or as though any King in any realm will not use the advice and direction of his prudent and sage councillors, as well concerning war and peace as also concerning religion. And these tender years of your King should move all good and true hearted subjects the more peaceably to obey all things that his Majesty might not in any wise be troubled or disquieted till he came to mature age and discretion to order all things himself.

[l. 40.] And a towarder prince (God be lauded therfor) in all points of virtue, goodness, learning, wisdom, policy, and justice never was in England. Why then should ye, good Devonsheir men and Cornishmen, be led by so slender a sort of traitorous rebellers and a few malicious papists to murmur against the godly proceedings of so noble a King? Thus much (if God have not clean forsaken you and utterly pluckt his grace from you) may suffice to make you leave your camping, and with most humble submission to cry to God and to your king for mercy and pardon. But in case ye be so desperate and past all cure and hope that this will not serve, then care I no more but as your countryman borne, and in all goodness your friend as far as God's cause and the King's cause may suffer me, and one that much bewaileth your fall, and most earnestly tendereth your wealth: I can no more (I say), but on the one side advise and exhort you to beware of the vengeance and punishment of God; and on the other side pray for you to Almighty God that ye may have grace to remember and reconcile yourselves before it light upon you, when neither your traitorous captaines nor Popish ceremonies shall be able to save or help you. Which thing that ye may have grace to do I beseech the most blessed Trinity, the father, the son, and the holy ghost, from whom cometh all grace, comfort, and goodness. Amen.

INDEX TO THE PREFACE.

Alasco, John, minister of the Dutch Church in London, xxix. xxx.
Anatomia of Geminus, Nicholas Udall's translation of, xxiv.
Antiquaries' Library, Society of, xvii.
Apophthegmata of Erasmus, xxv.
Arber, Edward, his English Garner and Reprints, xxiii.
Archæologia, Society of Antiquaries', xxix.
Arundell, Humphrey, governor of the Mount, and others, xxv. xxvi.

Baptism, Micron's Instruction on, xxxix.
Bishops, faintly resisting, v.; alleged to be in agreement, x.
Boleyn, Anne, Verses on her Coronation, xxii.
Bowyer, alias Braye, xxvii.
Braye, Henry, Mayor of Bodmin, his death, xxvii.
Brewer, the Rev. John Sherren, i. ii.
Bristowe (=Bristol), riots at, xvi.
Browne, Rawdon, his Venetian Calendar, xiv.
Bucer, Martin (1491-1551), xxix.
Burnet, Gilbert, his Reformation, xxix.

C., T., translator of Micron's Instruction, xlvi.
Cheney, Thomas, xxiii. xxiv.
Commandments, Instruction on the Ten, xxxiii.
Common Prayer (1549), Book of, iv. xiii.
Common Prayer (1552), Book of, iv.
Commons of Cornwall and Devonshire, v. xvi.; of Essex, Kent, Norfolk, and Suffolk, xvi.

Communion, Order of the Holy (8 March, 1548), iv.
Cornwall, the Commons of, v. xvi.
Correction or Discipline, Micron on Christian, xlix.
Cottonian Library, papers available, ii. iii. xvii.
Cranmer, Thomas, Archbishop of Canterbury, v. xviii.; Letters from, xviii.

Dalaber, Anthony, xxi.
Devonshire, the Commons of, v. xvi.
Durham (Cuthbert Tunstall), Bishop of, v.
Dutch Church at London, xxix. xxxi.

Edward VI., documents of his reign, i. *passim*
Ely (Thomas Goodrich), Bishop of, v.
Erasmus, Desiderius, his paraphrase of the New Testament, xx.; his Apophthegmata, xxv.
Essex, Commons of, xvi.
Eton, robbery of plate at, xxiii.; headmastership at, *ibid.*
Excepted names of ringleaders (1548), xvii.

Fabyan, Robert, his Chronicle quoted, xxvi.
Fœdera, Thomas Rymer's, iv.
Foxe, John, his Acts and Monuments, xvii. xviii. xxv. xxvii.
French translation of Reply by the Commons, xviii.

Gairdner, James (Cal. Papers Dom.), xxii.
Gardiner, Stephen, *see* Winchester, xv.
Garner, An English, xxii.

INDEX TO THE PREFACE. 195

Garret, Thomas, fellow of Magdalen College, xxii.
Geminus, Thomas, his Anatomia translated, xxiv.
Goodrich, Thomas, Bishop of Ely, v.
Grafton, Richard, his Chronicle quoted, xxvi. xxvii. xxviii.
Green, Mary Anne Everett, ii.
Gregory, ... , servant of N. Udall, xxiv.
Grenville Library, British Museum, xviii.

Hallam, Henry, v.
Harberte, Sir William, xvi.
Henry VII. and the Earl of Warwick, xv.
Henry VIII., documents of his reign, i. ii.; his wife Anne, xxii.
Holinshed, Raphael, his Chronicles, xvii. xxv.
Homilies alluded to by Udall, xxi.
Hoorde or Horde, John, an Eton scholar, xxiii. xxiv.

Instruction, A short and faithful, xxx.; reprinted, xxxi.
Insurrection in the year 1548, xvii.
Insurrection in the year 1549, xv. *et seqq.*

Jelf, . . . , his edition of Cranmer's Works, xviii.
Jenkyns, Professor H., his edition of Cranmer (1833), xxix.
Judgment of Paris exhibited, xxii.

Kempe (Alfred John), his Loseley Manuscripts, xxiii. xxiv.
Kingstone, Sir Anthony, xxvii.

Leland, John, xxii.
Lemon, Robert (editor of Domestic Papers), ii.
Letter from Cardinal Pole to Somerset, epitomised, xiv. to xvi.
Letter from Protector Somerset to Pole, vi.
Letters from Cranmer, xxviii.
Loseley Manuscripts, xxiii.; quoted, xxiv.
Lowndes's Bibliographer's Manual, xxix.

Macaulay, Thomas Babbington, his account of Cranmer, v.
Malet, Dr. Francis, xxi.
Martyr, Peter, xxv.
Mary Tudor, documents of her reign, iii.; warrant to Nicholas Udall, xxiv.
Micron, Michael, his Short Instruction, xxix. xxx.
Mountain, Thomas, xxiv.

Nichols's Narratives of the Days of the Reformation, xxv.
Nicolas, Sir N. Harris, Proceedings of the Council, xxiv.
Northumberland (John Dudley), Duke of, iv.

Parker, Dr. Matthew (Archbishop of Canterbury), xxviii.
Parker Society's Edition of Cranmer, xxviii. xxix.
Pole, Reginald (Cardinal), v.; letter to him from Somerset, vi.; reply to Somerset, epitomised, xiv. xv.
Pope's name reported to be odious, the, xii.
Prayer, Book of Common, 1549, iv. xiii.
Prayer, Book of Common, 1552, iv.
Prayer, Micron's Instruction concerning, xlvi.
Proclamation by the King, iv.

Ralph Roister Doister, Udall's comedy of, xxiii.
Records of the Reformation (Clarendon Press, 1870), i.
Reformation, Gilbert Burnet's History of the, xxix.
Reformation, Nichols's Narratives of the Days of the, xxiv.
Reformation, Records of the, i.
Reply to accusations made by the Commons, xviii. to xx.
Reply to the requisitions of insurgents, xvii.
Restoration of the Catholic religion proposed by Pole, xvi.
Review, The Saturday, on Cranmer, v.
Robbery of plate at Eton, xxiii.
Rymer, Thomas, his Fœdera, iv.

Sacrament of the Lord's Supper, Peter Martyr on the, xxv.
Sacraments, Micron's Instruction on the, xxxix.
Sadleyr, Sir Ralph, Secretary, xxiii.
Somerset (Edward Seymour), Duke of, iii. iv. v.; his letter to Cardinal Pole, vi.; its reply, epitomised, xiv. xv.
Stourton, Lord, xvi.
Subscribers to the articles, executed, xxv.
Suffolk, the Commons of, xvi.
Suffolk, the Duke of (1541), xxiii.
Supper, Michael Micron on Christ's Holy, xxxix.
Supper, Peter Martyr on the Lord's, xxv.

Terence, Udall's Floures gathered out of, xxiv.
Tunstall, Cuthbert, Bishop of Durham, v.
Turnbull, William B. (editor of Cal. State Papers, Foreign), ii.
Turner, Dr. William (Somerset's physician), xxix.
Tytler, Patrick Fraser, v. xvii.

Udall, Nicholas, xviii. xx.; his verses on Anne Boleyn's Coronation, xxii.; his Ralph Roister Doister, and career, xxiii.; his translations, from S. Luke, Erasmus, Geminus, Terence, and Peter Martyr, xxi. to xxv.

Venetian Calendar of State Papers, Rawdon Browne's, xiv.
Venice, Library of St. Mark's at, xiv.

Warrant from Queen Mary to Udall, xxiv.
Warwick, Earl of (temp. Henry VII.), xv.
Warwick, Earl of (1549), vi.
Westminster School, xxiv.
Winchester (Stephen Gardiner, imprisoned), Bishop of, xv.
Wood, Anthony à, his Athenæ Oxonicuses, xxiii.
Wriothesley, Sir Thomas, Secretary, xxiii.
Wriothesley's Chronicle, cited, xvi.
Wykeham, Udall's family at, xxiii.

INDEX.

[These Indices have been prepared by J. W. E., Member of the Council, Camden Society.]

Aaron murmured against, 166
Abbey-lands, proposed restoration of, 183
Abergavenny, Lord, 106
Abirou (= Abiram), 189
Abraham's lap, Lazarus in, 173
Adam and Eve, 143, 185
Alderney, 60, 61
Aleurj (doubtful), Mr. . . . , 35
Almayne hill, near Boulogne, between Boulogne and Ambletue, 68
Ambassador at Brussels (Sir William Paget), 19, 24. *See* Paget
Ambassador, French, 38
Ambassadors to France, various, 43, 53 85, 135. *See* Cheney, Paget, Petre, Wotton, etc.
Ambletue, or Hambletue, near Boulogne, 115
Ambrose (Saint), quoted, 159
Among Us, 132. *See* Magnus and York
Amos, 191
Amsdorf, 110
Andover, 92
Anne. *See* Boleyn, Bourchier, Parr, and Seymour
Anne of Cleves, 72, 101, 103, 111, 135, 136
Answer to the Commoners of Devonshire and Cornwall, 141 to 193
Antichrist, Udall's references to, 142, 143, 176, 191
Antiquaries, Proclamations belonging to the Society of, 43, 95, 96, 108
Apocalypse, the, 174
Apostles Ordinances, the, 176
Archaeologia, 22
Argentina (Strasburg), 110, 111

Arragon, Catharine of. *See* Catharine
Arrendell. *See* Arundel
Arundel (Henry Fitzalan), Earl of, 7, 14, 20, 21, 42, 53, 54, 81, 82, 85, 86, 88, 93, 100, 101, 106, 129
Arundel, Humphrey, leader of the insurrection, 37, 49, 54, 63, 65, 66; executed, 126
Arundel, Sir John, 26, 28, 29, 38
Articles, Law of the Six, 152
Articles, Udall's answer concerning the Sixteen, 148 to 193
Athenæ Cantabrigienses, 129
Auder, George, alderman of Cambridge, 4
Auder, Jane, daughter of George, 4
Audley, Thomas, Lord Chancellor, 50
Augmentations, Court of, 124 ; Chancellor of the, 139
Augsburg, 111
Austin vel Augustin (Saint), quoted, 159, 160

Baal, false priests and ministers of, 144
Baker, Sir John, 24; his career, 39, 42, 51, 52, 67, 100, 106, 119, 134, 135, 137
Bangor (John Bird, 1539 to 1542), Bishop of, 136
Bangor Use, Service-books, 128
Baptism, on week-days, 16, 163
Barlow, Matthew, his wife's bigamy, 72
Barlow, William, Bishop of Bath and Wells, 133
Barne *alias* Bocher or Butcher, *alias* Knell, *alias* Joan of Kent, condemned and sentenced by Cranmer to be burnt alive for heresy, executed at Smithfield, 139

198 INDEX.

Barret, Roger, priest and subscriber, 188
Barron, Patrick, imprisoned, 124
Bartevile, Captain, imprisoned, 126
Basing, Baron St. John of, 34
Bath and Wells (William Barlow), Bishop of, 133
Bath and Wells (John Goodman), Dean of, 133; (Wm. Turner), 134
Beasts, two sorts of them (ruffians and papists), according to Udall, 146
Beauchamp (Edward Seymour), Viscount, 2. *See* Somerset
Beaudesert (William), Lord Paget of, 53   *See* Paget, Sir William
Bedall, the Rector of, 132
Beddington, 121
Bedford, Earl of, 7, 12, 21, 53, 86, etc. *See* Russell (Sir John and Baron), Lord
Bedfordshire, Commissioner for, 48
Bell, Robert, imprisoned, 125
Bell, William, imprisoned, 126
Bells to be taken down from churches, 73
Bergottus, signature of Mount, 112
Berry, Bery, or Bury, John, 126, 188
Berwick, one of Somerset's men, 123
Bible to be called in again, the English, 175
Bird, Dr. John, Bishop of Chester, 136
Blackness, inland from Boulogne, 115
Blackwell, Walter, Somerset's footman, 121
Blackston, Mr. . . . , Ecclesiastical Commissary, 18
Blakemore, 11
Bluet of Exeter, Mr. . . . , 51
Bodmin (Henry Braye), Mayor of, 63, 184, 188
Boleyn, Anne, 86, 95, 119
Boleyn, George (Lord Rochford), 119
Bonner, Dr. Edmund, Bishop of London, 43, 75, 136, 137
Book of Common Prayer re-affirmed as displacing Latin Service-books, 127
Boucher, Joan (of Kent), executed, 139
Boulogne, 2, 26, 79, 82, 115
Bourchier, Ann, 81
Bourchier, Henry (Earl of Essex), 81
Bowers, Edward, imprisoned, 124, 126. *Cf.* Bowes
Bowers, John, imprisoned, 126
Bowes, Edward, 124. *See* Bowers

Bowyer (*see Preface*, xxv., xxvii., and Braye), 63, 184, 188
Brandon, Charles, Duke of Suffolk, 2
Brandon, Frances, 2
Braye (=Braie, Bray, or Bowyer), Henry, Mayor of Bodmin, 63, 184, 188
Bread for the Sacrament, dispute regarding, 165
Brentwood, 74
Bridge at Staines, supplication concerning the, 19
Bridgenorth Castle, 132
Bridgewater, 11
Bristol or Bristowe, 25, 33; the Mayor of, 139
Bromham, 123
Browne, Sir Anthony, 38
Brussels, 19, 24, 103
Bruton, Somersetshire, 11
Brystowe, the King's Receiver, 25
Bucer, Martin, his Gratulation, and Answer to Gardiner, 103; Cranmer's letter to him, 130
Buckinghamshire, 26, 27, 29
Bullenberg, English fort in the Boulonnais, on the hill at the back of Boulogne, 68, 115
Burleigh (William Cecil), afterwards Baron, his career, 31, etc. *See* Cecil, William
Burnet, Gilbert, his Reformation (Pocock's edition), 75, 84; quoted, 104, 129
Bury (Berry), John, in the Tower, 126; signatory, 188

Caath, the sons of, 143
Cæsar, the Emperor Charles V., 110, 111
Calais, 14, 26, 81, 88, 135
Cambridge, 4, 50, 54, 75, 129, 130, 136
Cambridge, Queen's College, 75
Cambridge University, 75, 136
Cambridgeshire, Commissioner for, 48
Camps in the West, 41, 145
Canterbury, Archbishop of (Matthew Parker), 133
Canterbury, Archbishop of (Reginald Pole), 138, etc. *See* Pole
Canterbury, Archbishop of (Thomas Cranmer), 20, 30, 36, 37, 39, 42, 43; absent from Council, 45; 51, 62, 64, 65, 67, 72, 73, 77, 81, 82, 88, 90, 102, 119, 129, 130, 133, 136, 137, 185

INDEX. 199

Canterbury, Archdeacon of (Dr. Nicholas Harpsfield), 3
Canterbury, Dean of (Dr. Nicholas Wotton), 106, 135
Cappe, Robert, imprisoned, 125
Cardiff, 23
Carew, Sir Gawen, 26
Carew, Sir Peter, 26
Carlisle (Owen Oglethorpe, 1557-1561), Bishop of, 132
Carmelites (Dr. John Bird), Provincial of the, 136
Catharine of Arragon, the pretended divorce, 75, 88, 119, 136
Cavy, . . . (Somerset's clerk-controller), 121
Cecil, William, afterwards Baron Burleigh, his career, 3, 7, 48, 55, 73, 75, 134, 135
Charles V. (Cæsar), 75, 110, 111
Cheke, Mary, 3
Cheke, Sir John, 3
Chester (John Gibbs), Archdeacon of, 136
Chester (John Bird, 1542—1554), Bishop of, 136
Cheyne, or Cheyney, Sir Thomas, 81, 82; his career, 85; 88, 100
Chichester (William Barlow), Bishop-elect of, 133
Cholwell, 75
Cholwyn, 75
Chore, or Corah, 189, 190
Christ, as considered by Udall, 148 to 173
Christmas, receiving the Sacrament at, 158
Chronicle, Wriothesley's, quoted, 1, 51
Chryspine, or Crispin, Dr., 125, 177 to 179
Church History, Dod's, 21, 22
Cinque Ports (Sir Thomas Cheney, 1540—1558); Warden of the, 85
Clere, Sir John, reported slain, 59
Cleves, Anne of, 72, 101, 103, 111, 135, 136
Clinton, Edward (Lord), governor of Boulogne, 60
Cobham, Elizabeth, 81
Cobham, George (Lord), 21, 81, 86
Colle, Richard, a prisoner, 125
Cologne, 111
Concilium, Agathense, 158

Confinement of Somerset's servants ordered, 120
Conspirators against Somerset, 43, 72, 81, 82, 85, 88, 94, 101, 103
Constable of the Tower, Sir John Gage, 126
Cook, Sir Anthony, King Edward's tutor, 3
Cook, Mildred, 3
Corah, or Chore, 189, 190
Corfe Castle, 59
Corinthians, First Epistle to the, cited, 142
Cornishmen, 147, 157, 162, 169, 171, 188, 192
Cornwall, troubles in, 1, 8, 19, 29, 32, 33, 36, 37, 41, 42, 44, 46, 64, 70, 71, 73
Cornwallis, Sir Thomas, reported slain, 59; fetches Elizabeth to Court, 101
Cotton and Woolcombe's Gleanings, 62, 73
Cotton MSS., 110, 134
Coulthurst, . . . one of Somerset's men, 123
Councillors, the twenty-six, 39, 43
Courtenay, Edward, in the Tower, 124
Courtenay, Peter, justice of peace, 13
Coverdale, Miles, afterwards Bishop of Exeter (Aug. 14, 1551), 7, 75, 119
Cox, or Kokks, John, prisoner, 125
Cox, Richard (Bishop of Ely, 1559 to 1599), 4
Cranmer, Thomas, Archbishop of Canterbury (1533 to 1556). *See* Canterbury
Crispin, Dr. . . . , 125, 177 to 179
Croche, . . . , Somerset's receiver, 25
Cromwell, Thomas, 72, 81, 103, 111, 129
Croydon, 121

Dacre, William, third Lord (1534), 14
Dakyn, Dr. John, Archdeacon of the East Riding, 132
Dathan, 189
David, King and Psalmist, 173, 175
David, Somerset's porter, 121
Declaration of War by the French King, 46
Deleway or Kellaway, 123
Denny, Sir Anthony, 19
Derby, the sheriff of, 82
Devall, Lewis or Lavys, 125

INDEX.

Devonshire, troubles in, 4, 11, 13, 19, 24, 29, 32, 41, 44, 46, 47, 51, 64, 70, 73, 126, 147, 150, 162, 166, 172, 188, 192

Diary, Machyn's (1550 to 1563). *See* Machyn, Henry

Dod's Church History, edited by Canon Tierney, 21, 22

Dorchester, 11

Dorset, Henry Grey, afterwards Duke of Suffolk, 129, &c. *See* Grey, Henry; and Suffolk

Dorsetshire, troubles in, 8, 11, 32, 46, 47, 49, 54, 56

Douglas, David, 124

Dover, 135

Drury, Captain, 73

Dudley (Mr.) . . . , 12, 30

Dudley, Sir Andrew, 27, 52

Dudley, Edmund (executed in 1510), 31

Dudley, Lord Guildford (grandson of Edmund and husband of Lady Jane Grey), called King, 104

Dudley, Sir John, Lord Lisle, Earl of Warwick, his career, 31. *See* Northumberland, Duke of

Dunstable, 88

Durham (Duresme: Cuthbert Tunstall), Bishop of, 77, 136

Dyer, Sir Thomas, 27

Easter Celebration, 157 to 163

Ecclesiastical Memoirs, Strype's, 95, &c. *See* Strype

Edward L, King (Preface), viii.

Edward VI., 34, 36, 38, 64, 72, 77, 82, 88, 94, 101, 103, 109, 119, 129, 135, 136, 186; his device for the limitation of succession, 53, 85, 94, 101; Letters from him, 76, 77, 79, 102, 127; his burial, 82

Egypt, bondage of, 166, 191

Elizabeth, Princess, afterwards Queen, 23, 26, 34, 38, 43, 72, 82, 86, 89, 101, 103, 108, 116; crowned by Oglethorpe, 132, 135, 136, 138

Ellis, Sir Henry, his Collection of Letters, 86

Elmer, Mr. . . . . . , 37

Ely, Bishop of (Richard Cox), 4

Ely, Bishop of (Thomas Goodrich), 129, 135, 137

Ely House, 38

Enclosures, redress of, 1, &c.

England under the Reigns of Edward VI. and Mary, P. F. Tytler's, 19

Esai = Isaiah, 190

Essex, county of, 24, 32, 45, 82

Essex, Henry Bouchier, fifteenth Earl of, 81

Essex, William, 125

Eve deserved to be expulsed Paradise, 143

Excester. *See* Exeter

Execution of Henry Braye (*Preface*, xxvii.), 63, 84, 88; of Essex and More, 74; of Joan of Kent, 139; of Humphrey Arundell, Wyndslow, Bury, and Holmes, 126; of many persons in Oxfordshire, 26; at Exeter, 51; of Somerset, 42; of Sir T. Seymour, 72, 85

Executors of the Will of Henry VIII., 23, 31, 34, 38, 39, 43, 53, 72, 81, 85, 94, 101, 135, 136

Exeter, 15, 40, 43, 44, 47, 48, 51, 53, 54, 62, 70, 73, 75, 141, 145

Exeter, Miles Coverdale, Bishop of, 7, 75, 119

Exeter, Simon Haynes or Heynes, Dean of, 75, 103

Exeter, the Mayor of (John Shillingford; *vide* Camden Society's New Series, No. 1, 1871), 62

Exodus, 166, 168, 189

Extracts from Council Books on Church Matters, 135

Fabian, Bishop of Rome (A.D. 236 to 250), quoted, 157, 158

Fane, Sir Ralph, 123, 126. *See* Vane

Feckenham or Feknam, Mr. . . . . . , 125

Ferdinand, the Archduke, 35

Fisher, John, Bishop of Rochester. 36

Fitzalan, Henry, Earl of Arundel, 14. *See* Arundel

Flanders, English ambassador in, 103, 104. *See* Hoby

Fleet Prison, 75, 101, 133, 135, 138

Foskewe or Foster, Anthony, 124

Foster or Foskewe, Anthony, late Marshal of Ireland, 124

Foxe, John, his Acts and Monuments, 21, 22, 80, 83

France, ambassadors to. *See* Ambassadors

France, invasion threatened from, 46, 56

Francis I., 119

INDEX. 201

Frankfort, 112
Fuller, John, a prisoner, 125
Pysher, Thomas, a prisoner, 126

Gage, Sir John, 81, 82, 85, 88, 100, 106, 119; Constable of the Tower, 126
Galatians, Epistle to the, 149
Gardiner, Dr. Stephen, deposed Bishop of Winchester, 43, 50, 82, 85, 103, 125, 136
Gates, Sir John, 123
George, Sir William, 14
Gibbs, John, Archdeacon of Chester, 136
Glastonbury, 123
Gleanings, Cotton and Woolcombe's, 62, 73
Gloucestershire, 23, 35, 44
Godolphin, Sir William, 33, 61
Godwin (William?), 129
Golding, ... Somerset's servant, 78
Goodman, John, Dean of Bath, 133
Goodrich, Thomas, Bishop of Ely, 129
Gosnalde, Mr. . . . ., 135
Grafton, Richard, 101
Grafton's Collection of Proclamations, 96
Graie or Graye, Lord. *See* Grey of Wilton, William
Gratianus, 159
Gray, Lord John, of Kirkby Bellews, 139
Gregory, Mr. . . . ., licenced preacher, 6, 7
Grey, Lady Catherine, 23
Grey, Henry, third Marquis of Dorset, afterwards Duke of Suffolk, 1, 2, 129
Grey, Lady Jane, afterwards Queen, 2, 3, 23, 31, 34, 38, 43, 72, 82, 86, 89, 94, 129, 135
Grey, Thomas, second Marquis of Dorset, 2, 38, 43, 72, 82, 86, 89, 94, 119, 129, 135
Grey, William, 106; prisoner in the Tower, 126. (Probably Grey of Wilton)
Grey of Wilton, William, Lord, 20 to 29, 33, 37, 51, 52, 68, 106, &c.
Guernsey, 59, 60
Guildford, 14
Guines, 88

Hackney, the Manor of, 119
Hadington, seventeen miles from Edinburgh, 116
Hales, 124
Halfield, yeoman of the scullery, 151
Hambletue or Ambletue, in vicinity of Boulogne, 115
Hamme, James Lawrence of, 122
Hampnes Castle, 26
Hampshire, troubles in, 24
Hampton Court, 36, 76, 79, 117, 121
Harberte, properly Herbert, Sir William, *see* Herbert
Harleian MS., 20
Harpsfield, Nicholas, LL.D., Archdeacon of Canterbury, 3; his Treatise of Marriage, on the divorce (Camden Society's New Series, 1878), 3
Harrington, John, prisoner, 125
Harvy, Anthony, Justice of the Peace in Devon, 13
Hastings, Lord (*i. e.* Sir Edward), 101
Hastings, Francis, second Earl of Huntingdon, 1, 2
Hastings, George, first Earl of Huntingdon, 2
Hatfield, 38
Haynes or Heynes, Simon, Dean of Exeter (1537), 75
Heath, Nicholas, Archbishop of York (1555), 54, 111
Hebrews, Epistle to the, 191
Hedley, diocese of Winchester, 125
Helen, third wife of William Parr, 81
Helvetii, the Swiss, 111
Henry VI., 192
Henry VIII., 2, 12, 23, 31, 34, 38, 39, 43, 53, 72, 81, 85, 88, 94 to 96, 101, 135, 136, 151, 168, 181
Herbert, Lord Henry, second Earl of Pembroke (1570), 23
Herbert, Mr. . . . . probably Sir William, 52
Herbert, Sir Richard, 23
Herbert, Sir William, afterwards Baron Herbert and Earl of Pembroke (1551). 1, 21, 23, 26, 29, 35, 44, 52, 63, 64, 66, 76, 78 to 80, 90, 93, 100, 102, 112, 113
Herbert, William, Earl of Pembroke (1468; beheaded by the Lancastrians in 1469), 23
Hereford Use, Service-books, 128
Hertford, Earl of (1537), afterwards Lord Protector, 114, 115. *See* Somerset
Hesse, the Landgrave of (1544), 112
Hobbie, Mr. 36
Hobbie or Hobby or Hoby, Sir Edward, 103

INDEX.

Hoby, Sir Philip, 103, 104
Hoby, Sir Thomas, 103
Hoby, Sir William, 103
Holbein, Hans, 103
Holborn, 104
Holgate, Robert, Archbishop of York (1544) 3, 132
Holinshed, Raphael, 83, 90, 149,
Holmes, Thomas, insurgent leader, executed, 126
Honnengs, William, 102
Hooper, John, Bishop of Gloucester (1550), and afterwards of Worcester, 130
Hopton or Hoptun, Dr. John, Princess Mary's chaplain, 20, 21
Hopton or Hoptun, Sir Ralph, the knight marshall, 112
Hostages or pledges demanded by the insurgents, 185
Howard, Lord William, 26
Howard, Queen Catharine, 88
Huddy, ... surgeon to Protector Somerset, 122
Huntingdon, Francis Hastings, second Earl of. 1, 2
Huntingdon, George Hastings, first Earl of, 2
Huntingdonshire, 48
Hyckoke, William, a prisoner, 126

Isaiah or Esai, 190

Jane the Queen. *See* Grey, Lady Jane
Jermyng, 62
Jersey, captain of (1542), 2. *See* Somerset
Jersey, Channel Island, 60
Joachim, 110
Joan of Kent, burnt for heresy, 139
John of Kent. *See* Joan and Barne
John the Baptist, Saint, 152
John the Evangelist, Saint, 174
Joseph, Dr. . . Cranmer's chaplain, 45
Jugge, Richard (printer), 103
Julius, an imprisoned Italian, 125
Justices of the Peace, proclamation to, 43

Kellaway or Delaway, ... 123
Ken, 4
Kendal, Baron Parr of, 81
Kent, Joan of, 139. *See* Barne and Boucher

Kent, Sheriff of (Sir Robert Southwell), 101
Kent, troubles in, 24, 32, 81
Kett, Robert, insurgent, afterwards executed (1549), 59, 126
Kett, William, brother and companion of Robert, 126
Kew, Dr. Turnor's house at, 121, 122
King, Thomas, 125
King's Bench Prison, 136
Kirkby Bellews, in Leicestershire, 139
Kyngesmyll, William, Dean of Winchester, 4

Lambeth, 130, 131
Lamport, 11
Lancaster, Chancellor of the Duchy of, 53
Latin services demanded to be restored, 169 to 172
Lawrence of Hamme, James, a warrener, 122
Laycoke, ..., 123
Lazarus the beggar, 173
Le Grand, 86
Lee, Edward, Archbishop of York (1531 —1544), 3
Lee, Henry, Mayor of Toreiton (*sic*), 188
Leeze (*qy.* Leighs?), in Essex, 36
Leicestershire, 2, 139
Lemonyall, a French prisoner, 125
Leominster, 103
Lermouth, a Scot, 137
Levy, the tribe of, 143
Leyson, Dr., 135
Limitation of the Crown, 72, 85, &c. *See* Edward VI.
Lincoln Use service books, 128
Lincolnshire troubles in, 1
Lisle, Viscount, 31
London, Bishop of (Cuthbert Tunstall), 136
London, Edmund Bonner, deposed bishop of, 130, 137, 138, &c. *See* Bonner
London and Westminster, nominated bishop of (Dr. John Poynet), 137
London, Nicholas Ridley, substituted bishop of, 3, 43, 81
Longer, Pierre, a French prisoner, 125
Lovel, Alice, sister and heiress of Henry Lovel, 95
Lovel, Henry, eighth Baron Morley, 95
Lutheranism, declared progress of, 110, 111

INDEX. 203

Machyn, Henry, merchant taylor of London, his Diary from 1550 to 1563 (Camden Society, 1st Series, No. 42), 95, 138
Magdalen College, Oxford, 131
Magdeburg, 110, 111
Magnus, Dr. Thomas, 132
Malle, Robert, Lord of Palmure, 124
Maltravers, Lord Henry Fitzallan. *See* Arundell, Earl of
Mary, Princess and afterwards Queen, 3, 4, 20, 21, 23, 31, 34, 38, 42, 43, 54, 72, 82, 86, 89, 104, 116, 119, 129, 133, 135, 136, 138
Mary Queen of Scots, 72
Mary Tudor, the French wife of Charles Brandon, 2
Mason, Sir John, Dean of Winchester (1549), 4, 43, 53
Mass said openly for Princess Mary, 20
Maunder (*qy.* James Mourton, priest), 63
Maurice, Elector of Saxony, 110
Maxfield, Robert Lord, 124
May, ..., 43
Mayor of Bodmin, Cornwall (Henry Braye), 63, 184, 188
Mayor of Bristol, 139
Mayor of London (1554, Sir Thomas White or Sir John Lion), 81
Melancthon, Philip, 111
Memorials, Ecclesiastical, and Memoirs, by John Strype, 73, 74, 95
Michias or Micah, 191
Middlesex, grievance at Staines in, 19
Milan, Duchess of, 103
Mildmay, Sir Walter, 124
Mint, in Southwark, 138
Montaborinus, 111. *See* Mount, Christopher
Montague or Mountague, Sir Edward, councillor, 7, 8, 82, 85, 86; his career, 93, 94; Chief Justice of the Common Pleas, 100, 106, 119, 135
Montius, 112. *See* Mount, Christopher
More, ... one of the insurgents, 74
More, Sir Thomas, 36
Moreman, Dr. 125, 177, 179
Moreton, James, Earl of, 124
Morley, Henry Lovel, eight Baron, 95
Morley, Henry Parker, ninth Baron, 94, 95
Morysine, Sir Richard, 104
Moses, 149, 166, 189, 190
Moundere als de loyes, 125

Mount, Christopher, 110 to 112
Mullinax, Sergeant, 124

Newark on Trent, Notts., 132
Noble, James, Scotch prisoner, 124
Norfolk, Thomas Howard, third Duke of (1539), 101, 123, 124
Norfolk, troubles in, 27, 32, 48, 57, 58, 119
Norman and his wife, 3
North, Sir Edward, treasurer and chancellor, of the Court of Augmentations, 20, 21; his career, 37, 38, 73, 81, 85, 88, 100
Northampton, 48
Northampton, William Parr, first Marquis of (1546), 21, 28, 36, 38, 48, 50, 58; his career, 81, 82, 85, 88, 93, 119
Northumberland, Sir John Dudley, Lord Warwick, &c., Duke of, 3, 20, 21, 30; his career, 31, 36; his eldest son mentioned (Lord Guildford Dudley) 53, 54, 57, 59, 72, 73, 81, 82, 85, 88, 93, 94, 100, 101, 106, 119, 129, 135
Norwich, 48, 59; dean and chapter of, 101
Nottingham, Sheriff of, 38
Nottinghamshire, 132
Nuremburg, 111

Oglethorpe, Owen, afterwards Bishop of Carlisle (1557), 132
Olyver, Dr. 135
Oriel College, Oxford, 133
Our Lady and the Holy Angels Chapel, York, 132
Oxford, 131 to 134, 136
Oxfordshire, 26, 27, 2)
Oza, otherwise Uzzah, 143

Paget, Robert, the insurgent brother of William, 53, 55, 74
Paget, Sir William, afterwards Lord Paget of Beaudesert, 19, 24, 39, 42; his career, 53, 60, 64, 65, 67, 73, 85, 90, 102, 119, 134, 135
Palladen, Richard, a prisoner, 126
Palmure, Robert Malle, Lord of, 124
Papists, Udall's description of, 146
Pardons for the rebels, 65
Paris, 192
Parker, Henry, ninth Baron Morley, 94
Parker, Henry, tenth Baron Morley, 95

204 INDEX.

Parker, Dr. Matthew, afterwards Archbishop of Canterbury, 130, 133
Parker, Sir William, 94
Parr, Anne, sister of Catherine, 23
Parr, Catherine, Queen, 23
Partridge, Sir Miles, 122
Paternoster, to be used in the vernacular and understood, 164
Paul, St., 142, 143, 180, 190, 191
Paulet, Sir Hugh, 52, 63, 64
Paulet, Sir John, 52
Paulet, Sir William, Baron St. John of Basing, afterwards Marquis of Winchester, his career, 34. *See* St. John
Paulle, Pietro, Italian prisoner, 126
Paul's Cross, 130, 136. *See* St. Paul's
Peckham, Sir Edmund, high treasurer of the Mint (1549), 96
Pembroke, William Herbert, first Earl of (1468), 23 (second creation 1551), 1, 23, &c. *See* Herbert
Penbroke, Symon, prisoner, 125
Penrith, John Bird, Suffragan Bishop of, 136
Peter, Sir William, 107, &c. *See* Petre, Sir William
Petre, William, secretary, 14, 19, 20, 21, 24, 34, 39; his career, 42, 43, 45, 49, 51 to 53, 55, 62, 64, 72, 73, 80, 84, 85, 88 to 90, 93, 102, 106, 107
Petyt MSS., here printed, from the originals at the Inner Temple, 6, 7, 15, 20 to 22, 25, 27, 30, 34, 35, 37, 38, 44, 46, 47, 50, 52, 53, 60, 63, 67, 68, 73, 74, 82, 88, 112
Pharao, 166, 191
Philip of Spain, husband of Queen Mary, 38, 43, 54, 82
Philippe, Mr. . . . . of Cornwall, 37
Piers, probably William, 29
Plymouth, the Mayor of, 33, 35
Plymouth, relief of, 61
Pocock, Nicholas, his edit. of Burnet's Reformation, 75, 84, 104, 129
Pole, Reginald, Cardinal, afterwards Archbishop of Canterbury, 38, 82, 138, 180, 181
Pomeray, Sir Thomas, concerning his pardon, 49; to be searched for, 63
Poole, in Dorsetshire, 29, 47, 49
Portsmouth, 29
Poynet, Dr. John, Bishop of Rochester, afterwards of Winchester, 137
Privy Seal, Lord. *See* Russell, Sir John

Proclamations in Cornwall and Devonshire, 41 to 43, 69 to 71, 95, 96, 108. *See* Antiquaries Society and Grafton
Protector, the Lord, *passim*. *See* Somerset, Edward Seymour
Purbeck, 29

Reading, 123
Rebellion in Norfolk, 27, &c. *See* Norfolk
Receiver, the King's (Brystowe), 25
Receiver, the Protector's (Croche), 25
Record Office, Domestic Papers of Edward VI. at the, 1, 3, 4, 8, 11, 12, 14, 19, 77 to 80, 83, 86, 92, 94, 102, 104, 106, 108, 113, 118, 120, 123, 127, 131, 133
Reformatio Legum Ecclesiasticarum, 72, 108
Reformation, Burnet's, 75, 84, 104, 129
Reynolds, Dr. . . . ., 7
Rich, Richard, Baron Rich, of Leeze, chancellor, 7, 8, 20, 24, 30, 34; his career, 36, 37, 39, 42, 45, 49, 51, 52, 60, 62, 64, 72, 81, 82, 85, 88, 93, 100, 101, 129
Richardson, Thomas, cleric and prisoner, 125
Richmond, 6, 7, 19, 20, 33, 121
Ridley, Nicholas, Bishop of London, (1550—1553), 3, 43, 81
Ringleaders to be sent for trial, 63
Rochester, Bishop of (John Fisher, 1504), 36
Rochester, Bishop of (Nicholas Heath, 1540), 138
Rochester, Bishop of (John Poynet, 1550), 137
Rochford, George Boleyn, Lord, 119
Rome, 157, 180
Rose, Richard, pursuivant, 129
Rosshampton, 121
Rouvett, Jacques, imprisoned Frenchman, 125
Russell, Sir John, Baron Russell, Lord Privy Seal (1542), and Earl of Bedford, 6, 8 to 11; his career, 12, 15, 22, 29, 38, 40, 42, 44, 46, 47, 50, 51, 53, 62, 63, 65, 73, 74, 78 to 80, 82, 86, 90, 92, 100, 102, 129, 134
Rutland, Henry Manners, second Earl of (1545), 26
Rutter, a carter, 121

INDEX. 205

Rybald, Sir John, prisoner, 124
Rymer, Thomas, his Foedera, 43

Sadleyr or Sadler, Sir Ralph, 20, 24, 72, 73, 82, 85, 88, 93; signs proclamation against Somerset, 100
Safe conduct demanded for Humphrey Arundel and Henry Braye, 184
Sainga, Pierre, 62
St. Asaph's, Bishop of (1536, William Barlow), 133
St. David's, Bishop of (1536, William Barlow), 133
St. John, Sir William Paulet, Baron St. John, of Basing, 7, 8, 20, 24, 30; his career, 34, 36, 37, 39, 42, 45, 49 to 52; created Earl of Wiltshire, 53, 60, 62, 64, 65, 67, 72, 73, 81, 85, 88, 93; signs proclamation against Somerset's evil government, 100, 119, 129; made Lord Treasurer, 134, 135
St. Leonard's, York, 132
St. Mary-le-bow, 45
St. Mary Magdalene, Bridgnorth Castle, 132
St. Mary Overy's Church, Southwark, 136
St. Paul's Church, the old cathedral, 45, 51
St. Paul's Cross, preaching station, 130, 136
St. Stephen's College, Westminster, 123
Salisbury, 15, 23
Sampford Courtney, 15
Sark or Serk, Channel Island, 60
Sarum Use, Service-books, to be destroyed, 128
Saxony, Duke Henry of (1544), 112
Saxony, Elector Maurice of (1541), 110
Scotland, Somerset's expedition into, 82; loss of Hadington, 116, 149
Scots disaffected during Protectorate, 13, 124, 137, 149
Seckendorff's History, 112
Segar, William, a chief captain and subscriber of the articles, 188
Semaryall, a French prisoner in the Tower, 125
Semere, Andrew, French prisoner in the Tower, 125
Sempringham, Monks of the Order of, 3
Serk or Sark, 60
Servants in attendance to be limited in number, 182

Sessay, in Yorkshire, 132
Sety, a yeoman usher, 122
Severn estuary, 61
Seymour, Lady Anne, daughter of Lord Protector Somerset, 31
Seymour, Edward, Lord Protector of England, Duke of Somerset, his titles and career, 1, 2, etc. *See* Somerset
Seymour, Sir Edward otherwise Lord Edward (son of the Protector Somerset), afterwards Baron Beauchamp and Earl of Hertford, 79, 80
Seymour, Sir Harry, 77, 78
Seymour, the Lady Jane, third Queen of Henry VIII., 2
Seymour, Sir Thomas (brother of Edward the Lord Protector Somerset, and of the Queen Jane Seymour), Lord Seymour of Sudelye, High Admiral of England, 38, 39, 42; committed to the Tower, 50; executed after attainder, 72, 85; Sudeley mentioned, 123
Sheep, payment for, 16
Sheffield, Edmund, first Baron (1547), slain at Norwich by a butcher, 48, 59
Sherburn, in Dorset, 11
Sherrington or Sharington, Sir William, treasurer of the King's Mint at Bristol, 123; a prisoner, and pardoned, 125
Shrewsbury, Francis Talbot, eighth Earl of, 7; his career, 81, 82; 85, 86, 88, 93; signs proclamation against Somerset, 100, 119
Shyne grounds, 121, 122
Sibthorp, 132
Sion or Syon, 13, 24, 27, 74, 121 to 123
Sloeman, John, a chief captain of the insurgents, and subscriber to their Articles, 188
Smith or Smyth, George, brother of Sir Thomas, 106
Smith or Smyth, Sir Thomas, Secretary, 34, 42, 45, 53, 55, 90, 102; sequestered from the Council and Secretaryship, 106; his career, 107 to 109; one of his perquisites, on alum, 123; imprisoned as adherent of Somerset, 126; but released in the following February, 108
Smith, William, a Richmond carter, 121
Somerset, Anne (daughter of Sir Edward Stanhope, of Shelford, Notts.), Duchess of, 121

CAMD. SOC. 2 E

206 INDEX.

Somerset, chief conspirators against the Lord Protector, Warwick and Southwell, first organizers. *See* Arundel, Baker, Cheney, Gage, Herbert. E. Montague, Edward North, Northampton, Petre, Rich, Russell, Sadler, Shrewsbury, Southampton, Sir Richard Southwell, Warwick, Wentworth, the Wottons, Edward and Nicholas, Yorke; to whom may be added Wingfield

Somerset: Edward Seymour, Viscount Beauchamp, Captain of Jersey, Earl of Hertford, Great Chamberlain for life, Lord Protector of England in minority of Edward VI., Baron Seymour, and Duke of Somerset (1547), 1 to 3, 5, 7, 8, 11, 14, 19 to 21, 24, 25, 27, 28, 30, 34, 36, 37, 39, 42, 43, 45, 46, 49, 52, 53, 55, 60, 62, 64, 65, 67, 72 to 74, 76 to 90; falls into discredit, 92 to 94; is proclaimed, 95 to 98; 101; 102, 103, 105, 107 to 110, 112; denounced to the ambassadors, 113 to 118; declared to be in custody, 119; as also his servants, 120; inventory of his removed chattels, 121 to 124; confined in the Tower, 126, 127; 129; the conspirators against him (*See* Somerset, Conspirators), 135, 138; limited restitution proposed for his benefit, 139; described by Nicholas Udall as the King's "most dear uncle Edward," 149, 187

Somerset House, near Strand Bridge

Somersetshire, troubles among the Commons in, 1, 8, 11, 31, 32, 47, 54, 56

Soter, Bishop of Rome (168, martyred under Marcus Antoninus), 158

Southampton, Thomas Wriothesley, Earl of, 42; formerly Secretary of State (1538), his career, 49 to 52; Baron Wriothesley of Titchfield, Lord Chancellor (1544), and Earl of Southampton, 50; 51, 60, 72, 83, 85, 88, 93; signs the proclamation against Somerset, 100; driven from the Council, 101, 119; 126

Southwark, 136, 138

Southwell, Sir Richard, 85, 88; his career, including the signing proclamation denouncing the Protector Somerset, against whom he was a chief contriver and conspirator, 101; announces him to be in custody, 119

Southwell, Sir Robert, brother of Richard, Master of the Rolls and Privy Councillor in the reign of Henry VIII., 101

Speke, Sir Thomas, 52

Spinola, 32

Staines, the bridge and town of, 19

Stanhope, Sir Michael, 106; imprisoned, 126

Stanhope's house at Bedding, Mr. (probably Sir Michael), 121

Stephenson, John, imprisoned, 125

Stepney manor, 119

Stourton, Lord (probably Charles Stourton, seventh Baron, who was in 1551 executed at Salisbury for murder of the Hargills, father and son), 1. *Cf. Preface*, xvi.

Stow, John, 90

Stowell, bringer of news, 15

Strasburg or Argentina, 110, 111

Strype, John, his Ecclesiastical Memorials, &c., 7, 8, 24, 73, 74, 95

Succession, Edward VI.'s device for the, 53, 85, 94, 101, &c. *See* Edward VI.

Sudeley, a former residence of High Admiral Thomas Seymour, 123

Suffolk, Charles Brandon, first Duke of (1514—1545), 1; his career, 2, &c.; at reception of Anne of Cleves (1539), 135

Suffolk, Henry Brandon, second Duke of (1545—1551), who died on the same day as his brother Charles, both being sons of Catherine Baroness Willoughby d'Eresby, and the first Duke of Suffolk, 2

Suffolk, Henry Grey, Duke of (1551), successor to the Brandons, his career, 2, his downfall, 101, 129

Suffolk, troubles in, 24, 32, 48, 58

Sunday Baptisms, 16, 163

Supplication of the Commons of Devon and Cornwall, to which the king sent answer, 19, 20

Surrey, commotions in, 24

Surrey, Henry Howard (judicially murdered in 1646: son of Thomas, third Duke of Norfolk), Earl of, 101

Sussex, Sir Henry Ratcliffe, second Earl of, 81, 106

Syon, 13, 24, 27, 74, 121 to 123

INDEX. 207

Talbot, Francis, fifth or eighth Earl of Shrewsbury (1541), his career, 81, 82
Talbot, George, fourth or seventh Earl of Shrewsbury (1473), 82
Talbot, John, first or fourth Earl of Shrewsbury (1442—1453), 82
Thanks officially rendered to helpers against the insurgents, 65
Thirsk, Yorkshire, 132
Thistleworth, 122
Thompson (perhaps Richard), the Pirate at the Severn, 61
Thompson or Tompson, John, priest, and one of the four governors of the insurgents' camp, 188
Thompson or Tomson, Richard, a prisoner in the Tower, 125
Thyn or Thynne, Sir John, 106, 123, 126
Tierney, Canon, his edition of Dod's Church History, 21, 22
Tomson, Richard, and John Tompson. *See* Thompson
Toreiton (probably Torrington, Devon), 188
Travers, Mr. . . . ., 12, 30, 34, 41, 50
Treatise on Marriage, occasioned by the Pretended Divorce of Henry VIII. from Catherine of Arragon, by Dr. Nicholas Harpsfield, edited by Nicholas Pocock, 3 (Camden Society, New Series, No. 21).
Trenchard, Sir Thomas, 28
Troubles at Frankfort quoted, 7
Tunstall, Cuthbert, Bishop of London (1522), afterwards of Durham (1530), 77, 136
Turner (afterwards Cox), Mrs. Jane (née Auder), wife of William, 4
Turner, Dr. William, Somerset's domestic physician, 3, 4, 122; begs the Presidentship of Magdalen College, Oxford, 131, 132; seeks some other preferment, and becomes Dean of Bath and Wells, 133, 134
Tyburn, execution of the insurgent leaders, Humphrey Arundel, John Wyndslow, John Bury, and Thomas Holmes, at, 126
Tytler, Patrick Fraser, his England under the reigns of Edward VI. and Mary (1839), 19, 64, 76, 78, 80, 90, 102, 109, 116, 119, 124

Udall, Nicholas (for account of his career see the *Preface*, separately indexed, xviii. to xxv.), his Answer to the Commoners of Devonshire and Cornwall (printed complete from Royal MS. 18 B. xi. fol. 1 to 40), with consideration of their Sixteen Articles, 141 to 193
Underhill, Thomas, a chief captain among the insurgents, 49, 54, 188
Unthanke, the imprisoned parson of Hedley, 125

Vane or Fane, Sir Ralph, 123; imprisoned in the Tower, 126
Vaughan, Sir Stephen, 11

Walden in Essex, 45
Wales, 1, 35, 44
Warden of the Cinque Ports (1540—1558), 85. *See* Cheney, T.
Warwick, John Dudley, Earl of (afterwards Duke of Northumberland), 20, 21, 30; his career, 31, 34, 36, 39, 48, 50, 57, 59, 73, 81, 82, 85, 93, 100, 101, 106, 118, 129, 134, 135. *See* also Dudley, John, and Northumberland
Wells. *See* Bath and Wells
Wentworth, Thomas, first Lord (1529—1551), 119
Wentworth, Thomas, second Lord (1551), Deputy of Calais (1559 trial), 81; one of the earliest adherents of Princess Mary, 119
West, Nicholas, Bishop of Ely (1515—1534), 129
West, William, a prisoner, 125
Westminster Abbey, burial of Edward VI. in, 82
Westminster, Bishop of London and (Dr. John Poynet proposed), 137
Westminster, Letters of Council, &c. sent from, 21, 28, 30, 36, 37, 39, 42, 45, 46, 48, 55, 64, 65, 67, 72, 73, 82, 106, 129
Westminster, St. Stephen's College, 123
Wetherhedd, . . ., Surveyor of Works, residing at Thistleworth, 122
Whaly, Mr. . . . ., at Wimbledon, 121
Whelps of the Romish litter (Udall's amenities of literature and theological controversy), 141; Antichrist's whelps (ditto), 191

INDEX.

Whitsuntide acceptance of the Holy Communion recommended, 158, 159
Will of Edward VI. for the succession of Lady Jane Grey, 94, &c. *See* Edward VI. and Succession
Will of Henry VIII. appointing sixteen executors, 38, 42, 72, 81, 85, 88, 101, 135, 136
Willoughby d'Eresby, Catharine, Baroness (mother of Henry and Charles Brandon, who died of the plague, both on one day), 2
Willoughby d'Eresby, Peregrine Bertie, Lord, 26
Wilton, 113
Wilton, William, Lord Grey de, 25; his career, 26, 27 to 29, 32, 33
Wiltshire, William Paulet, Earl of, 21; his career, 34; 53, 134, etc. *See* St. John, W.
Wiltshire, commotions in, 11, 23, 32, 44
Wimbledon, Surrey, 121
Winchester, Bishop of (Stephen Gardiner, 1531—1551 and 1553—1557)
Winchester, Bishop of (John Poynet, 1551—1553)
Winchester, Bishop of (Thomas Wolsey, 1529—1531), 12, 86
Winchester, Deanery of, 3, 4
Winchester, Marquis of (Sir William Paulet, Baron St. John of Basing, Earl of Wiltshire), 21; his career, 34. *See* St. John
Windsor, Council letters sent from, 36 42, 53, 75, 83, 86, 88 to 91, 94, 104 to 107, 118, 119, 121, 122, 132
Wingfield, Sir Anthony, 7, 9, 34, 36, 39; his career, 42, 43; 45, 96, 119
Wittenburg, 110
Wolf or Wulf, Edward, 106; imprisoned, 126
Wolsey, Thomas, Cardinal, Bishop of Winchester, and Archbishop of York, 12, 86
Wood, Anthony à, his Athenæ Oxonienses, &c., 103, 132
Woolcombe's Gleanings, Cotton and, 62, 73
Worcester, Bishop of (Nicholas Heath, 1544—1552 and 1553—1555), his career, 138
Worcester, Bishop of (John Hooper, 1552—1553), 130

Wotton, Sir Edward, brother of Nicholas, 135; his career, 73, 101;
Wotton, Dr. Nicholas, Dean of Canterbury, 86, 88, 93, 101; his career, 135
Wriothesley, Charles, Windsor Herald, his Chronicle of England during the Reigns of the Tudors (Camden Society's New Series, Nos. 11 and 20). *See* Wriothesley's Chronicle.
Wriothesley of Titchfield, Sir Thomas, Baron Wriothesley, Lord Chancellor, afterwards Earl of Southampton, 34, 38, 42; his career, 49 to 59; 60, 72, 83, 85, 88, 90, 93, 100, 110, 119, 126. *See* Southampton
Wriothesley's Chronicle, quoted, 1, 51, 125, 138
Wulf or Wolf, Edward, 106, 126
Wyatt, Sir Thomas, his rising in Kent (1553—1554), 81, 89, 101
Wyncestlo (probably the same as John Wyndslow), 54, 126
Wyndslow, John, imprisoned, 126. *See* Wyncestlo, 54

York, Archbishop of (Nicholas Heath, 1555—1560)
York, Archbishop of (Robert Holgate, 1544—1555)
York, Archbishop of (Edward Lee, 1531 —1544)
York, Archbishop of (Thomas Wolsey, 1514—1531)
York, Archdeacon of the East Riding (Dr. John Dakyn), 132
York, Archdeacon of the East Riding (Dr. Thomas Magnus, known as " Among Us "), 132
York, Chapel of Our Lady and the Holy Apostles, 132
York, Dean of (Dr. Nicholas Wotton, 1544), 135
York, Hospital of St. Leonard, 132
York, Prebendary of (Dr. William Clayburgh, 1549—1554), 132
York, Visitation in the Province of (June 24, 1559), 82
Yorke, Sir John, Sheriff of London (1549, with Augustine Hind), his career, 138

Zacharie or Zacharias, father of St. John the Baptist, 152

January 1885.

Camden Society,

FOR THE · PUBLICATION OF

Early Historical and Literary Remains.

The Members marked (c.) *have compounded for their Subscriptions.*

President.

THE RIGHT HON. THE EARL OF VERULAM, F.R.G.S.

(c.) Right Hon. Lord Acton, Aldenham Park, Bridgenorth, Salop.
G. H. Adshead, Esq. Fern Villas, 94, Bolton Road, Pendleton, Manchester.
William Aldam, Esq. Frickley Hall, Doncaster.
Lindsey M. Aspland, Esq. LL.D. 4, Elm Court, Temple.

Jonathan E. Backhouse, Esq. Darlington.
J. E. Baer, Esq. Frankfort.
Right Hon. Lord Bagot, Blithfield House, near Rugeley, Staffordshire.
(c.) John Eglington Bailey, Esq. F.S.A. Egerton Villa, Stretford, Manchester.
Franklin Bartlett, Esq. 161, Nassau Street, New York.
Wynne E. Baxter, Esq. F.R.G.S. 9, Laurence Pountney Hill, Cannon Street.

M. H. Beaufoy, Esq. South Lambeth.
Miss Eliza Bell, Borovere, Alton, Hants.
William Bethell, Esq. Rise, Hull
S. R. Bird, Esq. F.S.A. Public Record Office, London.
(c.) John Birkbeck, Esq. Anley House, Settle, Yorkshire.
(c.) Very Rev. Joseph William Blakesley, B.D. (Dean of Lincoln), The Deanery, Lincoln.
William H. Bliss, Esq. 13, Via Gregoriana, Rome.
Rev. Wm. Borlase, M.A. Zennor Vicarage, St. Ives, Cornwall.
Mr. Thomas Bosworth, 66, Great Russell Street, Bloomsbury.
W. H. Bothamley, Esq. 1, Cavendish Square, W.
William Jerdone Braikenridge, Esq. 16, Royal Crescent, Bath.
F. A. Brockhaus, Esq. Leipzig.
Francis Capper Brooke, Esq. Ufford, Suffolk.
Henry Thomas Brown, Esq. Roodeye House, Chester.
Rev. W. E. Buckley, Middleton Cheney Rectory, Banbury.
Professor Montagu Burrows, Oxford.

Frederick Caldwell, Esq. 4, Hanover Terrace, Regent's Park.
W. Henry Pole Carew, Esq. Anthony, Torpoint, Devonport.
(c.) Sir Stafford Carey, M.A. Candie, Guernsey.
Rev. Henry A. Cartwright, M.A. Whitestaunton Rectory, Chard, Somerset.
James J. Cartwright, Esq. M.A. F.S.A. (*Treasurer*), Public Record Office, London.
(c.) William Chappell, Esq. F.S.A. Strafford Lodge, Oatlands Park, Weybridge.
(c.) Right Rev. the Lord Bishop of Chester, Dee Side, Chester.
(c.) John Walbanke Childers Esq., Cantley, Doncaster.
Thomas Chorlton, Esq. 32, Brasenose Street, Manchester.
J. W. Clark, Esq. 1 Scrope Terrace, Cambridge.
Right Hon. Lord Clermont, 35, Hill Street, Berkeley Square.
Right Hon. Lord Coleridge, 1, Sussex Gardens, Bayswater.
John Coode, Esq. Polcarne, St. Austell, Cornwall.
Robert Humphrey Cooke, Esq. F.R.C.S. 73, Church Street, Stoke Newington.

William Henry Cooke, Esq. M.A. Q.C. 42, Wimpole Street., W.
Dr. George Elwes Corrie, D.D. Master of Jesus Coll. Camb. Jesus College, Cambridge.
(c.) Fred. Wm. Cosens, Esq. F.S.A. 7, Melbury Road.
(c.) John Ross Coulthart, Esq. Greenlaw Park, Castle Douglas, Kirkcudbright.
Right Hon. Earl Cowper, 8, Grosvenor Square.
Hon. Henry Frederick Cowper, M.P. 4, St. James's Square.
(c.) James T. Gibson Craig, Esq. Edinburgh.
W. H. Crawford, Esq. Lakelands, Cork.
(c.) George Cubitt, Esq. M.P. 123, St. George's Square, Pimlico.

Thomas M. Dalton, Esq. Iridge Place, Hurst Green, Sussex.
R. S. Longworth Dames, Esq. 21, Herbert Street, Dublin.
Francis Robert Davies, Esq. Hawthorn, Blackrock, Dublin.
Rev. J. Silvester Davies, M.A. F.S.A. St. James's Vicarage, Enfield Highway.
Right Hon. Lord Delamere, 13, Carlton House Terrace, S.W.
(c.) Right Hon. the Earl of Derby, K.G. 23, St. James's Square.
Miss J. A. L. De Vaynes, 15, Dalby Square, Cliftonville, Margate.
His Grace the Duke of Devonshire, K.G. D.C.L. 78, Piccadilly.
Sir C. Wentworth Dilke, Bart. M.P. 76, Sloane Street.
Hon. Harold Dillon, F.S.A. 3, Swan Walk, Chelsea.
C. E. Doble, Esq. 12, Park Crescent, Oxford.
James E. Doyle, Esq. 54, Clifton Gardens, Maida Vale.
(c.) Sir William R. Drake, F.S.A. 12, Prince's Gardens, S.W.
Sir George F. Duckett, Bart. F.S.A. Newington House, Wallingford.

Rev. Joseph Woodfall Ebsworth, M.A. F.S.A. Molash Vicarage, Ashford, Kent.
Rev. Henry Thomas Ellacombe, M.A. F.S.A. The Rectory, Clyst St. George, Topsham.
John Evans, Esq. F.R.S. F.S.A. Nash Mills, Hemel Hempstead.
Mr. J. R. Evans (late Rivington and Co.) Oxford.

(c.) John Leman Ewen, Esq. Southwold, Wangford, Suffolk.
George Edward Eyre, Esq. M.A. F.S.A. 59, Lowndes Square.

(c.) Right Hon. Lord Viscount Falmouth, 2, St. James's Square.
(c.) Sir Walter R. Farquhar, Bart. 18, King Street, St. James's.
Chas. Harding Firth, Esq. M.A. 33, Norham Road, Oxford.
A. Fitzgibbon, Esq. Moorside, Bushey Heath, Herts.
(c.) John Lewis Ffytche, Esq. Thorpe Hall, Louth.
(c.) Rev. William Fletcher, D.D. The Vicarage, Ulceby, Lincoln.
(c.) Thomas William Fletcher, Esq. F.R.S. F.S.A. Lawneswood House, Stourbridge.
Cyril Dudley Fortescue, Esq. Boconnoc, Lostwithiel, Cornwall.
Francis F. Fox, Esq. Yate House, Chipping Sodbury, co. Gloucester.
J. J. Freeman, Esq. 2, Poets' Corner, S.W.
(c.) Frederick J. Furnivall, Esq. M.A. 3, St. George's Square, Primrose Hill, N.W.

James Gairdner, Esq. Public Record Office, London.
S. Rawson Gardiner, Esq. M.A. LL.D. (*Director*), South View, Widmore Road, Bromley, Kent.
Rev. Francis Aidan Gasquet, St. Gregory's College, Downside, Bath.
Henry H. Gibbs, Esq. 15, Bishopsgate Street, E.C.
William Gilbert, Esq. The Close, Salisbury.
William Bulkeley Glasse, Esq. Q.C. 35, York Place, Portman Square.
(c.) Henry Gough, Esq. Sandcroft, Redhill, Surrey.
E. Leigh Grange, Esq. M.A. LL.M. Lansdowne House, Great Grimsby.
Benjamin Wyatt Greenfield, Esq. 4, Cranbury Terrace, Southampton.

Edward Hailstone, Esq., F.S.A. Lond. & Scot., Walton Hall, Wakefield.
Professor John W. Hales, M.A. 1, Oppidan's Road, Primrose Hill, N.W.

William Douglas Hamilton, Esq. F.S.A. Public Record Office, London.
(c.) Joseph Alfred Hardcastle, Esq. 54, Queen's Gate Terrace, S.W.
Miss Lucy Harrison, 161, Haverstock Hill, N.W.
Henry Gay Hewlett, Esq. 24, Spring Gardens.
(c.) Rev. Herbert Hill, M.A. 2, Old Square, Warwick.
(c.) Right Hon. Viscount Holmesdale, Montreal, Sevenoaks.
Miss Holt, Balham House, Balham Hill, S.W.
Right Hon. A. J. B. Beresford Hope, M.A. M.P. 1, Connaught Place, Edgware Road.
(c.) Richard Hussey, Esq. F.S.A. Harbledown, Canterbury.

(c.) Rev. L. W. Jeffray, Wynlass Beck, Windermere.
Rev. Augustus Jessopp, D.D. Scarning Rectory, East Dereham, Norfolk.
James Jones, Esq. Stoneleigh Rosset, near Wrexham.
(c.) Joseph Jones, Esq. Abberley Hall, Stourport, Worcestershire.

William Kelly, Esq. F.S.A. Ivy Lodge, Alexandra Road, Leicester.
Alfred Kingston, Esq. (*Secretary*), Public Record Office, London.

Philip Lang, Esq. Ivy Cottage, Poltimore, Exeter.
W. N. Lawson, Esq. 6, Stone Buildings, Lincoln's Inn, W.C.
F. de M. Leathes, Esq. 17, Tavistock Place, W.C.
(c.) F. Kyffin Lenthall, Esq. F.S.A. 122, Mount Street, Grosvenor Square.
D. Lewis, Esq. Arundel, Sussex.
Messrs. Lockwood and Co. 7, Stationers' Hall Court.
Rev. Henry Richards Luard, M.A. 4, St. Peter's Terrace, Cambridge.

R. Bownas Mackie, Esq. M.P. F.S.A. St. John's Wakefield.

(c.) David Mackinlay, Esq. 6, Great Western Terrace, Hillhead, Glasgow.
D. J. Maclagan, Esq. 6, North St. David Street, Edinburgh.
Sir John Maclean, F.S.A. Glasbury House, Richmond Hill, Clifton, Bristol.
Alex. Macmillan, Esq. F.S.A. 29, Bedford Street, Covent Garden, W.C.
Robert Malcomson, Esq. Bennekerry Lodge, Carlow, Ireland.
W. T. Marriott, Esq. Sandal Grange, Wakefield.
Alfred Trice Martin, Esq. Clifton College, Clifton, Bristol.
Charles A. J. Mason, Esq. 29, Emperor's Gate, S.W.
Alexander B. McGrigor, Esq. 172, St. Vincent Street, Glasgow.
W. J. Mercer, Esq. 12, Marine Terrace, Margate.
Mr. Michaelowsky, Moscow.
W. J. C. Moens, Esq. Tweed, near Lymington.
Right Hon. Lord Monson, 29, Belgrave Square, S.W.
Professor Henry Morley, LL.D., University Hall, Gordon Square, W.C.
Stuart A. Moore, Esq. F.S.A. 1, Serjeant's Inn, Chancery Lane.
Jerom Murch, Esq. Cranwells, Bath.

(c.) George Whitlock Nicholl, Esq. The Ham, Cowbridge, Glamorganshire.
Robert Cradock Nichols, Esq. F.S.A. F.R.G.S. 5, Sussex Place, Hyde Park.
Francis Morgan Nichols, Esq. M.A. F.S.A. Lawford Hall, Manningtree, Essex.
(c.) Rev. William L. Nichols, M.A. Woodlands House, near Bridgwater.
Martinus Nihjoff, Esq. The Hague.
Most Honourable the Marquis of Northampton, Castle Ashby, Northampton.
Messrs. Nutt and Co. 270, Strand.

Richard Oliverson, Esq. 37, Gloucester Square, Hyde Park.
Rev. Sir Frederick A. Gore Ouseley, Bart. Mus. Doc. M.A. St. Michael's, Tenbury, Worcestershire.

William Dunkeley Paine, Esq. Reigate.
Rev. Fielding Palmer, M.A. East Cliff, Chepstow.
Messrs. James Parker and Co. Broad Street, Oxford.
(c) Anthony Parkin, Esq. Sharrow Bay, Penrith.
R. J. H. Parkinson, Esq. Ravendale Hall, Grimsby.
George Peel, Esq. Brookfield, Cheadle, Cheshire.
Right Hon. Lord Penrhyn, Penrhyn Castle, Bangor, North Wales.
(c.) James Orchard Halliwell Phillipps, Esq. F.R.S. F.S.A. Hollingbury Copse, near Brighton.
Rev. William Poole, M.A., Hentlands, near Ross.
F. W. L. Popham, Esq., Littlecot, Hungerford,
Right Hon. the Earl of Powis, LL.D. 45, Berkeley Square.
(c.) Osmond de Beauvoir Priaulx, Esq. 8, Cavendish Square.
S. E. Bouverie Pusey, Esq. Farringdon, Berks.

James Rae, Esq. 32, Phillimore Gardens, Kensington.
Frederick John Reed, Esq. Hassness, Cockermouth.
Henry Reeve, Esq. C.B. F.S.A. Privy Council Office, Whitehall, S.W.
Walter Charles Renshaw, Esq. 5, Stone Buildings, Lincoln's Inn.
Herbert Richards, Esq. Wadham College, Oxford.
(c.) Ralph Richardson, Esq. M.D. 10, Roland Gardens, South Kensington.
Robert Rigby, Esq., The Grove, Lawton, Stoke-upon-Trent.
The Most Hon. the Marquess of Ripon, K.G. D.C.L. F.R.S. 1, Carlton Gardens, S.W.
(c.) Very Rev. the Dean of Rochester, The Deanery, Rochester.
Thomas E. Rogers, Esq. care of B. B. Rogers, Esq. 8, Old Square, Lincoln's Inn, W.C.
J. Anderson Rose, Esq. 11, Salisbury Street, Strand.
(c.) Right Hon. the Earl of Rosebery, Lansdowne House, Berkeley Square.
Henry Ross, Esq. Chestham Park, Henfield, Sussex.
Joseph Carne Ross, Esq. Shian Lodge, Penzance.

Thomas Bush Saunders, Esq. M.A. Priory, Bradford-on-Avon, Wilts.

William Scott, Esq. Kington House, Perry Street, Gravesend.
Thomas W. Scott.
R. M. Short, Esq. 34, Lansdown Crescent, Great Malvern.
F. S. Seebohm, Esq. Hitchin, Herts.
(c.) Edward Simpson, Esq. Walton, Wakefield.
(c.) Rev. William Sparrow Simpson, D.D. F.S.A. 9, Amen Court, E.C.
Miss L. Toulmin Smith, Wood Lane, Highgate.
William Smythe, Esq. Methven Castle, Perth.
Samuel Spalding, Esq. 147, Drury Lane.
R. B. Stewart, Esq. 11, Crown Terrace, Dowanhill, Glasgow.
Robert Stoneham, Esq. 5, Philpot Lane.
Miss Stokes, Tyndale House, Cheltenham.
John Sykes, Esq. M.D. Doncaster.

Rev. Wm. Hepworth Thompson, D.D. F.S.A. Master of Trinity College, Cambridge, Trinity Lodge, Cambridge.
William John Thoms, Esq. F.S.A. 40, St. George's Square, Pimlico.
Miss Adelaide Thrupp, Merrow House, near Guildford.
John Tolhurst, Esq. 60, Tooley Street, S.E. and Glenbrook, Beckenham, Kent.
John Tomlinson, Esq. 31, St Sepulchre Gate, Doncaster.
Geo. Montgomery Traherne, Esq. Coedriglan, Cardiff.
Sir John S. Trelawny, Bart. Trelawny, Liskeard, Cornwall.
Sir Charles E. Trevelyan, Bart. K.C.B. 8, Grosvenor Crescent, Belgrave Square.
K. I. Trübner, Esq. Strasburg.
Robert Samuel Turner, Esq. A 5, Albany, Piccadilly.

(c.) Sir Harry Verney, Bart. M.P. Claydon, Bucks.

(c.) Henry Wagner, Esq. F.S.A. 13, Half Moon Street, Piccadilly.
Edward Walmisley, Esq. 25, Abingdon Street, Westminster.
Charles Walton, Esq. Manor House, East Acton.

(c.) Right Hon. the Earl of Warwick, 1, Stable Yard, St. James's.
John Weld, Esq.
Eugene R. Wethey, Esq. 10, Eldon Place, Bradford, Yorkshire.
James Whatman, Esq. M.A. F.R.S. F.S.A. Reform Club, Pall Mall.
F. E. Wheeler, Esq. Westmorland House, Lordship Park, N.
Ignatius Williams, Esq. The Grove, Bodfary, Denbigh.
Richard Henry Wood, Esq. F.S.A. Penrhos House, Rugby.
Sir Albert W. Woods, Garter King of Arms, F.S.A. 69, St. George's Road, Pimlico.
Henry Workman, Esq. Great Hampton, Evesham.
Messrs. D. Wyllie and Son, Aberdeen.

LIBRARIES.

Belfast, Queen's College.
Birmingham Library.
    Free Library.
Bolton Public Free Library.
Bradford Subscription Library.
Bristol Museum and Library (Bishop's College).
Cambridge, Christ's College.
    King's College
    St. Catharine's College.
    St. John's College.
    Trinity College.
Canterbury, Dean and Chapter Library.
Cheltenham Permanent Library.
Dublin, King's Inns Library.
    National Library of Ireland.
    Royal Irish Academy.
Durham University.
Edinburgh Free College.
    University.
    Library of the Writers to the Signet.
Exeter, Devon and Exeter Institution.
Glasgow University Library.
    Mitchell Library.
Hull Subscription Library.
Leeds Library.
    Public Libraries.
Leicester Free Library.
Liverpool Free Library.

London:—
    Athenæum Club.
    Bank of England.
    City of London (Guildhall)
    Gray's Inn.
    House of Commons.
    Inner Temple.
    Lambeth Library.
    Law Institution.
    Lincoln's Inn.
    London Institution.
    London Library.
    London University.
    National Portrait Gallery.
    New University Club.
    Oxford and Cambridge Clu
    Reform Club.
    Royal Historical Society.
    Royal Institution.
    St. Paul's Cathedral Librar
    Science and Art Depar
        South Kensington.
    Sion College Library.
Manchester, Chetham's Library
    Free Library.
    Owen's College.
Newcastle-on-Tyne Literary an
    losophical Society.
Norwich, Dean and Chapter Li

LIBRARIES.

Norfolk and Norwich Literary Institution.
Nottingham Free Public Libraries.
Oxford, All Souls College.
    Queen's College.
    Union Society.
Preston Library (Dr. Shepherd's).
Rochdale Free Public Library.
Rugby, Temple Reading Room.
St. Andrew's University.
Sheffield Free Library.
Stonyhurst College.
Warwick, Warwickshire Natural tory and Archæological Socie
Windsor, Royal Library.

Adelaide, South Australian Institute.
Baltimore Peabody Institute.
Berlin, Bibliothek des Deutschen Reichstages.
    Royal Library.
Boston (U.S.) Athenæum.
    Free Library.
Breslau University Library.
Chicago Public Library.
Connecticut., Watkinson Library.
Copenhagen Royal Library.
Cornell University.
Göttingen University.
Hamburg City Library.
Heidelberg University.
Königsberg Royal Library.
Marburg University.
Massachusetts, Harvard College
    Wellesley College.
Melbourne Public Library.
Michigan University.
Münich Royal Library.
New York, Astor Library.
    Brooklyn Library.
    State Library.
Paris, National Library.
Philadelphia Library Company.
Prague Imperial University.
St. Louis Mercantile Library.
Sydney Free Library.
Tübingen University Library.
Vienna Imperial Library.
Washington, Congress Library.
Yale College.

REPORT OF THE COUNCIL

OF

THE CAMDEN SOCIETY,

READ AT THE GENERAL MEETING

ON THE 2ND MAY, 1884.

THE Council of the Camden Society have to regret the loss, by death, of the following Members—

>Right Rev. LORD BISHOP OF ARGYLE.
>Sir GEORGE BOWYER.
>JAMES CROSSLEY, Esq. F.S.A.
>SAMUEL EDWARDS, Esq.

The following have been elected Members of the Society during the past year:—

>BOSTON, U.S.A., FREE LIBRARY.
>Rev. ALEXANDER COOKE.
>W. N. LAWSON, Esq.
>WM. JOHN MERCER, Esq.
>D. J. MACLAGAN, Esq.
>FRANCIS WM. LEYBOURN POPHAM, Esq.
>HENRY ROSS, Esq.
>Rev. THOS. W. SCOTT.
>Rev. Canon WM. STUBBS, D.D., F.S.A. (now Bishop-elect of Chester).
>EUGENE R. WETHEY, Esq.

The volumes promised in the last Report are now all in the hands the Members, or will reach them in a few days.

The books for the year 1884-5 will be:—

1. Papers relating to issue of the Second Prayer Book of Edward VI. Edit by the Rev. N. POCOCK.
2. Political Memoranda of the fifth Duke of Leeds, 1774, &c. Edited by Osc BROWNING, Esq.
3. Selections from the Lauderdale Papers, Vol. II. Edited by OSMUND AIR Esq.

Of these, the first two are already in the press.

The Council have added to the list of works in preparation an accoun of the war in Ireland after the rebellion of 1642, from the pen of Colon Plunket, a Catholic officer serving under the Marquis of Ormond, to edited by Miss Mary Hickson, which will add to our knowledge of Iri history during the period which has recently been illustrated by the work edited by Mr. J. T. Gilbert.

The forthcoming publications will show that the Council have bee glad, by breaking what is to them the new ground of the latter half of t eighteenth century, to extend the sphere of their labours, and thereby render the work of the Society still more attractive than it has hither been.

On the whole, the Council may congratulate the Society on a year steady progress, the fruits of which, it is to be hoped, will be seen in t additional Members who may be attracted to it.

By order of the Council,

SAMUEL RAWSON GARDINER, *Director.*
ALFRED KINGSTON, *Secretary.*

REPORT OF THE AUDITORS.

We, the Auditors appointed to audit the Accounts of the Camden to the Society, that the Treasurer has exhibited to us an Account of t Expenditure from the 1st of April 1883 to the 31st of March 188 have examined the said accounts, with the vouchers relating thereto, an to be correct and satisfactory.

And we further report that the following is an Abstract of th Expenditure during the period we have mentioned:—

Receipts.	£	s.	d.	Expenditure.
To Balance of last year's account...	382	16	6	Paid for printing 500 Copies Camden M Vol. VIII..
Received on account of Members whose Subscriptions were in arrear at last Audit	64	3	0	Do. do. Voyage to Cadiz .... Do. do. Letter Book of Gabrie
The like on account of Subscriptions due on the 1st of May, 1883......	233	2	0	Paid for Miscellaneous Printing .... Paid for delivery and transmission of Bo
The like on account of Subscriptions due on the 1st of May, 1884......	17	1	0	paper for wrappers, warehousing expen cluding Insurance)....................................
To two Compositions in lieu of Annual Subscription	20	0	0	Paid for Binding.. Paid for making various Transcripts..,...........
One year's dividend on £466 3 1 3 per Cent. Consols, standing in the names of the Trustees of the Society, deducting Income Tax..	13	14	0	Paid for postages, &c................................. Legal Expenses ....
To Sale of Publications of past years..	15	4	9	
To Sale of Promptorium Parvulorum (3 vols. in 1)	2	5	0	By Balance ....
	£748	6	3	

And we, the Auditors, further state, that the Treasurer has repor over and above the present balance of £428 3s. 3d. there are outst subscriptions of Foreign Members, and of Members resident at a London, which the Treasurer sees no reason to doubt will shortly be re

JA

April 25th, 1884.

REPORT OF THE COUNCIL

OF

THE CAMDEN SOCIETY,

READ AT THE GENERAL MEETING

ON THE 4TH MAY, 1885.

IT is with the greatest regret that the Council of the Camden Society announce that the Secretary of the Society, Alfred Kingston, Esq., died on April 24. Some of them have lost in him a warm personal friend. All of them can bear witness to the devotion with which he studied the interests of the Society, and the good judgment and unfailing courtesy and tact which have for many years made him so valuable both as a counsellor and in his more immediately official capacity. Since the death of Mr. Bruce no such loss has befallen the Society.

The Council have also to regret the loss, by death, of the following Members—

>The Very Rev. J. W. BLAKESLEY, D.D. Dean of Lincoln.
>The Right Rev. Dr. JACOBSON, Bishop of Chester.
>HENRY CHAS. COOTE, Esq. F.S.A.
>Mrs. R. J. HOLLOND.
>JOHN W. MACKENZIE, Esq.
>Dr. N. ROGERS.

Of these Dr. Blakesley, Dr. Jacobson, and Mr. Mackenzie had been Members of the Society since its establishment in 1838.

REPORT OF THE COUNCIL, 1885.

The following have been elected Members of the Society during t past year:—

    Miss LUCY HARRISON.
    Professor HENRY MORLEY, LL.D.
    ROBERT RIGBY, Esq.
    PERCY M. THORNTON, Esq.
    MERTON COLLEGE, OXFORD; and
    BROOKLYN LIBRARY, NEW YORK.

Of the volumes promised in the last Report, two are already in tl hands of the Members, and the third, consisting of Papers relating to t Troubles caused by the issue of the second Prayer Book of Edward V will follow in a few days.

For the year 1885-86, the Council proposed to issue :—

1. Proceedings in the Courts of the Star Chamber and High Commission in t years 1631-2. To be edited by S. R. GARDINER, LL.D. Director.

2. Custumals of Battle Abbey, temp. Edward I., from a MS. in the Pub Record Office. To be edited by SAMUEL R. BIRD, Esq. F.S.A.

3. Selections from the Lauderdale Papers, Vol. III. To be edited by OSMU AIRY, Esq.

In their last Report the Council announced their intention of printi an account of the war in Ireland after the rebellion of 1642, from the p of Colonel Plunket. Further inquiry has, however, shown that the amou of unpublished matter contained in the MS. was insufficient to justify 1 issue at the expense of the Society, and it has therefore been withdra from the list of suggested publications.

There is, however, no lack of material for the operations of the Societ and the Council are able to look forward to much useful work in tl future.

    By order of the Council,

        SAMUEL RAWSON GARDINER, *Director.*

REPORT OF THE AUDITORS.

WE, the Auditors appointed to audit the Accounts of the Camden to the Society, that the Treasurer has exhibited to us an Account of t Expenditure from the 1st of April 1884 to the 31st of March 188 have examined the said accounts, with the vouchers relating thereto, an to be correct and satisfactory.

And we further report that the following is an Abstract of th Expenditure during the period we have mentioned:—

RECEIPTS.	£	s.	d.	EXPENDITURE.
To Balance of last year's account...	428	3	3	Paid for printing 500 Copies Lauderdale Vol. I. ....
Received on account of Members whose Subscriptions were in arrear at last Audit	12	0	0	Do. do. Memoranda of Duke Do. do. Lauderdale Papers, V
The like on account of Subscriptions due on the 1st of May, 1884......	230	3	0	Paid for Miscellaneous Printing .... Paid for delivery and transmission of Boo
The like on account of Subscriptions due on the 1st of May, 1885......	18	1	0	paper for wrappers, warehousing expens cluding Insurance)..............................
One year's dividend on £466 3 1 3 per Cent. Consols, standing in the names of the Trustees of the Society, deducting Income Tax*				Paid for paper.. .... Paid for Binding................................... Paid for making various Transcripts............. Paid for postages, &c.................................
To Sale of Publications of past years......................................	9	5	6	Clerical Assistance ....
To Sale of Promptorium Parvulorum (3 vols. in 1)	3	15	0	
Interest on deposit of £200 for two years	9	10	5	By Balance ....
	£710	18	2	

* NOTE.--This dividend has not been collected during the current year, owing to the d Trustees, and consequent delays in getting the stock transferred to fresh Trustees.

And we, the Auditors, further state, that the Treasurer has repor1 over and above the present balance of £237 8s. 8d. there are outst subscriptions of Foreign Members, and of Members resident at a London, which the Treasurer sees no reason to doubt will shortly be rec

JAMES
WYNN

April 25th, 1885.

RETURN TO ➡ **CIRCULATION DEPARTMENT**
202 Main Library

LOAN PERIOD 1 **HOME USE**	2	3
4	5	6

ALL BOOKS MAY BE RECALLED AFTER 7 DAYS
1-month loans may be renewed by calling 642-3405
6-month loans may be recharged by bringing books to Circulation Desk
Renewals and recharges may be made 4 days prior to due date

DUE AS STAMPED BELOW

NOV 1 5 1981		
RET'D APR 7 1982		
AUTO. DISC.		
MAR 1 1 1992		
CIRCULATION		

UNIVERSITY OF CALIFORNIA, BERKELEY
FORM NO. DD6, 60m, 12/80   BERKELEY, CA 94720

Lightning Source UK Ltd.
Milton Keynes UK
UKOW01f0939180717
305535UK00001B/49/P